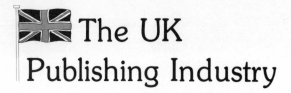

The UK Publishing Industry

Other Titles of Interest

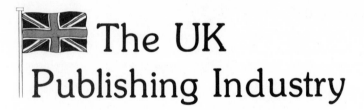

The UK Publishing Industry

by

PETER J. CURWEN
Senior Lecturer in Economics
Sheffield City Polytechnic

PERGAMON PRESS

OXFORD · NEW YORK · TORONTO · SYDNEY · PARIS · FRANKFURT

U.K.	Pergamon Press Ltd., Headington Hill Hall, Oxford OX3 0BW, England
U.S.A.	Pergamon Press Inc., Maxwell House, Fairview Park, Elmsford, New York 10523, U.S.A.
CANADA	**Pergamon Press Canada Ltd., Suite 104, 150 Consumers Rd., Willowdale, Ontario M2J 1P9, Canada**
AUSTRALIA	Pergamon Press (Aust.) Pty. Ltd., P.O. Box 544, Potts Point, N.S.W. 2011, Australia
FRANCE	Pergamon Press SARL, 24 rue des Ecoles, 75240 Paris, Cedex 05, France
FEDERAL REPUBLIC OF GERMANY	Pergamon Press GmbH, 6242 Kronberg-Taunus, **Hammerweg 6, Federal Republic of Germany**

First edition 1981

British Library Cataloguing in Publication Data

Curwen, Peter J
The UK publishing industry.
1. Publishers and publishing
Great Britain
I. Title
338.4'70705'0941   Z323   80-42045
ISBN 0-08-024081-X

In order to make this volume available as economically and as rapidly as possible the typescript has been reproduced in its original form. This method has its typographical limitations but it is hoped that they in no way distract the reader.

Printed in Great Britain by A. Wheaton & Co. Ltd., Exeter

To Gabrielle and Benjamin

Preface

It may come as something of a surprise to many readers to learn that this book constitutes the first attempt to conduct a comprehensive survey into the affairs of the UK publishing industry. True there have previously been a number of books about the art of publishing, but these have been written by practising publishers and have generally said little about anything other than the publishing and printing of books. One of the consequences of this shortage of information has been a lack of understanding about each others' positions by the various sectors of the book trade, and more especially an almost total ignorance of the economics of publishing by the general public. This book therefore constitutes a first attempt to satisfy a need which the author believes is becoming increasingly acute, namely the provision of a survey of the entire spectrum of the UK publishing industry, incorporating not merely publishers but printers, booksellers, libraries and learned societies, and encompassing journals as well as books.

There are a number of reasons why it is particularly appropriate that this survey should be published at this point in time. In the first place we have recently witnessed a supposedly thorough investigation of the industry by the Price Commission, whose conclusions, let alone methods of investigation, were not all they might have been. In the second place the industry is undergoing yet another of its alleged periods of impending doom, as manifested by generally poor profitability in 1979. In this respect the industry is something of its own worst enemy because it cries wolf so often that one is inclined to assume that its difficulties will soon disappear as they have done in the past. Finally almost all of the sacred cows of the industry have been given a public airing over the past two or three years, for example the Net Book Agreement, closed markets, Public Lending Right and copyright, and the dust has just about settled sufficiently for these issues to be re-assessed in a relatively calm and dispassionate manner.

The publishing industry is excessively defensive about its trade practices, for reasons analysed by Sutherland (1978) in his introduction. However, both he and other commentators believe that the book industry is in bad shape compared, say, to the audio industry. In the <u>Guardian</u>, Martin Lightfoot (1976) wrote about, among other things,

"the failure to develop an industry-wide system of stock control; the unco-ordinated, ragged and inefficient distribution system; ... the failure to confront realistically the publishing consequences of outdated copyright legislation; ... the reluctance to consider standardisation of formats, paper and typesetting; ... the failure ... to produce books quickly ...;"

To the outsider the publishing industry's unwillingness or inability to come to terms with these and other problems is surprising to put it mildly. Some issues, it seems, may never be put to rest. When one reads that "it can be argued that by any criterion book production at present is excessive", or that "if any book is going to suffer it will be the novel ... it is the young or unestablished novelists who will be harder hit", one might well imagine that one was reading the President's address at the 1980 Booksellers' Conference. In fact the quotations come from P.E.P. (1951). This author acknowledges in advance that this book is unlikely to lay any of these issues to rest once and for all. Nevertheless this book should serve as a timely reminder to the powers-that-be that action is long overdue, and offer them an analysis on which to base such action.

The format and scope of this book have been dictated by a number of considerations. In the first place the book concentrates upon economic rather than sociological material. A good deal of work has been done on such matters as author-publisher relationships and book reading habits, and appropriate references are to be found in the bibliography, but these topics are explicitly excluded from consideration in this book. Secondly, because the primary market for this book is seen as lying within the publishing industry itself, the contents are expressed in terms more to the taste of members of the industry than of professional economists. This has, among other things, served the cause of brevity, and in a further attempt to keep the book concise an explicit decision has been made not to qualify generalisations. All books are indeed different to a degree, as are all publishing houses, printers, booksellers and libraries. This book, however, is concerned with the analysis of the underlying principles and issues which determine the behaviour of the <u>typical</u> rather than of the individual organisation. Finally, a substantial section has been included on the economics of journals and learned societies, as these areas of publishing have in the past been greatly neglected. Because of the specialised nature of this information it has been supplied by Alan Singleton of the Leicester University Centre for Communications Research.

Readers of this book will discover that it consists primarily of factual analysis. Wherever possible this is based upon available statistics set out in tabular form. Occasionally, however, it has been necessary to stray from fact to opinion. Opinions expressed in this book have been arrived at in the time-honoured academic manner, namely through reading and evaluating everything previously published about each topic, and showing the early drafts to referees for their opinions. Unfortunately certain members of the book trade do seem to find this approach disagreeable, as evidenced, for example, by the remark made anonymously in <u>The Bookseller</u> that "when economists tangle with the book trade there is an enjoyable tendency for a spectacular pratfall to take place." Whether this book constitutes a pratfall is, ultimately, for members of the publishing industry to decide for themselves, but it is to be hoped that the experience of reading this book will provide a source of pleasure one way or another.

Finally it is to be hoped that the comprehensive bibliography will prove useful to all those wishing to conduct further research into the book industry, or indeed to those wishing simply to acquire more detailed knowledge in specific areas. Despite opinion to the contrary, the tracing, acquiring, reading and assimilating of information takes much longer than the process of writing, especially where a list of references has virtually to be prepared from scratch, and in this respect, at least, those who follow on should now find their lives made a little easier.

Although I must be held wholly responsible for the contents of this book, I would like to take this opportunity to express my gratitude to some of those who have assisted me in various capacities during the five year period which led up to the writing of the book, together with a general brickbat for all those who appear to believe that releasing a statistic about their affairs is comparable to the release of a state secret. My thanks firstly to Shaie Selzer of Macmillan, Colin Day of C.U.P., John Hitchin of Penguin, David Whitaker of <u>The Bookseller</u>, John Duffield of Hartley Seeds Booksellers, Tim Godfray of the Booksellers' Association, Miss Daphne Connolly of the British Printing Industries Federation, and above all to Professor Frank Livesey of Preston Polytechnic for information and constructive criticism of the book in draft form; to my editors Tom Dalby and Simon King of Pergamon Press; to <u>The Journal of Industrial Economics</u> for permission to reproduce parts of articles published in that journal; to the ladies of the Sheffield City Polytechnic inter-library loan section for their invaluable help in obtaining many of the items listed in the bibliography; and finally to my wife Gabrielle for her valiant efforts in typing this manuscript.

Sheffield City Polytechnic   Peter Curwen
          November 1980

Contents

LIST OF TABLES   xi

1. STATISTICAL OVERVIEW
   Introduction   1
   The Census of Production   1
   Turnover   4
   Publishers' Association Sales Statistics   13
   Consumers' Expenditure   15

2. PUBLISHING
   Introduction   16
   Competition in Publishing   16
   Titles Published   18
   The Size Distribution of Firms   21
   The Publisher's Role   22
   Breakdown of Costs   22
   Royalties   24
   Elasticity of Demand   26
   Financial Accounts   27
   Valuation of Stock   30
   Print Runs   31
   Technical Books   31
   Fiction   33
   Paperbacks   33
   The Price Commission Report on Books   38

3. THE NET BOOK AGREEMENT
   Introduction   41
   Historical Retrospect   41
   The Agreement   42
   The Judgement   43
   Reflections on the Judgement   45
   The Net Book Agreement in the 1890's   47
   Price Maintenance in the Record Industry   47
   Overseas Experience   47
   Recent Criticism of the Net Book Agreement   48
   The Number of Titles and Consumer Detriment   49
   Book Prices   50
   Stockholding Bookshops   50
   Conclusion   51
   Appendix: The Net Book Agreement 1957   51

4. INNOVATION AND COPYRIGHT
   Introduction   53
   On-Demand Publishing   53
   The Future of the Printed Word   55
   Copyright   56

5. PRINTING
   Introduction   60
   Size of Firms   61
   Scale of Production   61
   Expenditure on Plant and Machinery   64
   Capacity   64
   Competition   65

Financial Performance   65
Costs and Prices   67

6. MARKETING AND DISTRIBUTION
   Introduction   71
   Wholesaling   71
   Teleordering   73
   The British Market Agreement   75
   Closed Markets   76
   Current Export Problems   77
   Book Promotion   79
   Book of the Season   82
   Book Clubs   84

7. BOOKSELLING
   Introduction   86
   Structure and Competition   86
   Discounts   87
   Financial Analysis   88
   Small Order Surcharges   92
   Delivery   93
   School Books   95
   Libraries   96
   Public Lending Right   101

8. PRICE INDICES
   Price Composition   104
   Price Indices   104
   Conversion of Money Values to Real Values   112

9. QUANTITATIVE ASPECTS OF JOURNAL PUBLISHING
                              By Alan Singleton
   Definitions   114
   Number of Journals   115
   Journal Size   116
   Journal Prices   120
   Conclusions   124

10. JOURNAL PRODUCTION
                              By Alan Singleton
    Introduction   126
    Authors, Editors and Referees   126
    Publishers   130
    Learned Societies and Co-operation   132

11. JOURNAL PUBLISHERS
                              By Alan Singleton
    Publisher Types and Roles   136
    Growth and Diversification   137
    Printers   141
    Subscription Agents   141
    Markets and Libraries   143
    Conclusion   147

  BIBLIOGRAPHY   148

  AUTHOR INDEX   161

  SUBJECT INDEX   163

List of Tables

1	Analysis of Establishments by Size 1977	2
2	Output, Employment, Wages and Salaries, and Capital Expenditure	5
3	Sales and Receipts of UK General Printers and Publishers. £ million	6
4	Sales and Receipts of UK General Printers and Publishers. £ million at 1971 Prices	7
5	Proportion of Total Receipts Earned by Exports %	9
6	Export Sales and Receipts of UK General Printers and Publishers. £ million at 1971 Prices	11
7	Home Sales and Receipts of UK General Printers and Publishers. £ million at 1971 Prices	12
8	Annual Cumulation - Subject Analysis. Net Revenue. £ million	13
9	Annual Cumulation - Quarterly Regional Analysis. Net Revenue. £ million	14
10	Consumers' Expenditure at Constant 1975 Prices. £ million	15
11	Titles Published 1950 - 1979	19
12	The 100 Largest Publishers, Ordered According to the Number of New Books Published in 1979 in the UK	20
13	Size Distribution of Large Publishers 1978 and 1979	21
14	Concentration Ratios	22
15	Costs, Prices and Profits	24
16	Financial Results for 29 Large Publishers 1974 - 1977	28
17	Financial Ratios. Large Publishers	29
18	Sales Per Volume Per Year	31
19	Sales and Employment in the Printing Industry	60
20	The Size Distribution of Printing Firms	61
21	Large Printer/Binders. Financial Results 1974 - 1977	66
22	Real Rates of Return on Capital Employed %	67
23	Printers' Non-Material Costs	68
24	International Comparisons in Printing	69
25	Exchange Rates: US Dollars to the £	78
26	Overseas Trade Statistics. Books. £ million	79
27	Average Discounts Allowed to Booksellers	88
28	Overall Results 1972 - 1978	89
29	Net Profit as a % of Total Sales	91
30	Average Time Lapse of Delivery	94
31	Expenditure by Public Library Authorities. England and Wales %	97
32	Percentage of UK Library Expenditure by Category 1971 - 1977	98

33   Average Prices Recorded in The Bookseller. £   105

34   Price Indices. July 1964 - June 1965 = 100   106

35   Average Prices of Books in Selected Price Ranges 1965 - 70. £   107

36   Price Indices. July 1969 - June 1970 = 100   108

37   Price Indices. July 1974 - June 1975 = 100   109

38   Annual Price Indices. All Titles. 1975 - 1979   110

39   Annual Price Indices. Sub-Categories. 1975 - 1979   111

40   Retail Price Index. Annual Series   112

41   Retail Price Index. Books. January 1975 = 100   113

42   Size Changes of 62 UK Serials 1960 - 1973. Text Pages   118

43   Changes in Price and Size of Some Physics Journals 1959 - 75   119

44   Average Price of Periodicals in the UK   121

45   Average Price of Journals Published in the UK   121

46   Average Prices of Journals in the UK According to Country of Origin   122

47   Average Prices of Journals by Subject 1972 to 1980   122

48   Turnover and Pre-Tax Profit for Five Commercial Publishers
       1977 and 1978. £000's   123

49   Rejection Rate of Papers in a Sample of UK Journals   129

50   Largest UK Journal Publishers as Measured by
       Number of Journals Published   131

51   Journals Scanned by Physics Abstracts According to Publisher Type   131

52   Distribution of Number of Journals Produced by or with Societies
       in the UK   132

53   Subject Areas of Co-operating and Non-Co-operating Societies   133

54   Breakdown of Co-operative Journals by Publisher Type   134

55   Geographical Circulation of 8 Institute of Physics Journals and 56
       Pergamon Journals   144

56   Exports of Journals 1971 - 1977 %   144

57   Trends in Total Number of Subscriptions 1971 - 1977   145

58   Circulation Trends of UK Journals in Different Subject Fields.
       1971 = 100   145

59   Circulation Data for UK Learned Journals Produced by,
       or in Association with, Learned Societies 1979   146

CHAPTER 1

Statistical Overview

INTRODUCTION

In the course of this chapter we will be examining and interpreting three sets of
statistics obtained primarily from government publications. Their biggest drawback
is that they are collected at too high a level of aggregation in that both Census
of Production and <u>Business Monitor</u> statistics refer to a category known as General
Printing and Publishing. In later chapters we will need to examine printing and
publishing as separate categories. Nevertheless government statistics are useful
as a means of obtaining an overview of the publishing industry especially from the
point of view of identifying trends over a long period of time. There is typically
a shorter span of years covered in the tables elsewhere in this book either because
statistics are available only for recent years or because of the particular nature
of the circumstances which they are intended to illustrate. One practice is, however,
commonplace, and that is the conversion of a statistical series originally published
in money terms, that is measured according to the prices ruling in each individual
year, on to a constant price basis, that is measured according to the prices ruling
in some base year. The purpose of this conversion is to take account of inflation
which erodes the real purchasing power of money over time. The Retail Price Index
which has, with certain exceptions, been used to implement this conversion is set
out at the end of the chapter on book prices together with a text explaining its
use.

THE CENSUS OF PRODUCTION

The Size Distribution of Establishments

Census of Production data are available for 1963, 1968, 1970 and annually thereafter.
In this section we will be analysing Minimum List Heading 489 covering General
Printing and Publishing. At a later stage we will be examining financial data which
was supplied by firms to the Price Commission, and also published company accounts.
These latter accounts present especial difficulties because so few large publishers
are completely independent, and there is great variability in the amount of detail
supplied. Census information, on the other hand, is collected at individual establishments whose principal activity can be assigned to a specific minimum list heading.
The size distribution of establishments in M.L.H. 489 appears as Table 1 below. As
can readily be seen the industry operates on a small scale, and we will return to
this matter in the subsequent·chapters covering individual parts of the industry.

TABLE 1   Analysis of Establishments* By Size 1977

Size Group**	Establishments	Enterprises***
1 - 10	6886	6655
11 - 19	1341	1312
20 - 49	1035	997
50 - 99	356	328
100 - 199	165	140
200 - 299	67	59
300 - 399	31	28
400 - 499	15	15
500 - 749	22	21
750 - 999	9	9
1000 - 1499	5	5
1500 and over	4	4
TOTAL	9936	9173

*All UK establishments classified to the industry including
estimates for establishments not making satisfactory returns,
non-response, and employing less than 20 persons.
** Average number employed (full and part-time) during the
year including working proprietors.
*** Some enterprises control establishments in more than
one size group: the sum of the figures for the size groups
therefore exceeds the total for the industry.

Census Data in Money and Real Terms

In Table 2 below a selection of data drawn from Census reports is presented for the
years 1963 to 1977, the most recent year for which detailed information is available.
The structure of the table is based upon, and updates, the earlier work of Wood
(1977). The top half of the table contains data at current prices, and the bottom
half the same data at constant 1970 prices. Gross output broadly represents total
turnover (also incidentally available in Census reports) adjusted to take account
of changes in the stock of finished goods. Net output equals gross output less the
cost of purchases such as materials, and is thus a close approximation to the concept
of value added, although the latter's precise definition of wages, salaries and
other employment costs, plus depreciation, interest charges and net profit before
tax means that its scope is slightly narrower than that of net output. Operatives
are essentially manual workers whereas other employees are essentially white collar.
To these are added working proprietors in order to obtain figures for total employment. Total wages and salaries, however, exclude working proprietors. Net capital
expenditure represents the purchase of construction work, land, buildings, plant,
machinery and vehicles less income received from disposal of the same.

The first ratio, net divided by gross output, broadly represents the industry's
gross margin, and therefore fluctuates according to, for example, relative movements
in material costs and selling prices. Net output per head is the nearest that one

can get to a measure of labour productivity, whereas net output per £ of wages and
salaries indicates whether or not employees are being rewarded for all or part of
their improved productivity in the form of higher rates of pay. Finally, capital
expenditure per head should move broadly in line with net output per head given the
widespread assumption that increased capital intensity goes hand in hand with a rise
in labour productivity.

We will be concerned below with the analysis of the real rather than the money values
in the table. In this particular case the deflators used to convert the top half
of the table into the bottom half are taken from the National Income and Expenditure
'Blue Book' 1977 as follows. Gross output is deflated by figures for Total Final
Expenditure; net output by figures for Gross Domestic Product at Factor Cost; wages
and salaries by figures for Income and Employment; and capital expenditure by figures
for Gross Domestic Fixed Capital Formation. If we turn to the real output series
we can see that both gross and net output grew at almost identical rates between
1963 and 1977, indicating that the real cost of purchases such as materials and fuel
varied very little as a proportion of gross output. By the standards of manufacturing industry in general the growth performance of General Printing and Publishing
was very much middle-of-the-road, since 1 in 6 of the manufacturing industries which
Wood examined grew by at least 100% between 1963 and 1974. The modest growth of
M.L.H. 489 was accompanied, as was true of manufacturing industry in general, by a
decline in numbers employed, although again in typical fashion the decline was primarily in the category of operatives. Indeed white collar employment actually rose
between 1963 and 1977. Overall, therefore, the pattern of employment, like the
pattern of growth, was in no way out of the ordinary, although one must not lose
sight of the fact that General Printing and Publishing is one of the largest employers amongst all of the manufacturing industries, with the result that relatively
small proportional changes in numbers employed have a relatively large absolute
impact.

When one considers the apparently large amounts of material used up in the process
of publishing it is a little surprising to discover that the net to gross output
ratio was one of the highest for all manufacturing industries. Aside from the sharp
increase in 1973 which was itself in part clearly a reaction to the downturn in 1972,
the real ratio remained stable, having the same value in 1976 as in 1968. This
stability was in line with manufacturing industry as a whole, although it was to be
found in few individual industries.

We have already referred to the expectation that net output per head and capital
expenditure per head would move in line with one another. Certainly this has been
the typical experience of industries with either a relatively high or a relatively
low capital expenditure per head. General Printing and Publishing, however, falls
into neither category since it has a rate of investment a little below the average
for manufacturing industry, and year by year variations in the relationship between
these two magnitudes such as we find in the table were fairly typical of industries
whose capital expenditure per head was of approximately average size. As can be
seen in the above table net output per head fell in 1972 and 1975, the former year
being one in which capital expenditure per head rose significantly. The most
alarming fall in the latter magnitude occurred in 1975 as a result of a collapse in
investment. This provides a good indication of the seriousness of the alleged
crisis at that time. Unfortunately we are as yet unable to compare this fall with
the situation in the current crisis.

The rest of the table is essentially concerned with manpower productivity. Between
1963 and 1974, 22 of the 750 manufacturing industries exhibited below average manpower productivity combined with above average wage levels, amongst them General
Printing and Publishing. However, the relationship for this industry was far from
extreme. In all other respects M.L.H. 489 was strictly middle-of-the-road. As
compared to all other manufacturing industries net output per £ wages/salaries was

neither very high nor very low, nor was it rising at above average speed. Real
wages and salaries were very much run-of-the-mill, and in neither employment category were they either rising or falling at an unusual rate. The best year for
operatives was 1973 closely followed by 1977, whereas for white collar workers the
1973 figure was slightly below that of 1971 with 1977 some distance behind. If we
examine changes in productivity we find that noticeably more was translated into
higher real wages and salaries in 1973 than in 1977. Clearly operatives in General
Printing did not do as well as those in newspaper publishing. Over the entire
seventeen year period real wages and salaries rose by 27% for employees as a whole,
but by only 5% between 1970 and 1977 as a result of the no-growth period from 1974
to 1977.

This three year period 1974 to 1977 provides evidence of a significant adjustment
to a crisis of some kind although the radical improvement in real wages and in
capital expenditure during 1977 does indicate the industry's ability to bounce back
once any immediate crisis is past. A final point arising from the table is that
whereas we have already noted that the proportion of total employment consisting
of operatives fell almost continuously throughout the 1970's, not merely was this
proportion never either very high or very low as compared to the rest of manufacturing industry, but its rate of decline was close to the average for all industry.

                    TURNOVER

Definitions

Until recently the only comprehensive data on publishing turnover was to be found
on a quarterly basis in the **Business Monitor** series, among which PQ 489 covers
General Printing and Publishing. Until the end of 1972 coverage was of establishments in the UK, having a turnover of £10,000 or more, classified to Minimum List
Heading 489 of the Standard Industrial Classification by virtue of their main business activity, viz. all printing and publishing other than the printing and publishing of newspapers and periodicals. These establishments were thought to account
for 70% of the employment of all establishments classified to the industry. Turnover figures in Table 3 below also include the sales of principal products of
Minimum List Heading 489 by establishments, classified to other industries, which
are contributing to the quarterly inquiries. From the beginning of 1973 the
criterion for inclusion was changed to one of employment of 25 or more persons, or,
in the case of book publishers, to one of employment of 6 or more persons. At the
beginning of 1978 the employment threshold for book publishers was also raised from
6 to 25. Table 3 expresses turnover at current prices, whereas Table 4 converts
these figures on to a constant 1971 price basis.

Several general observations are in order. In the first place it must be noted
that years 1973 to 1977 inclusive are to some degree incompatible with both earlier
and later years. The significance of the change in 1973 was probably small, but it
has been estimated that had the 1978 change not taken place, 1978 turnover figures
would have been some 10% higher than reported. In the second place it may be argued
that the division of school textbooks into hardback and paperback is somewhat arbitrary. Finally it must be observed that over a quarter of all turnover is labelled
'other' which is none too helpful for analytical purposes.

Trends in Real Turnover

If we concentrate on 'real' rather than on money turnover we can see that it rose
by 6% in 1972, by $6\frac{1}{2}$% in 1974, by 2% in 1976, and by 4% in 1978. However the reductions during the odd-numbered years resulted in an overall rise of $12\frac{1}{4}$%, or $1\frac{1}{2}$%
per annum. If we assume that 1979 figures should be 10% higher in money terms in

TABLE 2 Output, Employment, Wages and Salaries, and Capital Expenditure

	Total Gross Output	Total Net Output	Total Employees Operatives	Total Employees Other	Total Employment	Total Wages/ Salaries	Total Net Capital Spending	Net ÷ Gross Output	Net Output Per Head	Net Output Per £ Wages	Wages/Salaries Per Employee Operatives	Wages/Salaries Per Employee Other	Capital Spending Per Head
	£ mill	£ mill	000s	000s	000s	£ mill	£ mill	%	£	£	£	£	£
1963	483.1	286.8	168.9	50.3	228.6	169.5	24.4	59.4	1255	1.693	728	924	107
1968	668.4	386.6	152.4	52.4	212.7	216.9	29.5	57.8	1817	1.782	1003	1221	139
1970	810.3	476.8	152.8	56.5	213.9	269.7	31.4	58.8	2229	1.786	1221	1471	147
1971	924.8	529.8	147.0	55.8	211.1	299.9	31.1	57.3	2509	1.767	1385	1726	147
1972	975.0	552.4	132.1	52.7	192.3	299.6	37.1	56.7	2872	1.844	1544	1816	193
1973	1071.7	656.9	138.2	49.3	194.8	335.6	48.0	61.3	3372	1.957	1705	2031	246
1974	1375.7	812.8	137.6	54.0	204.1	408.6	59.1	59.1	3982	1.989	2065	2430	308
1975	1597.8	935.4	139.7	52.7	200.2	504.2	57.8	58.5	4673	1.855	2481	2988	289
1976	1980.2	1155.7	133.5	58.1	199.5	581.0	67.6	58.4	5792	1.989	2871	3404	339
1977	2384.7	1351.7	126.8	58.6	193.7	638.6	98.2	56.7	6977	2.116	3305	3747	507

TABLE 2 Data Adjusted to Constant 1970 Prices

	Total Gross Output	Total Net Output	Total Employees Operatives	Total Employees Other	Total Employment	Total Wages/ Salaries	Total Net Capital Spending	Net ÷ Gross Output	Net Output Per Head	Net Output Per £ Wages	Wages/Salaries Per Employee Operatives	Wages/Salaries Per Employee Other	Capital Spending Per Head
	£ mill	£ mill	000s	000s	000s	£ mill	£ mill	%	£	£	£	£	£
1963	662.7	379.4	168.9	50.3	228.6	233.1	31.3	57.2	1660	1.627	1002	1272	137
1968	752.7	432.0	152.4	52.4	212.7	249.3	33.1	57.4	2030	1.733	1153	1404	156
1970	810.3	476.8	152.8	56.5	213.9	269.7	31.4	58.8	2229	1.786	1221	1471	147
1971	856.3	480.3	147.0	55.8	211.1	273.9	28.5	56.1	2274	1.754	1265	1576	135
1972	845.6	454.3	132.1	52.7	192.3	250.3	31.4	53.7	2361	1.815	1289	1517	163
1973	841.8	498.4	138.2	49.3	194.8	257.6	34.8	59.2	2558	1.934	1308	1559	178
1974	898.5	528.8	137.6	54.0	204.1	255.5	35.8	58.8	2591	2.070	1291	1520	187
1975	840.5	473.4	139.7	52.7	200.2	239.2	28.2	56.3	2365	1.979	1178	1418	141
1976	892.8	512.7	133.5	58.1	199.5	246.5	28.0	57.4	2570	2.080	1218	1444	141
1977	945.9	538.5	126.8	58.6	193.7	251.7	37.1	56.9	2780	2.139	1303	1477	192

Source: Census of Production

TABLE 3 Sales and Receipts of UK General Printers and Publishers. £ million

Category of Book	1971	1972	1973	1974	1975	1976	1977	1978	1979
Hardback									
Bibles	5.20	5.25	4.48	5.20	7.06	9.67	10.34	10.09	8.83
School Textbooks	16.03	16.82	19.71	22.88	26.19	28.49	30.44	34.35	37.08
Technical and Scientific	34.49	38.75	37.59	45.42	49.14	54.88	60.82	65.27	73.16
Fiction, Literature and Classics	23.00	24.56	28.03	30.93	39.34	46.33	53.83	58.19	59.83
Children's	15.07	17.22	17.64	23.59	26.88	27.05	28.27	32.02	36.59
Other	34.06	39.18	45.37	58.16	73.11	88.14	103.51	126.09	146.76
Paperback									
School Textbooks	14.41	17.25	17.17	22.64	29.13	38.70	48.80	50.41	55.82
Technical and Scientific	5.37	6.50	7.50	9.15	11.90	13.65	16.08	17.27	21.01
Fiction, Literature and Classics	18.58	21.16	23.10	30.11	40.99	49.32	56.05	66.59	69.17
Children's	4.37	5.72	7.02	8.84	10.28	11.39	11.84	12.29	14.68
Other (incl. Bibles)	9.99	12.83	13.95	14.94	18.14	25.57	32.21	32.53	38.56
Total	180.59	205.27	221.56	271.85	332.18	393.20	452.19	505.10	561.49
Royalties	6.04	6.26	8.54	9.66	10.23	15.10	14.85	16.33	18.89
TOTAL	186.63	211.53	230.10	281.51	342.41	408.30	467.04	521.43	580.38

Source: Department of Industry. Business Monitor PQ489

TABLE 4 Sales and Receipts of UK General Printers and Publishers. £ million at 1971 Prices

Category of Book	1971	1972	1973	1974	1975	1976	1977	1978	1979
Hardback									
Bibles	5.20	4.90	3.83	3.87	4.23	4.95	4.59	4.14	3.19
School Textbooks	16.03	15.70	16.85	17.01	15.68	14.58	13.50	14.08	13.40
Technical and Scientific	34.49	36.20	32.13	33.77	29.43	28.09	26.98	26.75	26.41
Fiction, Literature and Classics	23.00	22.93	23.96	23.00	23.56	23.71	23.88	23.85	21.59
Children's	15.07	16.08	15.08	17.54	16.10	13.84	12.54	13.12	13.21
Other	34.06	36.58	38.78	43.24	43.78	45.11	45.92	51.68	52.98
Paperback									
School Textbooks	14.41	16.11	14.68	16.83	17.44	19.86	21.65	20.66	20.15
Technical and Scientific	5.37	6.07	6.41	6.80	7.13	6.99	7.13	7.08	7.58
Fiction, Literature and Classics	18.58	19.76	19.74	22.39	24.55	25.24	24.86	27.29	24.97
Children's	4.37	5.34	6.00	6.57	6.16	5.83	5.25	5.04	5.30
Other (incl. Bibles)	9.99	11.98	11.92	11.11	10.86	13.08	14.29	13.35	13.92
Total	180.59	191.66	189.37	202.12	198.91	201.23	200.61	207.00	202.70
Royalties	6.04	5.84	7.30	7.18	6.13	7.73	6.59	6.74	6.82
TOTAL	186.63	197.50	196.67	209.30	205.04	208.96	207.20	213.74	209.52

Source: Table 3 as amended by author to take account of inflation

order to be consistent with earlier years this raises the average annual rate of growth to just under 3%. Overall the picture would appear to be incompatible with the generally accepted notion of crisis despite the industry's fondness for this expression.

Taking paperback sales as a proportion of total turnover we find that there was a steady increase from around 29% in 1971 to over 36% in 1977. 1978, however, saw this figure fall marginally to $35\frac{1}{2}$% where it remained in 1979. If we examine individual paperback categories we find that the only category which was significantly out of line taking the period as a whole was that of children's books. This is compatible with evidence shown elsewhere that the prices of most children's books failed to keep pace with inflation more or less consistently throughout the 1970's. However this was the only paperback category where the improvement in terms of real turnover was markedly below 40% over the eight year period. Thus it comes as no surprise to discover that only one category of hardback books, namely 'other' showed an improvement in real turnover. The increase in the 'other' category was, however, larger than for any paperback category. Unfortunately this category is too ill-defined to provide an obvious explanation for this result. It may be that an increasing proportion of hardback books published during the 1970's could not readily be assigned to the other categories, although there is no evidence to support this hypothesis in the case of paperbacks where growth in the 'other' category was not outstanding. One probable contributory factor was that this category includes most reference books the prices of which rose faster than for any other book category between 1974 and 1979.

The reduction in real turnover of the other four hardback categories was fairly uniform, being most marked for 'technical and scientific' until 1978 and for 'bibles' when the 1979 results are taken into account. The former point is particularly interesting because the Price Commission found that the profitability of technical books (on its own definition) was unreasonably high between 1975 and 1978 and one would not have expected to find this linked with falling real turnover. Over the period 1974 to 1977 the decline in the 'school textbook' and 'childrens' categories was also severe. Taking hardback and paperback sales together the 'school textbook' category grew slowly as did 'fiction, literature and classics'. On the other hand 'childrens' books declined slightly and 'technical and scientific' more noticeably. Raising 1979 figures by 10% would leave this latter category as the only one in decline taking the period as a whole.

Exports

In view of the unusually significant role of exports in the publishing industry it is appropriate to move on next to examine information on exports on the same basis as above. Before doing this, however, it is helpful to examine the proportion of total turnover which is exported year by year, and this is presented as Table 5 below. From this table it would appear that the proportion of total turnover exported has not fluctuated all that much during the 1970's, the highest figure being less than 10% greater than the lowest if 1979 is excluded. Historically the export percentage was only some 30% during the early post-war years, but by 1969 it had risen to 47%. Experience in the 1970's gave the impression that an equilibrium level had been reached but the 1979 figure casts doubt upon this conclusion. It is further alleged that recent export figures are increasingly understated due to a rising number of books produced, sold and distributed by overseas subsidiaries set up or acquired, or by overseas companies in which a controlling interest is held. In support of this hypothesis it is argued that in 1975 the Business Monitor index of general printing and publishing production was lower than in 1973 whereas the number of books published was noticeably higher; that financial reports of publish-

TABLE 5 Proportion of Total Receipts Earned by Exports %

Category of Book	1971	1972	1973	1974	1975	1976	1977	1978	1979
Hardback									
Bibles	75.3	72.1	64.0	61.1	60.0	65.0	64.1	62.1	55.2
School Textbooks	38.7	38.1	40.4	41.0	38.5	41.8	43.0	39.8	40.3
Technical and Scientific	51.4	45.4	45.0	50.1	45.9	47.1	43.0	43.4	41.8
Fiction, Literature and Classics	31.5	31.0	33.2	28.0	26.9	31.4	30.9	33.8	19.9
Children's	29.2	24.3	25.4	28.9	27.3	27.0	30.9	30.3	23.4
Other	32.5	28.1	33.6	30.8	29.1	32.3	34.1	28.8	26.0
Paperback									
School Textbooks	44.0	43.5	39.9	46.0	44.1	50.1	55.1	47.4	46.9
Technical and Scientific	38.2	36.5	33.8	33.4	37.5	42.5	45.0	44.1	43.5
Fiction, Literature and Classics	37.8	35.9	40.9	40.1	39.2	38.3	39.5	38.3	34.4
Children's	24.8	21.1	23.4	27.4	26.7	26.5	26.0	26.2	28.1
Other (incl. Bibles)	21.0	17.1	20.4	20.0	20.5	24.2	24.8	27.3	25.9
Total	38.1	34.8	36.2	36.7	34.9	37.6	38.5	36.7	32.5
Royalties	52.6	49.8	52.6	56.7	57.0	59.8	56.1	49.1	49.6
TOTAL	38.6	35.2	36.8	37.3	35.6	38.4	39.0	37.1	33.0
Plus Exports by Principal Retail and Wholesale Booksellers	43.2	39.9	41.7	42.4	40.5	43.0	43.7	40.6	37.1

Source: Department of Industry. Business Monitor PQ489

ers in 1975 indicated a switch from home to export markets; and that profitability was good in 1976 despite a very modest improvement in real turnover* The Publishers' Association and The Bookseller estimated in 1977 that total turnover in 1976 was understated by 25%. On that basis the 1976 export percentage rises from 43% to 54%, which suggests that publishers' export drive did not slacken during the 1970's.

With this proviso in mind we can see from the table that sales of bibles, school textbooks and books for higher education are particularly dependent upon export

*See The Bookseller (July 17th, 1976) and (June 25th, 1977)

markets, a none too surprising discovery when one remembers how widely dispersed
is the English-speaking world. However it is also clear that the fortunes of every
category of book are heavily dependent upon export markets, a matter to which we
will again turn our attention in a later section.

In Table 6 are to be found details of real turnover in each category on a comparable
basis to Table 4. Once again 1978 and 1979 were not wholly compatible with earlier
years. Unlike figures for total turnover, figures for export turnover did not rise
in even-numbered years and fall in odd-numbered years but followed a random pattern
peaking in 1977 and declining sharply in 1979 back to the 1972 level. Paperback
exports rose as a proportion of all exports from $27\frac{1}{2}\%$ in 1971 to 39% in 1977, fell
back slightly to 37% in 1978, but rose again to 40% in 1979. Most individual
paperback categories did well in averaging at least 6% growth per annum, with the
exception of childrens' books where the growth was a more modest $4\frac{1}{2}\%$ per annum,
and of fiction if 1979 is included although progress was very good up to 1978.
Sales of 'technical and scientific' books were especially buoyant, as were sales in
the 'other' category. This latter category was, however, one of only two categories
to do better in 1978 than in 1977 and only two different categories did better in
1979 as compared to 1978, although raising 1978 and 1979 figures by 10% makes things
look noticeably healthier. The overall picture for hardback exports was much less
happy. Only two categories showed any improvement over the period 1971 to 1978,
although 1978 was not too bad a year except for sales of bibles, and only one category was higher in 1979 than in 1971. Given relatively high rates of inflation
in the UK one would have expected some switching by overseas customers from hardbacks to paperbacks. But if we combine hardbacks with paperbacks this still leaves
all categories bar school textbooks with a negative growth rate although the picture
is much healthier if 1979 is excluded. Furthermore if exports are as seriously
under-reported as was suggested above then one must be careful not to be too pess-
imistic about categories identified in the Business Monitor as being in decline
unless there is evidence elsewhere to support this viewpoint.

The Home Market

In the home market annual variations in total real turnover were also rather erratic.
The most notable feature was that whereas the export market suffered after 1977, the
home market achieved record levels both in 1978 and in 1979. If we combine hardback
and paperback sales in each category we discover that whereas 'technical and scientific' declined overall and 'children's' remained static, the 'other' category rose
by 60% and, more interestingly, 'fiction etc' rose by 23%. Thus although this
latter category is in difficulties in export markets, it is somewhat ironic in the
light of the much heralded death of fiction that it should be responsible for so
much of the prosperity of the home market.

As a proportion of total home market turnover paperbacks rose fairly steadily from
30% in 1971 to a peak of 35% in 1977, but fell back to 34% in 1978 and to 33% in
1979. Every individual paperback category improved over the period as a whole
although in two cases, 'technical and scientific' and 'children's', the peak year
was 1974 after which in the latter case it was more or less downhill all the way.
The performance of 'school textbooks' and 'fiction etc' during 1978 and 1979 was,
all things considered, especially meritorious, and as a consequence these two categories showed the highest rates of growth over the period as a whole, although
only in the latter category was the rate above 5% per year on average.

Of the hardback categories three declined between 1971 and 1979 and only one, namely
'other' grew significantly. Somewhat curiously the latter's growth was especially
rapid during 1978 and 1979 although these years were by no means as bad in general
as one would have expected with 'fiction etc' also peaking in 1979. Also somewhat
surprisingly the peak year for 'technical and scientific' was as early as 1972 and

TABLE 6 Export Sales and Receipts of UK General Printers and Publishers. £ million at 1971 Prices

Category of Book	1971	1972	1973	1974	1975	1976	1977	1978	1979
Hardback									
Bibles	3.92	3.54	2.45	2.37	2.57	3.20	2.94	2.57	1.76
School Textbooks	6.20	5.99	6.81	6.97	6.57	6.08	5.81	5.60	5.40
Technical and Scientific	17.74	16.42	14.47	16.92	16.02	13.24	11.60	11.60	11.05
Fiction, Literature and Classics	7.25	7.10	7.95	6.44	7.08	7.44	7.39	8.07	4.29
Childrens'	4.40	3.90	3.83	5.06	4.38	3.75	3.88	3.97	3.10
Other	11.07	10.28	13.05	13.32	11.72	14.56	15.68	14.90	13.75
Paperback									
School Textbooks	6.34	7.01	5.85	7.75	7.79	9.92	11.93	9.80	9.46
Technical and Scientific	2.05	2.22	2.17	2.27	2.66	2.93	3.21	3.12	3.30
Fiction, Literature and Classics	7.02	7.09	8.07	8.98	9.61	9.66	9.81	10.46	9.58
Childrens'	1.08	1.13	1.41	1.80	1.66	1.57	1.36	1.32	1.49
Other (incl. Bibles)	2.09	2.05	2.43	2.22	2.15	3.16	3.55	3.65	3.61
Total	68.81	66.73	68.48	74.10	72.21	75.50	77.16	75.06	65.79
Royalties	3.18	2.91	3.84	4.07	3.60	4.63	3.70	3.31	3.38
TOTAL	71.99	69.64	72.32	78.17	75.81	80.13	80.86	78.37	69.17

Source: Department of Industry. Business Monitor PQ489

TABLE 7   Home Sales and Receipts of UK General Printers and Publishers. £ million at 1971 Prices

Category of Book	1971	1972	1973	1974	1975	1976	1977	1978	1979
Hardback									
Bibles	1.28	1.36	1.38	1.50	1.66	1.75	1.65	1.57	1.43
School Textbooks	9.83	9.71	10.04	10.04	9.11	8.50	7.69	8.48	8.00
Technical and Scientific	16.75	19.78	17.66	16.85	13.41	14.85	15.38	15.15	15.36
Fiction, Literature and Classics	15.75	15.83	16.01	16.56	16.48	16.27	16.49	15.78	17.30
Children's	10.67	12.18	11.25	12.48	11.72	10.09	8.66	9.15	10.11
Other	22.99	26.30	25.73	29.92	32.06	30.55	30.24	36.78	39.23
Paperback									
School Textbooks	8.07	9.10	8.83	9.08	9.65	9.94	9.72	10.86	10.69
Technical and Scientific	3.32	3.85	4.24	4.53	4.47	4.06	3.92	3.96	4.28
Fiction, Literature and Classics	11.56	12.67	11.67	13.41	14.94	15.58	15.05	16.83	16.39
Children's	3.29	4.21	4.59	4.77	4.50	4.26	3.89	3.72	3.81
Other (incl. Bibles)	7.90	9.93	9.49	8.89	8.71	9.92	10.74	9.68	10.31
Total	111.78	124.93	120.89	128.02	126.70	125.73	123.45	131.94	136.91
Royalties	2.86	2.93	3.46	3.11	2.53	3.10	2.89	3.43	3.44
TOTAL	114.64	127.86	124.35	131.13	129.23	128.83	126.34	135.37	140.35

Source: Department of Industry. Business Monitor PQ489

for 'school textbooks' it was 1973. It would appear, therefore, that whereas the heyday for hardback sales in institutional markets is but a distant memory, there is a surprisingly bright future for hardbacks in other markets.

PUBLISHERS' ASSOCIATION SALES STATISTICS

In the summer of 1977 the Publishers' Association decided to undertake a study of sales statistics complementary to that undertaken by the Department of Industry.

TABLE 8   Annual Cumulation - Subject Analysis. Net Revenue. £ million

Type of Book	Home			Export			Total		
	1978	1977	% change	1978	1977	% change	1978	1977	% change
1.School									
Primary	11.0	9.1	20.2	4.2	6.1	-32.1	15.1	15.3	- 0.9
Secondary	19.0	15.8	20.6	13.0	13.0	Nil	32.0	28.8	11.3
Non-Book	2.4	2.2	7.3	0.4	0.3	23.5	2.7	2.5	9.1
E.L.T.	2.4	1.9	27.7	12.4	10.7	16.4	14.8	12.6	18.1
2.University									
Science/Tech.	8.7	7.1	22.5	10.0	8.2	22.2	18.7	15.3	22.4
Medicine	4.3	3.7	18.6	6.5	5.6	17.1	10.9	9.2	17.7
Business/Ind.	2.4	2.2	10.2	2.7	2.3	17.8	5.1	4.5	14.1
Law	8.5	7.0	21.0	2.6	2.5	4.9	11.1	9.5	16.8
Humanities/ Soc. Sci.	6.1	6.7	- 9.9	8.1	7.3	10.9	14.2	14.0	1.0
Journals	7.1	5.7	25.2	6.0	4.7	28.6	13.1	10.3	27.1
3.Mass Mkt. Paperback									
Children's Fiction	5.0	4.2	17.6	1.7	1.5	15.0	6.7	5.7	16.9
Children's Non-Fict.	0.8	0.7	16.7	0.2	0.2	-14.4	1.0	0.9	9.9
Adult Fict.	22.1	16.5	34.0	14.6	12.0	22.5	36.8	28.5	29.2
Adult Non-Fict.	7.5	7.2	4.6	4.6	4.3	8.2	12.1	11.4	5.9
4.Specialised									
Encycs./Dicts.	9.4	7.7	22.5	3.8	2.9	31.5	13.1	10.5	25.0
Atlases	1.5	1.1	33.3	0.3	0.2	17.4	1.7	1.3	30.6
Bibles etc.	3.1	3.3	- 6.1	1.4	1.2	12.4	4.4	4.5	- 1.0
Other Relig.	2.4	2.3	6.1	1.7	1.5	8.4	4.1	3.8	7.0
5.General									
Child. Fict.	7.8	6.1	27.7	4.2	3.8	8.7	12.0	9.9	20.4
Children's Non-Fict.	3.6	2.0	80.4	1.3	0.9	43.6	4.9	2.9	68.8
Adult Fict.	12.6	10.3	23.1	3.2	3.0	6.9	15.9	13.3	19.4
Adult Non-Fict.	42.7	33.1	29.0	15.2	14.4	5.9	57.9	47.4	22.0
TOTAL	190.3	155.7	22.3	118.0	106.5	10.8	308.4	262.2	17.6

The first fruits of this exercise, entitled the Statistics Collection Scheme and Business Monitor, appeared in October 1979 in the form of a series of tables which compared 1977 net revenue with that of 1978 on a quarterly basis for 22 categories of books. Table 8 above contains the cumulated annual data for 1977 and 1978.

The data was supplied by 71 core members of the PA accounting for nearly 90% of the turnover of UK books, although only a proportion of these publishers are active in any individual subject category*. The 22 subject categories are divided into five groups, four of which correspond to the main divisions of the PA. It was felt that the Business Monitor categories were either too broad, too vague or too rigid, and that the PA categories were a better reflection of the scope of current UK publishing. The total net revenue in 1978 of £308 million represents approximately 60% of the equivalent Business Monitor figure of £510 million, so that conclusions drawn from the PA figures can be considered to be representative of UK publishing as a whole. The percentage changes in the table must be treated with caution until such time as data are available covering a period of several years. Nevertheless, the overall picture in 1978 was fairly promising and indeed was rather better than the 12.8% improvement recorded by the Business Monitor. Tertiary education was generally buoyant as were paperback adult fiction and hardback adult non-fiction.

However, as also shows up in the Business Monitor figures, export sales only just kept up with inflation. The reasons for this can be found by examination of Table 9 below where export sales are split up into twelve regions.

TABLE 9 Annual Cumulation - Quarterly Regional Analysis. Net Revenue.
         £ million

REGION	1978	1977	% Change
Western Europe (excl. UK)	24.1	20.4	18.3
Eastern Europe	1.5	1.4	6.5
East and Central Africa	2.5	2.4	2.3
Western Africa	14.2	16.7	-14.8
Southern Africa	6.2	5.8	6.5
Middle East and North Africa	6.3	5.2	21.6
Caribbean	3.6	3.3	8.0
Latin America	2.9	2.4	25.3
North America	20.1	18.2	10.5
Indian Sub-Continent	3.8	3.4	11.8
East and South East Asia	9.3	7.7	21.8
Australasia and Oceania	22.6	18.9	20.1
Unidentified Sales	6.7	6.7	0.3
TOTAL	118.0	106.5	10.8

Source: PA Statistics Collection Scheme and Business Monitor

*For an introduction to the Scheme see Graham (1978b)

The table includes books published in the UK for exclusive use in other countries and all books imported into the UK for resale or for re-export, but excludes books published by British-owned companies outside the UK and subsidiary rights sales such as to book clubs. Over half of the export regions showed real gains in 1978, most notably Western Europe and Australasia. Nevertheless the overall increase was disappointing, and the important market of Western Africa showed serious signs of malaise, a problem reflected in Table 8 in the severe downturn in export sales of primary school publications.

CONSUMERS' EXPENDITURE

Information on consumers' expenditure can be found in the National Income and Expenditure 'Blue Book'. Selected information is presented in Table 10 below in the form of series of real index numbers.

TABLE 10   Consumers' Expenditure at Constant 1975 Prices.   £ million

	1969	1970	1971	1972	1973	1974	1975	1976	1977	1978
Books	100	108	121	138	138	143	148	144	135	142
Magazines	100	99	97	97	97	90	82	77	76	76
Newspapers	100	97	95	97	96	93	89	86	86	85
Cinema	100	89	82	71	63	66	59	50	48	56
Other Entertainment	100	100	106	121	135	151	162	178	181	192
Misc. Recreational	100	108	113	129	147	157	157	158	157	165
Total Consumers' Expenditure	100	103	106	112	117	115	113	114	113	119

If we compare the series for the three types of reading matter we can see at once that not merely has the book series risen while the others have fallen, but books have done roughly twice as well as magazines and newspapers over the past decade. Progress has been patchy, it is true, but these figures prove the falsity of the oft-heard assertion that the general public is turning away from books in large numbers in favour of other forms of entertainment. What appears to be the case is that expenditure on entertainment other than the cinema, and primarily one presumes on television, has risen faster than expenditure on books as one would expect, but not at the expense of book sales. The series on total consumers' expenditure shows that the general public has increased its real expenditure on books much faster than on competing goods and services in general. The prospects for further growth in the book series are obviously limited, and some decline in the series is to be expected for a year or two. Nevertheless the figures show the last so-called crisis to be more imaginary than real, so one may reasonably expect the book industry to weather the current difficulties rather better than one is being led to believe in many quarters.

CHAPTER 2

Publishing

INTRODUCTION

In this chapter are gathered together a disparate number of sections which shed
light upon the operations of book publishers in the UK. The primary concern is to
examine the key economic variables which are common to all industries. To this end
we begin by assessing the degree of competition within the industry concluding with
an attempt to measure concentration. Subsequently we move on to examine costs,
prices and profits, digressing where necessary to take a more detailed look at a
particularly interesting issue such as the royalty system for rewarding authors.
This then leads on naturally to an assessment of how publishers perform as reflected
in key financial ratios. The latter part of the chapter consists primarily of an
overview of a selected number of publishing categories such as technical books and
fiction. This limited selection reflects the cause of brevity rather than any implied assumption that other publishing categories are of insufficient importance to
warrant inclusion. The chapter concludes with a critique of the Price Commission
Report which if nothing else stirred the publishing industry into a phase of long
overdue self-examination.

COMPETITION IN PUBLISHING

We will have cause to refer not merely to publishing specifically but to all areas
of the publishing industry as competitive. For competition to occur several conditions must be satisfied, namely that new firms can enter the industry without
serious hindrance; that the economies of large-scale operation are not so great as
to render small-scale operation uneconomic; and that individual firms do not have
a persistent controlling interest in distinct segments of the overall market. On
the first point little need be said. Publishing, unlike printing, is not a capital-
intensive process, and it is extremely common for individuals or small groups of
staff to resign from a major publishing house in order to start up their own imprint.
There are nearly two thousand publishers in existence of whom the majority are small
entrepreneurial organisations. Indeed, and leading on to the second point, there
are positive advantages in being small, the main ones being that:
(1) overheads can be kept to a minimum especially where the publisher operates out
     of his own premises using members of his family as his staff
(2) the entrepreneur can concentrate on specialist markets in which he can develop
     greater expertise than any one individual in a larger publishing house
(3) The entrepreneur may be able to sell direct to his customers thereby simultan-
     eously holding down his prices and raising his profit margin.

However, it is by no means easy to remain small-scale if publishing is to provide an entrepreneur with his primary source of income. This is because each individual title has a limited sales-life and must be replaced by a new title as soon as sales begin to fall away if the entrepreneur's income is to be maintained. Thus a back-list very quickly builds up·which may provide a useful steady stream of income but which cannot be a substitute for a successful frontlist if the firm is to survive. Unfortunately the process whereby a list is built up brings problems in its wake. The publisher will, for example, have to tie up increasing amounts of capital in the maintenance of his backlist. He will need proper warehousing space. He will need to improve his channels of distribution. Furthermore he may be obliged to move out into markets in which his expertise is limited because of a shortage of publishable material in his original specialism.

Clearly this growth phase is critical for the continued success of the firm and it is during this phase that the entrepreneurial house may find it necessary to merge with an established house in order, for example, to obtain a guaranteed source of finance for expansion. Those entrepreneurs who survive the growth phase will eventually join the ranks of the large diversified publishing houses. Such houses can obtain economies of scale because, for example,
(1) they can bulk-purchase materials such as paper, and services such as printing capacity
(2) they can offer relatively high salaries to talented staff
(3) they have direct access to export markets through wholly-owned subsidiaries
(4) they have access to overdraft facilities and possibly to equity capital
(5) they are protected from the possibility of liquidation by virtue of their ability to cross-subsidise should any one area get into severe difficulties

Economies of Scale

Economies of scale, however, tend not to give the diversified publishing house a significant advantage over the entrepreneurial house. A major factor here is that management must deal with large numbers of individual titles, each of which absorbs a roughly equivalent amount of management time. Thus an editor, say, in a divers-ified house cannot be expected to be noticeably more productive than his entrepren-eurial equivalent.

The advantage of guaranteed access to printing capacity might lead one to suppose that a diversified house could maximise this advantage by setting up its own printing works. In practice publisher-printers are few on the ground, and, as the recent troubles of Wm. Collins seem to indicate, vertical integration in the industry does not have a lot to commend it. In fact, although a diversified house can obtain a quantity discount from printers, an entrepreneurial house may be able to obtain the lowest prices as a result of its ability to slot its work into any spare capacity which a printer may have available at short notice.

Another area in which a diversified house would appear superficially to have an advantage is to do with its ability to attract commercial manuscripts by virtue of its established reputation. At times this is undoubtedly the case. However, many smaller houses have the highest reputation in the fields in which they specialise, and they may offer more personal contact or better royalties both to aspiring authors and to those who are disenchanted with their treatment at the hands of diversified houses where editors come and go with great frequency.

Finally, it may be argued that a diversified house should be able to obtain consid-erable economies in distribution as a result, for example, of the bulking of orders from booksellers. The major publishers' warehouses are not, however, generally regarded in the trade as models of efficiency for reasons explained further on in this book, and a small publisher may provide a more efficient service by operating out of cheap rented storerooms using labour-intensive methods of despatch.

Monopoly power

The third condition for competition to exist namely, that individual firms do not
have a persistent controlling interest in distinct segments of the overall market,
raises a number of interesting issues. We have already observed that a publisher
cannot afford to rest on his laurels even if he has a comparatively successful
record for producing bestsellers. Since the bestsellers cannot be predicted with
confidence it is necessary for a publisher to produce a range of titles, each of
which, whether successful or not in practice, therefore contributes to the continued existence of the imprint. It is clearly somewhat inaccurate to say that publishers produce more and more books because the public has expressed a demand for
them, since although there is a known demand for books in general, it is the exception rather than the rule for there to be a known demand for a particular title.
Thus it is extremely difficult, though by no means impossible, for a publisher to
ensure that his titles in a particular field will continue to elicit a strong customer response over a period of years.

It is important to remember in this context that even bestsellers typically exhibit
a sales pattern which rises sharply to a peak within a matter of months after publication and then goes into steady decline. Furthermore, where a particular field
shows above-average profitability an increasing number of publishers are going to
examine the possibilities for muscling in on established imprints by the use of
such expedients as outbidding the latter for paperback rights. Our overall conclusion must therefore be that whereas a publisher can influence a particular field
of publishing by virtue of his monopoly vested in an individual title, this is
wholly insufficient for him to maintain control over a particular field of publishing other than in the very short term.

As we can see the tenor of these arguments is such as to suggest that we should
expect to find entrepreneurial houses co-existing happily alongside much larger-
scale operations. Since virtually nothing is known about the size distribution
of firms in publishing it is necessary at this juncture to provide some statistics
which we have chosen to derive, for the reasons stated below, from available data
on the number of new books published.

TITLES PUBLISHED

Statistics relating to the total number of books published in the UK during the
past three decades appear as Table 11 below which is based upon entries in The
Bookseller. Between 1949 and 1959 the total number of books increased by 21.5%;
between 1959 and 1969 by 56.6%; and between 1969 and 1979 by 29.5%. The overall
increase was 146%. Whereas the total fell four times during the 1950's and three
times during the 1970's, the 1960's was a decade of continuous growth. The figures
therefore suggest that the book industry is at least partially recession-proof.
This is particularly apparent when one considers the output of new books which
comprised 76% of total output during the late 1970's compared to 72% during the
late 1950's. However, the extremely high percentages recorded during the mid-1960's
suggest that caution is needed in attempting to interpret this as an ongoing trend.

The figures disguise a rapid expansion of US publishers in the UK. Thus it cannot
be assumed that UK publishing houses have all grown as fast as the overall figure
suggests. The issue of The Bookseller on January 5th, 1980 purports to demonstrate
this point using a random sample of UK publishers, but rather spoils the show by
using figures for the second half of the year only; by including Collins which was
in dire trouble during 1979; and by citing a total figure for O.U.P. in 1979 of

TABLE 11 Titles Published 1950 - 1979

Year	Total	New Books	%	Reprints/ New Editions	%
1950	17,072	11,738	68.8	5,334	31.2
1951	18,066	13,128	72.7	4,938	27.3
1952	18,741	13,313	71.0	5,428	29.0
1953	18,257	12,734	69.8	5,523	30.2
1954	18,188	13,342	73.4	4,846	26.6
1955	19,962	14,192	71.1	5,770	28.9
1956	19,107	13,805	72.3	5,302	27.7
1957	20,719	14,798	71.4	5,921	28.6
1958	22,143	16,172	73.0	5,971	27.0
1959	20,690	15,168	73.3	5,522	26.7
1960	23,783	18,794	79.0	4,989	21.0
1961	24,893	18,487	74.3	6,406	25.7
1962	25,079	18,975	75.7	6,104	24.3
1963	26,023	20,367	78.3	5,656	21.7
1964	26,154	20,894	79.9	5,260	20.1
1965	26,358	21,045	79.9	5,313	20.1
1966	28,883	22,964	79.5	5,919	20.5
1967	29,619	22,559	76.2	7,060	23.8
1968	31,420	22,642	72.1	8,778	27.9
1969	32,393	23,287	71.9	9,106	28.1
1970	33,489	23,512	70.2	9,977	29.8
1971	32,538	23,563	72.4	8,975	27.6
1972	33,140	24,654	74.4	8,486	25.6
1973	35,254	25,698	72.9	9,556	27.1
1974	32,194	24,342	75.6	7,852	24.4
1975	35,608	27,247	76.5	8,361	23.5
1976	34,434	26,207	76.1	8,227	23.9
1977	36,322	27,684	76.2	8,638	23.8
1978	38,766	29,530	76.2	9,236	23.8
1979	41,940	32,854	78.3	9,086	21.7

Source: The Bookseller

344 books when the February 16th issue shows the correct figure to be 480. Table
12 below lists the 100 largest publishers ordered according to the number of new
books published in 1979, with 1978 positions in brackets. As a result of delays

TABLE 12 The 100 Largest Publishers, Ordered According to Number of
New Books Published in 1979 in the UK*

1.	Hale	(1)	51.	Karger	(39)
2.	Academic Press	(2)	52.	Collier-Macmillan	(42)
3.	Oxford U.P.	(4)	53.	Addison	(58)
4.	Pergamon Press	(10)	54.	Octopus	(96)
5.	Macmillan Press	(12)	55.	Cassell	( )
6.	Wiley	(3)	56.	Blackie	(38)
7.	Cambridge U.P.	(5)	57.	Garland	(44)
8.	Collins	(8)	58.	Blackwell	( )
9.	Longmans	(6)	59.	Greenwood Press	( )
10.	Sangam	( )	60.	John Murray	(74)
11.	Hodder	(9)	61.	Stockwell	(56)
12.	Prentice-Hall	(7)	62.	Ward Lock Educational	( )
13.	McGraw-Hill	(18)	63.	New English Library	(54)
14.	Hamlyn	(16)	64.	Heinemann	(43)
15.	Van Nostrand	(45)	65.	Churchill Livingstone	( )
16.	Routledge	(13)	66.	Open U.P.	( )
17.	Batsford	(49)	67.	Johns Hopkins U.P.	(55)
18.	Mills and Boon	(15)	68.	Deutsch	(63)
19.	Edward Arnold	(11)	69.	Harvard U.P.	(87)
20.	Sage Pubns.	(90)	70.	W.H.Freeman	(78)
21.	Macmillan Educational	(27)	71.	Eyre Methuen	(91)
22.	Allen and Unwin	(36)	72.	Houghton-Mifflin	(22)
23.	Hamish Hamilton	(14)	73.	Sphere	(60)
24.	Nelson	(92)	74.	Dent	(80)
25.	Grosset and Dunlap	( )	75.	Yale U.P.	( )
26.	Croom Helm	( )	76.	Futura Pubns.	(88)
27.	Hutchinson	(17)	77.	Chicago U.P.	(68)
28.	Macmillan London	(25)	78.	Usborne	( )
29.	North-Holland	(19)	79.	Mansell	(84)
30.	Elsevier	(30)	80.	Ward Lock	(71)
31.	Heinemann Educational	(24)	81.	Michael Joseph	(73)
32.	Macdonald Educational	(62)	82.	Reidel	( )
33.	W.H.Allen	(21)	83.	Wheaton	( )
34.	Gollancz	(35)	84.	Mosby	(53)
35.	Faber	(28)	85.	Park U.P.	(82)
36.	Pan	(52)	86.	Scarecrow	(46)
37.	California U.P.	(26)	87.	Praeger	( )
38.	Lexington	(23)	88.	Cape	(79)
39.	David and Charles	( )	89.	Wayland	( )
40.	Penguin	(40)	90.	Halsted	(50)
41.	Macdonald and Janes	(28)	91.	Bodley Head	( )
42.	Central Books	(61)	92.	M.I.T. Press	( )
43.	Smithsonian I.P.	( )	93.	B.B.C.	(70)
44.	Harper and Row	(20)	94.	Phaidon	( )
45.	Weidenfeld	(34)	95.	J - K	( )
46.	Pitman	(64)	96.	Dobson	( )
47.	Harvester Press	(86)	97.	Methuen	(65)
48.	Evans Bros.	(81)	98.	Sidgwick and Jackson	(95)
49.	Thames and Hudson	(57)	99.	Harrap	(89)
50.	Corgi	(33)	100.	Butterworth	(77)

*1978 positions given in brackets
Source: Based upon half-yearly figures in The Bookseller

with production in 1978 a considerable number of books appeared in 1979 rather than
in 1978 as originally intended, thus accounting in part for the sharp upturn in
output in 1979. This may have produced one or two of the more significant changes
in position, although the biggest changes tend to be associated with American firms
which suddenly flood the UK market during a six month period and then more or less
disappear. Of these the most prominent example is Sangam which came from nowhere
in 1978 to 10th position in 1979. Equally Kodansha, 31st in 1978, and Rand McNally,
32nd in 1978, failed to merit a listing in 1979.

From 1975 to 1979 inclusive, five firms appeared consistently among the seven largest in terms of new books published. Furthermore, none of the largest ten firms in
1975 fell to a position below 20th in the list during that period. Thus there is
some evidence that large size offers a measure of protection against the forces of
free competition, although the recent experience of Wm. Collins provides a salutary
warning that large size can be accompanied by correspondingly large problems.

THE SIZE DISTRIBUTION OF FIRMS

Measuring size according to the output of new books is somewhat unorthodox, but has
certain obvious virtues. In the first place, although there is no Minimum List
Heading for publishers alone, a fact which makes it very difficult to estimate other
measures of size, statistical data on new books are readily available. In addition
the use of such data produces much more stable results than would be forthcoming
through the use of a more conventional measure of size such as value of sales. This
is because the erratic incidence of bestsellers would cause many firms to rise and
fall in the order in a way which would obscure the significance of those firms in
relation to the industry as a whole. The results of measuring the size distribution
of firms in the manner indicated are set out in Table 13 below for 1978 and 1979.

TABLE 13 Size Distribution of Large* Publishers 1978 and 1979

Number of New Books	Number of Publishers	
	1978	1979
600 - 700	1	2
500 - 600	3	1
400 - 500	0	4
300 - 400	5	6
200 - 300	6	4
100 - 200	46	45
50 - 100	60	60
TOTAL	121	122

*Producing at least 50 new books per year

As can be seen the same number of publishers produced more than 50 new books in
both years despite an overall increase of 11% in the total output of new books in
1979. The only significant change took place at the top end of the distribution
where the number of firms producing more than 400 new books rose from 4 to 7, and
where the dominance achieved by the top 4 firms in 1978 disappeared in 1979, as a

result primarily of a sizeable expansion in the output of Pergamon and Macmillan Press.

In Table 14 below are to be found a number of concentration ratios which measure the proportion of total new book production accounted for by the 3, 10, 50, and 100 largest firms in the industry in 1978 and 1979.

TABLE 14   Concentration Ratios

	1978	1979
3 Firm Concentration Ratio	5.8%	5.6%
10 Firm Concentration Ratio	14.3%	14.7%
50 Firm Concentration Ratio	35.1%	35.1%
100 Firm Concentration Ratio	49.4%	48.8%

No changes of any significance took place during the year in question so these ratios can be taken as a fair reflection of the current structure of the industry. The ratios clearly confirm, despite an element of understatement introduced as a result of certain firms appearing more than once, for example Macmillan, that the structure of the industry is competitive. Indeed publishing is one of the least-concentrated industries in the UK, a country which contains a surprisingly large number of highly-concentrated industries by the standards of comparable industrial economies. There are altogether roughly 2000 publishers in the UK, although not all of them publish in any given year. The 100th largest publisher in 1979 which was Butterworth, produced 64 new books, roughly one-tenth as many as the largest firm, although the great bulk of the remaining 1900 firms produced fewer than 10 books in that year.

THE PUBLISHER'S ROLE

Before coming on to examine the relationship between a publisher's costs and the price of a book, it may be as well to spell out the functions which are performed by a publisher. His first task is to obtain manuscripts in draft form, and if these are not sent to him voluntarily he must persuade potential authors to put pen to paper. He must decide whether the manuscript is worth publishing, and if it is he must advise and guide the author concerning desirable amendments to the draft version. Once the final manuscript has been received he must decide what format is to be employed, how many copies to print, the eventual selling price and the approximate date of publication. He must then purchase the needed printing capacity and issue instructions to the printer. Once the manuscript has been edited and seen through the printing press the bound copies must be stored in his warehouse and despatched in accordance with orders. Controls must be placed upon stock levels and a decision to reprint must be taken where desirable before stocks run out. Finally, contacts must be established with distributors and the media in order to promote sales of the book.

BREAKDOWN OF COSTS

There are numerous ways in which the breakdown of costs associated with publishing can be presented, and the paragraphs which follow are illustrative rather than definitive.

First-Copy Costs

It is common practice in publishing to begin by specifying the so-called first-copy
costs. These costs include those incurred in choosing which manuscript to publish;
origination costs incurred in preparing the manuscript for the printer, selecting
illustrations, designing the jacket, type-setting, proof-reading and correcting;
costing and price fixing; and the payment of advance royalties and research fees.
These costs can be treated as fixed costs because they are incurred prior to the
printing of the book. For this reason the larger the edition the smaller the first-
copy cost borne by each book. Although this obviously militates in favour of long
print runs an offsetting factor is the expense of holding books in stock prior to
being sold which includes both the cost of storage space and the interest charged
on working capital tied up in stock. The optimal size of the print run is therefore determined by the point at which the marginal increase in unit storage cost
exactly equates the marginal reduction in unit first-copy cost. This formula is,
of course, very difficult to apply in practice because so much depends upon the
rate at which stocks are used up, and this can only be estimated in a rough-and-
ready way at the time when the initial print run is fixed.

Manufacturing Costs

The second major category of cost covers materials, printing and binding and is
known as production or manufacturing cost. This is a variable cost because it is
dependent upon the size of the print run. Whereas a publisher can make only minor
savings in the field of first-copy costs, the field of production cost offers more
scope for flexibility in respect of, for example, the combination of printing process, paper quality and type of binding. For this reason a publisher may well do a
series of costings before reaching his final decision on these matters.

The other major category of variable cost is the author's royalty which is custom-
arily expressed as a percentage of retail price. However royalties earned on export
sales are generally expressed as a percentage of the publisher's net receipts because of the much larger discounts which are typically offered on such sales. No
royalty is payable where a book is out of copyright.

Overheads

Most other costs are subsumed under the general category of overheads. These costs
are incurred in producing the publisher's entire list of publications and are allocated to individual books on some agreed, and possible arbitrary, basis. The main
overheads are editorial, warehouse and despatch, advertising and promotion, selling
and interest. It is common in publishing to cross-subsidise, that is to cover the
losses arising from unsuccessful publications with the profits arising from the
successful, which in practice means that the latter bear a disproportionate share
of the burden of overhead recovery. However, all books as a matter of principle
are projected to recover the appropriate share of overheads when prices are fixed,
and the solution to the problem of overhead recovery is often found in the application of a multiplier to production costs. Some idea of how this operates and the
effects upon profitability can be seen by examining Table 15 below where it should
be noted that the term turnover refers to publishers' receipts net of the trade
discount. The range of multipliers used in the table is typical for adult books,
although the multiplier range for school books and children's books varies from
2.5 to 4.

TABLE 15 Costs, Prices and Profits

Trade Discount % Retail Price	Author's Royalty % Retail Price	Office Overhead % Turnover	Unit Production Cost % Retail Price	Retail Price As Multiple Of Production Cost	Net Profit Edition Fully Sold Out % Turnover
30	10	35	25 20 16.7	4 5 6	15.0 22.1 26.9
30	10	40	25 20 16.7	4 5 6	10.0 17.1 21.9
30	12.5	40	25 20 16.7	4 5 6	6.4 13.5 18.3
35	10	35	25 20 16.7	4 5 6	11.1 18.8 23.9
35	10	40	25 20 16.7	4 5 6	6.1 13.8 18.9
35	12.5	40	25 20 16.7	4 5 6	2.3 10.0 15.0
40	7.5	35	25 20 16.7	4 5 6	10.7 19.1 24.7
40	7.5	40	25 20 16.7	4 5 6	5.7 14.1 19.7
40	10	40	25 20 16.7	4 5 6	1.5 9.9 15.5

ROYALTIES

It is traditional to recompense an author for his efforts by means of a royalty expressed as a percentage of retail price. Indeed, it is so traditional that one is extremely hard-pressed to find any explanation for this practice or indeed any consideration of the alternative systems for rewarding authors which are available.

The most curious feature of a royalty payment is that it inevitably creates a conflict between author and publisher with respect to the ideal price for a book. We have observed elsewhere that authors generally consider demand to be elastic whereas publishers generally consider it to be inelastic. However this is not the entire story. It must also be remembered that a publisher is out to make profits and must therefore take account of both price and costs. An author, on the other hand, is indifferent to costs because his rewards are a function of price alone. Thus what he wants is for his publisher to maximise revenue (price times quantity sold) rather than profit. But where demand is elastic revenue is increased through a reduction in price, and an author's tendency to assume that demand is indeed elastic thus leads him to prefer a lower price than his publisher who has in mind the unprofitable consequences of over-production.

A related source of conflict has to do with book promotion. Since book promotion increases cost a publisher not unnaturally requires promotional expenditure to generate an increase in revenue of at least equal size. But publishers are not great optimists in this respect and generally commit very small sums to promoting individual titles. An author, on the other hand, is concerned solely with generating additional sales irrespective of the cost, and can therefore see no limit to the amount of promotional expenditure which will further that aim.

Thus an author typically wants review copies to be spread around like confetti since any review is better than no review where sales are concerned. A publisher, understandably, feels less expansive because he is counting the cost of the operation.

Authors are also greatly annoyed by the practice of paying royalties some six months or so after the end of their publisher's financial year. This common practice means that authors have to wait up to eighteen months to be paid their share of a publisher's sale to a bookseller, during which period the publisher earns interest on that share at the author's expense. There is no obvious reason why publishers should not pay to authors in the middle of each financial year a sum roughly equal to the previous half year's expected royalty, and a further sum at the end of the financial year. Any adjustments due to mis-estimation can then take place at each subsequent half-yearly settlement. Many American publishers pay in this way and may attract authors away from UK publishers because of it. Certainly there is something to be said for a publishers' royalty payment league table in addition to that already in existence to cover delivery times.

There are several other anomalies arising from the royalty system which need not concern us here. The interesting question is whether or not these anomalies are a function of this specific form of author reward or whether they can be overcome by recourse to other systems. It is possible, for example, for an author to assign copyright to a publisher for a lump-sum payment. If the book sells badly the author benefits at the expense of the publisher, and vice versa if it sells well. It may be argued that since neither party is sure of a book's potential this system has the merit of insuring the author against the possibility of earning a negligible return on his time and effort. The publisher on the other hand, can offset the losses against the gains and still come out on top provided he has done his sums right.

Although publishers frequently offer contracts to authors prior to delivery of a completed manuscript, delivery delays often occur because the effort of writing is a current cost whereas the reward under a royalty system only appears some considerable time into the future. Contracting to purchase the manuscript for a lump sum may therefore provide a stimulus to the author which is otherwise lacking. It may be argued that a middle-ground between these two systems is represented by the offering of a substantial advance combined with a low rate of royalty, and certain authors prefer to be paid in this way. In this case the publisher is technically entitled to redeem any unearned payment, although this is not generally done in practice.

A final alternative is to use a profit-sharing system. The simplest form is for
author and publisher to share equally in revenue net of certain specified costs.
The key to this system obviously is the need to reach agreement about which costs
are to be specified. There might also be some residual conflict over the optimum
price and promotional budget. However this conflict is likely to be considerably
less than that associated with a royalty system. Of course the author is required
to bear more risk than under a royalty system because if his book sells badly he
earns nothing at all. On the other hand, he does considerably better than he otherwise would if the book is a success.

In conclusion it would seem that where an author expects sales to be no better than
moderate his best interests are probably served by the royalty system, although his
relations with his publisher may be soured. On the other hand he is likely to earn
so little net of tax that it might still seem a better alternative to opt for a
profit-sharing agreement or for a lump-sum payment. For an author who expects to
be successful a profit-sharing agreement appears to be the best bet, or alternatively
a substantial advance combined with a low royalty.

ELASTICITY OF DEMAND

Elasticity of demand is an economic concept which is potentially useful to a publisher. It describes the relationship between a change in price and the resultant
change in demand. Demand is said to be elastic if a price reduction of 10% causes
demand to increase by more than 10%, and to be inelastic if as a result demand
increases by less than 10%. If demand is elastic a price reduction causes sales
revenue to increase, and, if inelastic causes sales revenue to fall.

Unfortunately a major difficulty in the publishing field is that no specific information exists about the elasticity of demand for different kinds of books. Given
that every book is an individual product it is unhelpful to talk about the demand
for books in general. Nevertheless, it is probable that all books within a specific
category exhibit fairly uniform elasticities. For example, whereas it is true that
much fiction is interchangeable in the eyes of the consumer since the objective of
the purchase is to be entertained, this is clearly not going to be true of technical
and scientific books where the market mainly comprises students on specific courses
of study. In every case, however, the publisher needs to know whether the optimal
strategy is to price high or low, which in turn requires a decision about the
optimal print run for the book in question.

It is interesting that authors invariably believe that a low price is preferable to
a high price. They argue that demand is typically elastic and that the much increased demand potentially stimulated by low prices makes long print runs feasible
and thus results in higher royalties. Publishers, on the other hand, often take
the contrary view on the grounds that since the product is obviously superior, which
is why they are publishing it rather than anyone else, it will sell nearly as many
copies at a high price as at a low price. The difference of opinion is vital because
of its implications for print runs. The authors' strategy relies upon long print
runs to keep down unit costs, thus permitting the low prices at which these print
runs will be absorbed by the market.

This is also, of course, the publishers optimal strategy for potential bestsellers.
In other cases publishers may opt for shorter print runs which result in higher
unit costs, relying upon the expectation that the higher prices made necessary by
these costs will not cause the market to shrink too much.

As suggested above the degree of competition between books is obviously important

when deciding upon a pricing policy. Nevertheless competitiveness is a hard concept to define in publishing because every book is a unique product. Consumers
tend to regard a price as acceptable provided that it falls within the fairly
narrow range associated with books of a similar kind. There is some evidence that
this leads to perceived price barriers which publishers break through with some
trepidation. During the early 1970's, for example, an academic book in paperback
could not easily be sold at more than £4.95. More recently the barrier for paperback fiction stood for some time at £1. This latter barrier now appears to have
been breached where the product is bulky and has a good jacket although price
resistance is still manifest in other areas, and especially in children's books
because, for example, of the constraint imposed by pocket money.

In the absence of obvious price barriers the preferred price strategy would currently appear to be in the upper realms of what the market will bear. It is possible
to demonstrate, using simple numerical examples, that in the majority of cases
higher prices go hand in hand with higher profits, although a good deal does depend
upon the importance of overheads relative to other costs of production.

At the present time the attitude of consumers towards book prices appears to be somewhat ambivalent. When considering the purchase of a book in isolation consumers
typically consider it to be overpriced. This is probably due to the fact that the
effects of inflation are only brought home when a particular product is purchased
at frequent intervals. When a purchase is infrequent consumers tend to remember
the price last time around. On the other hand at times like Xmas when a definite
decision has already been made to spend a given sum on say a child, consumers
suddenly realise how expensive toys have become and see books as a cheaper alternative. Thus there is little to be gained in trying to make books artificially and
unprofitably cheap.

FINANCIAL ACCOUNTS

In this section we will attempt to give an overview of the financial situation of
publishing houses in the UK. We do not propose to examine the position of individual firms in detail. Financial data is normally drawn from published company accounts. The first difficulty in the publishing field is that the accounts of some
large companies such as O.U.P. are not fully comparable to the accounts of truly
commercial publishers. In several other cases companies have been taken over by
conglomerates with the result that their accounts become difficult to disentangle
from those of the holding company. There is also the inevitable variation from
company to company with respect to the definition of key financial variables, and
with respect to methods of depreciation and stock valuation.

Price Commission Report

Analysis of published accounts is undertaken by several organisations, of whom the
most useful are Jordan Dataquest and Inter Company Comparisons Ltd. There is also
some analysis and tabular material in the Price Commission Report. This latter
document has the virtue of reporting data which is internally compatible, but presents a major difficulty to the reader in that he cannot discover which firms were
sampled by the Commission and thus cannot cross-check the reported results. The
Report concentrates on companies with a turnover of over £2.5 million per annum.
Its main findings are presented in Table 16 below.

The Report made several comments on the results shown in the Table. In the first
place it pointed out that whereas all kinds of publishers made roughly the same
profit margin in 1975, in 1976 the seven technical book specialists in the sample
did twice as well, at 15.4% on average, as the other twenty-two companies. We will

TABLE 16 Financial Results For 29 Large Publishers 1974 - 1977

	1974	1975	1976	1977
Sales Value £ million *	168.6	201.0	231.5	264.6
Direct Costs %	59.4	60.1	57.8	57.0
Contribution to Overheads and Profits %	40.6	39.9	42.2	43.0
Overheads %	33.1	32.6	32.6	32.4
Net Profit Before Tax %	7.5	7.3	9.6	10.6
Return On Capital % **	14.6	16.3	22.5	-

*Of which 85% is derived from sales of books
**Based upon 28 firm sample on an historic cost basis

Source: Price Commission Report, Tables 4.4 and 4.5

have more to say about this point in the subsequent critique of the Report. In the second place the four large paperback publishers sampled suffered a reduction in contribution from 46% to 44% between 1974 and 1977, and a corresponding reduction in net profit margin from 7.5% to 6.1%, primarily because of rising paper prices which affected them disproportionately. Finally, the eight hardback-only publishers sampled achieved an improvement in contribution from 42% to 47% between 1974 and 1977, and a corresponding improvement in net profit margin from 8.2% to 16.3%.

It was also observed that the return on capital in 1976 was roughly the same as in 1973. During the four year period 1973 to 1976 two firms consistently earned above-average rates of return, whereas four others did especially well in a single year as a consequence of sales from one or more bestsellers.

Inter Company Comparisons

The most recent offering from Inter Company Comparisons covers a sample of 60 firms during the financial years 1975-76, 1976-77, 1977-78. Some of the data is summarised in Table 17 below. A proviso to be borne in mind is that the figures in the Table are expressed in money rather than in real terms, requiring adjustments to be made where appropriate.

Thus whereas turnover grew by 22% between the first pair of years and by 17% between the second pair, equivalent to an annual rate of 19%, prices also rose on average by 15% per annum. The increase in real turnover during this period was therefore rather small. Of the 56 companies for which the data are reported 33 showed a rise in real turnover and 23 a decline. Total assets grew by 21½% between the first pair of years and by 20% between the second. Hence the value of real assets grew rather faster than real turnover. Nevertheless, the observed improvement in both the ratio of pre-tax profit to sales and of pre-tax profit to total assets largely resulted from the marked improvement in real profits between 1975-76 and 1976-77. Between 1976-77 and 1977-78, however, real profits improved only slightly and the ratios remained essentially unchanged.

Twenty of the fifty seven companies reporting consistently achieved above-average profitability (profits divided by assets) in all three years. Three companies,

TABLE 17 Financial Ratios. Large Publishers

	Pre-Tax Profit Sales			Pre-Tax Profit Total Assets			Return On Capital Employed		
	1975-1976	1976-1977	1977-1978	1975-1976	1976-1977	1977-1978	1975-1976	1976-1977	1977-1978
Mean Average	7.2%	10.0%	10.4%	8.6%	12.0%	12.0%	15.8%	23.0%	23.8%
Highest Value	24.0%	29.1%	34.3%	35.2%	38.5%	40.9%	78.2%	175.2%	245.0%
Lowest Value	-31.8%	-32.1%	-10.1%	-32.5%	-26.8%	-10.2%	-105.3%	-51.9%	-18.2%
Over 50%	0	0	0	0	0	0	6	12	11
40% - 50%	0	0	0	0	0	1	7	4	8
30% - 40%	0	0	1	3	4	3	9	11	7
20% - 30%	1	4	5	4	7	6	12	13	11
10% - 20%	18	25	23	22	24	25	13	12	13
0% - 10%	32	25	23	22	19	17	4	2	2
Negative	9	5	5	9	5	5	9	5	5
TOTAL	60	59	57	60	59	57	60	59	57

Source: Company accounts reported in ICC Business Ratios

Sphere Books, Futura Publications and notably Cassell, achieved the dubious distinction of making losses in all three years. Fifteen companies recorded an above-average profit margin (profits divided by sales) in all three years. Among them were several very large companies such as Heinemann, A.B.P. and Macmillan. None of these companies, however, were to be found among the twenty leaders in respect of return on capital employed in 1977-78, of whom eighteen were to be numbered among the twenty-four which were earning an above-average rate of return in all three years. Of the ten companies earning the highest rates of return in 1977-78 only two could be regarded as very large, namely Butterworth and Pergamon. If a company is to earn an exceptionally good rate of return on capital in publishing it clearly pays not to be too big. It clearly also pays to be specialised and to turn stock over quickly. In other respects the pattern among the companies is, however, considerably more varied.

It appears that whereas a company cannot guarantee to be successful merely by virtue of being very large, it can thereby ensure that it will earn above-average returns in the majority of years. The main inhibiting factor would appear to be the largest companies' inability to use capital efficiently in order to generate sales.

In three major respects publishers appear to have made little headway during the period 1975 to 1978. In the first place, liquidity became marginally worse whereas one would have expected the reverse. Somewhat curiously, by far the two most liquid companies were consistent loss-makers Cassell and Sphere, whilst the two companies earning much the highest return on capital, namely Michael Joseph and Allen and Unwin, were almost dangerously short of liquidity. Perhaps this is a pointer to the road to success in the industry. In the second place, stock turnover remained more or less constant throughout the period. Very few companies showed a marked improvement in stock turnover, although Mills and Boon, Michael Joseph and Pergamon improved steadily. The severest declines were exhibited by N.E.L., World Distributors and Guinness Superlatives, despite the fact that these latter two companies were among

est returns on capital. Finally, the credit collection period became
er than shorter, averaging over three months in each year. Interestingly,
slowest collectors were successful firms such as Michael Joseph and
3oon. If Pergamon can collect consistently in under two months, one is
given to onder why other companies need more than six.

VALUATION OF STOCK

The major difficulty which arises out of any attempt to measure profitability in
publishing is that of stock valuation. The traditional accounting approach is to
value stocks either at purchase price or at net realisable value, as compared to
the alternative approach of replacement cost. However, a publisher can manipulate
historical cost accounting techniques to his own advantage in such a way as to
disguise true profitability, as is shown by the examples below.

A publisher normally prints enough copies of a book to last for several years of
sales, although not all need to be bound at the same time. The bulk of all production costs are fixed rather than variable, and varying the print run by 10% either
way makes comparatively little difference to total costs. Let us assume for illustrative purposes that a print run of 2,000 copies would cost £1,000, whereas a print
run of 3,000 copies would cost £1,200. In the former case average cost is 50p,
whereas in the latter case it is 40p. Let us further assume that 2,000 copies are
printed and that over a period of three years total sales are 1,500 copies, each
sold for £2.50. Sales value therefore totals £3,750 which, with unsold stock valued
at cost totalling £250, amounts to £4,000. Production costs are £1,000 so total
profits are £3,000, arising from sales of 1,500 copies at a unit profit of £2.

But suppose 3,000 copies are printed. Sales value is £3,750 and the value of unsold
stock £600 (1,500 copies at 40p) totalling £4,350. Production costs are £1,200 and
total profits are therefore £3,150, arising from sales of 1,500 copies at a unit
profit of £2.10. At first light it appears that profitability can be improved by
increasing the print run (and if 4,000 copies were printed profitability would be
even better). However, this example presupposes that it is meaningful to value
stock at cost. A publisher may believe that the larger print run will eventually
be sold, in which case this practice is fair enough provided storage costs are not
excessive. But suppose that there are no real prospects of selling more than a
fraction of the unsold stock beyond year three. In that case the larger print run
is clearly less profitable than the smaller. If we assume in the extreme case that
the entire unsold stock has to be pulped the net profit of 2,000 copies is £3,750
less £1,000, making £2,750, whereas that of 3,000 copies is £3,750 less £1,200,
making £2,550.

Clearly if unsold copies can be remaindered at say 50p apiece the longer print run
once again becomes the more profitable alternative. But the point is that a publisher cannot be certain about the ultimate destination of unsold copies. More
importantly he cannot even be certain about how many will be sold during the initial
sales period. It would therefore appear prudent to ensure that sufficient copies
are available to provide for an unexpectedly high initial demand. Furthermore,
large quantities of unsold stock permit a publisher to manipulate his profitability
by recourse to variations in the amount of stock value to be written off in any
one financial year. If stock values are maintained then profitability looks a lot
better than if stock values are reduced at a stroke by a significant percentage.

In practice both over-valuing and under-valuing stock present dangers. Over-valuation
enhances current profitability but increases tax liability and reduces cash flow.
Under-valuation defers tax liability and enhances cash flow, but increases the risk
of take-over because declared profits are poor and saleable stocks are held in store
at below their true value. A publisher's attitude to stock valuation may therefore

vary over time, thereby presenting problems in interpreting the accounts.

PRINT RUNS

There is no readily available information about variations in print runs over time.
One indirect approach is to assume that print runs are expected to be sold out over
a limited number of years, so that the average expected sale per year will determine
the initial run. Clearly, expected annual sales will vary from one category of book
to another, but we will restrict ourselves here to an examination of the total annual output of new books and new editions. The somewhat rough and ready procedure
is to calculate an average sale per title per year by taking the figure for total
turnover, raising it by a factor of 1.5 in order to allow for the bookseller's one-
third discount, dividing by the appropriate average price and dividing again by the
number of titles published. This yields results as follows.

TABLE 18   Sales Per Volume Per Year

1955	305	1973	302
1960	274	1974	363
1965	233	1975	309
1970	248	1976	302
1971	254	1977	293
1972	297	1978	278

On the one hand these figures are over-estimates because a substantial part of
total turnover arises from the sale of backlist items or reprints. On the other
hand the average price is biased upwards by the very high prices of a limited number of titles, the great majority of titles in fact selling for less than the average figure. The most sensible policy, therefore, is to assume that these factors
cancel each other out to some extent, and to view the above sequence as an internally consistent trend on the grounds that these other factors do not vary much from
year to year.

On this basis we can see firstly that the 'average' author has a very limited market
for his work, although more people will typically read as against purchase it;
secondly, how dependent publishers are upon the occasional bestseller since the
'average' book is hopelessly unprofitable; and thirdly, that the 1970's did not
manifest a severe decline in sales per volume by historical standards despite the
continuous decline after 1974. Nevertheless, despite their imprecision, these
figures do point to the conclusion that the typical print run must have shrunk
quite sharply during this latter period.

TECHNICAL BOOKS

The term 'technical' is, for reasons explained below, more than a little difficult
to define, but is generally taken to refer to books intended for the academic and
professional markets. The general financial considerations governing the supply
of other types of books apply equally to technical books, but with the added provisos set out below.

In the first place, the print run for a technical book is typically rather small.

Such a book is generally produced in both hardback and softback editions, in which event it is known as a textbook. When only a hardback edition is printed the term monograph is used. The typical print run for a monograph is of the order of one to two thousand copies, and for a textbook of the order of 500 hardback and two to three thousand paperback. These print runs produce high unit production costs and hence relatively high prices. In many cases production costs are also raised by the need for tables, diagrams, formulae, footnotes and indexes which are normally wholly absent in a work of fiction. This factor is independent of the print run and may, therefore, cause wide variations in price between books of similar length aimed at the same market.

A further notable feature of technical books is their low elasticity of demand. In the case of fiction, there is a potential market of millions, whereas technical books are generally bought for specific reasons, for example by students pursuing a specific course of studies. Thus no matter how low the price, the market remains strictly limited for a textbook on, say, the anatomy of the worm. In addition, it is hard to penetrate a market where there is an established textbook merely by undercutting its price, and in the case of monographs the market is anyway now largely limited to institutional sales. Since textbooks are designed to perform specific functions, it is their quality in relation to these functions, rather than their price, which is the primary determinant of sales.

An obvious difficulty from the publisher's point of view is that quality is difficult to assess in the absence of specialised knowledge on his part, although this difficulty is overcome to some degree by the use of specialist external reviewers. Thus it is generally a sensible policy to keep prices on the high side in the expectation that quality will overcome all resistance, since low prices combined with poor quality is neither a necessary nor a sufficient condition for success.

Technical book sales are thus unusually dependent upon the opinion of a limited number of people, primarily academics and librarians. In the field of fiction reviewers exercise some power over sales, but whereas a novel may be successful despite poor reviews a textbook will not be successful unless recommended to students. For this reason the sales effort in the technical book field is directed towards those people with the power to recommend, utilising visits by representatives or direct mailing to this end. Advertisements appear only in the technical press and journals, and little effort is typically made in retail outlets to stimulate interest.

Technical books are also unusually dependent upon export markets. In this respect one of the greatest boons to technical book publishing in the UK has been the growing dominance of English as the language of scholarly communication. By and large, the more specialised the book the more likely it is that profitability is determined by overseas sales. But even where overseas markets can be secured, little profit can be made from the initial print run given the high set-up costs and high interest rates. Profitability is very much dependent upon the sort of regular annual demand which warrants a periodic reprint and perhaps an occasional new edition. It is not possible to produce reprints all that cheaply because the costs of paper and print rise inexorably year by year, and it is by no means unknown for a reprint to cost more than the original edition despite the absence of set-up costs. However, the price of a reprint can be pitched at a level comparable to that fixed for new books, thus providing a generous margin of profit. In the case of new editions the margin is less good because of the need to reset part or all of the text.

The fact that the shelf life of a technical book is very long compared to that of most fiction does have some disadvantages, however. In particular, the publisher faces the problem of how to raise the price of a book as it is pushed out of his warehouse over a period of years, in order to reflect, or perhaps to take advantage of, inflation and to recompense him for the costs of storage and tied-up capital.

Some years ago Macmillan decided to stop printing prices on books, and to induce the bookseller to mark the appropriate figure on each book when it was put on display. This practice proved unpopular with the booksellers, although some publishers do still appear to pursue this course of action. Nevertheless, the alternative policy, which is to over-stick the original price as it leaves the publisher's warehouse is extremely unpopular with customers who peel back the stickers and then complain that the bookseller is over-charging. One other possibility is to bind only one year's estimated sale at a time, altering the printed price as each batch is bound, though this in turn is by no means free from drawbacks.

Finally, it is worth remembering that unlike fiction, a part rather than the whole of a technical book may be recommended as useful for a potential purchaser, and he may therefore decide to rely either upon library copies, or increasingly upon the xerox copier, the consequences of which are discussed in a later section on photocopying.

FICTION

Whenever either recession looms or price rises are in the pipeline one can be sure that there will be an outcry to the effect that the final nail has been driven into the coffin of fiction. A lengthy description of this phenomenon is to be found in Sutherland (1978), and he himself concludes that salvation and security are not at hand, at least not for the literary novel. However, if one examines statistics of fiction publishing in The Bookseller one discovers a picture somewhat at odds with the popular view of the demise of fiction. The annual figures for fiction books published are as follows:

1973 - 4,145: 1974 - 4,154: 1975 - 4,198: 1976 - 4,025: 1977 - 4,487:

1978 - 4,379: 1979 - 4,551.

The overall number of publications fell in 1974 and 1976 whereas the first fall in the fiction category occurred in the latter year as a result of decisions taken in the light of the 'crisis' in 1974. However, this fall was neither severe nor prolonged and although a further slight fall occurred in 1978 the past three years have been buoyant ones for fiction, culminating in a record-breaking first quarter output of 1,325 titles in 1980 up 23% on the equivalent 1979 figure. It is also interesting to note that whereas the major impact of the alleged recession in fiction publishing was supposed to fall upon new authors, that proportion of total fiction output accounted for by new titles has remained consistently within the 50 to 60% range. Thus, since the total itself has grown, it would appear to be getting easier rather than harder to find a publisher for a fiction book.

PAPERBACKS

Up to 70% of the hardback edition of a novel is bought by libraries, a factor which may well have serious effects upon the viability of hardback fiction during the early 1980's. Paperback fiction, on the other hand, is largely bought by individuals. Although this enables the private buyer to obtain a book at a much reduced price, it also means that he has to wait, possibly for several years, before the hardback edition is joined by one in paperback. Under the circumstances many people are given to wonder why fiction is not published originally in paperback format.

In fact it is a matter of faith in the trade that fiction or books of general interest need to be published in hardback if they are to have any real chance of success as paperbacks. There are, of course, exceptions to this general rule, but experiments in original paperback publication, such as that conducted by Quartet books and Wildwood in 1973, have always proved to be failures. A number of reasons may account for this. Libraries, for example, are not keen on insecurely-bound books. Neither, for that matter, are book reviewers who like to keep or sell their copies, and authors who regard hard covers as a testimonial to the durability of their work, and who in general earn the greater part of their royalties from the hardback edition. For some readers the absence of a hardback edition may suggest a lack of quality, and for booksellers the contribution per hardback book sold is much superior. However, the ultimate consideration is invariably variations in the economics of publication. Under the existing system paperback rights are usually sold after a book has achieved at least modest success in hardback format. Thus the risk inherent in a long paperback print run is considerably less than would exist where no hardback edition has previously been on sale. Paperbacks are cheaper primarily because of the spreading of direct costs over a much larger quantity of books, although hardbacks also typically use a different printing process and better quality paper, and are much more expensive to bind. A hardback edition also tends to bear the great bulk of the advertising and publicity costs for the title, and each book is considerably more costly to distribute. In the absence of a hardback edition a publisher inevitably tends to be conservative in his estimation of market potential, and each paperback must therefore incur a much higher unit cost than where two editions are produced, which inevitably becomes reflected in a price which is high by the standards of paperbacks in general. In turn a high price may deter buyers and render the whole operation uneconomic.

Penguin

The hardback/paperback split for fiction dates back to the 1830's, although it only became truly significant with the appearance of Penguin in 1935. It is not the purpose of this book to examine detailed case histories. On this occasion, however, a more detailed look at a single firm is warranted by the fact that it enables us to examine the major trends operating within the paperback market generally. Whereas in America paperbacks were sold from the beginning in the same way as magazines, in drugstores and news-stands rather than bookshops, Penguins in the UK were not merely sold in bookshops but usurped space previously occupied by hardback fiction. It was to Penguin that we owe the now widespread willingness to put paperbacks on show in ones living-room. Furthermore, when the initial sales fling was over Penguins were not consigned to be turned into pulp but to an ever-lengthening backlist operating in exactly the same way as a backlist of hardback titles. As a result some 80% of Penguin turnover currently originates from the backlist of some 4,500 titles, and many are given a second lease of life by television or film tie-ins. A further historical virtue of the Penguin operation was the fact that the reputation of the list as a whole was such that it was sufficient to publicise a series rather than spend a lot of money on individual titles. Initially covers were left plain as a mark of quality to distinguish them from more luridly self-advertising competitors.

However, the success of Penguin not unnaturally bred competition which predominantly took the form of newer imprints concentrating on fast-selling titles with limited backlist potential. These newer imprints were assisted by the growing tendency for hardback publishers to seek the best possible price for paperback rights rather than the most eminent imprint, and Penguin's initial reluctance to compete strongly for such rights left it with an uncommercially weak frontlist. Furthermore, the strength of the backlist began to decline when paperback licences reverted back to hardcover imprints, who then resold the potentially most profitable among them to other paperback houses which were willing to outbid Penguin. Certainly, none of the newer imprints managed to usurp Penguin's postion as the pre-eminent publisher of quality paperbacks. On the other hand, the former were able to make a killing from less culturally-worthy authors whom Penguin disdained. The end-result for

Penguin was an unsurprising decline in the value of sales adjusted for inflation, starting in financial year 1975, and a sharp drop in profitability, commencing in 1977 and culminating in a loss in 1979, although this loss reflected in part the costs of the rationalisation process which Penguin were forced to introduce in order to stem the tide.

Rights

Inevitably one aspect of Penguin's hard road back to successful trading is a deter- mination to bid more agressively for paperback rights to potential bestsellers, since the frontlist is the weak-spot of the firm's operations. Furthermore, the reputation of the backlist is ultimately dependent upon the progressive addition of what are colloquially termed 'books with legs'. Unfortunately, the rights to potential bestsellers are rapidly becoming astronomically expensive.

In 1978 Futura published "The Thornbirds", the rights to which cost them £160,000, on top of which was added a promotion budget of £60,000. These sums seemed imposs- ible to justify in the eyes of most competing publishers, but in the event the book took off immediately and one million copies were sold by the beginning of 1980. With the eventual total sale almost certain to exceed two million copies Futura's decision has turned out to be very shrewd, and this has given other publishers the confidence to bid ever-larger sums for rights. In some cases, such as the £250,000 bid for the latest Frederick Forsyth, the author at least had an established rep- utation in the UK, but in other cases, such as the £200,000+ paid for Judith Krantz's "Princess Daisy", the offer appeared to reflect solely the extraordinary £1$\frac{1}{2}$ million paid for the US paperback rights. Whether a company such as Penguin should join in the rush is obviously a matter for their commercial judgement. There are obvious dangers in going down-market because a major consideration is to ensure that most publications warrant reprinting, a factor of less concern to their competitors. In their heyday 75% of Penguins were reprinted as against a current figure of about 33%, and Penguin now have several shops-within-shops which need to be filled with titles with at least modest sales potential.

Trade Paperbacks

Another option open to Penguin is to concentrate upon 'trade' paperbacks, sometimes referred to as 'midways'. In recent years publishers have been experimenting with larger formats than was the traditional norm. The print run for such titles is often below the 25,000 minimum needed for a standard paperback to break even, and the print and paper quality may be superior. As a result the price falls somewhere in-between the ranges customary for hardbacks and popular paperbacks. Trade paper- backs are common in the USA, and indeed have their own bestsellers' list. However, whereas they used to be handled much like hardbacks from the bookseller's point of view, being distributed by publisher rather than the wholesaler, they rely like popular paperbacks largely upon impulse buying.

There is uncertainty about prospects for trade paperbacks in the UK, but for Penguin at least they do have the virtue of a longer shelf life than is traditionally acc- orded to popular paperbacks. In the USA popular paperbacks have an average shelf life of only fifteen days. One direct consequence of this is that it is by no means uncommon for 50% of the print run to be returned to the publisher. The situation in the UK is rather better, with an average figure for returns of 10%, being rather higher for popular titles and rather lower for trade titles. The discrepancy be- tween the two countries incidentally reflects the much higher proportion of back- list to new titles in the UK, and the much greater dependence upon bookshops rather than other retail outlets.

The Omnibus Edition

A paperback edition is not the only way to breathe new life into a novel which has run out of steam in hardback format. An illustration of the potential for innovation is to be found in the Heinemann/Octopus omnibus editions, originally conceived in June 1975 and first marketed in September 1976. Packaging four or more complete backlist novels into a single hardback edition was in principle incompatible with low prices. But the real innovation in this case was not so much the return to the neglected omnibus edition, but rather the idea of selling exclusively through a single outlet, in this case W.H. Smith shops. By so doing, the publishers achieved a guaranteed sale of the entire print run combined with minimal distribution and selling costs, thus making it possible for each omnibus edition to sell at the same price as an average new novel without any sacrifices in quality. Despite this low price W.H. Smith could still make a good profit by buying at a 50% discount and selling in large quantities. Obviously a degree of risk was involved since W.H. Smith could not be certain of the potential market, but in the event it turned out very well with roughly 1.5 million copies sold during the first year, of which half were exported.

Anatomy of a bestseller

The man in the street tends to think almost exclusively in terms of bestsellers simply because those are the only books brought to his attention sufficiently often for him to remember their titles with any degree of accuracy. It happens that bestsellers are sometimes born and sometimes made. What is fascinating about bestsellers is not, however, the process by which they can be 'hyped' on to the market, but rather the much more mysterious process by which they occasionally amass considerable sales without any hyping at all, as was the case for the early works of Tolkien.

Even Tolkien, however, cannot match the performance of the book which has outsold all others during the past three years, and which was born some seventy years before its publication. I refer, of course, to "The Diary of an Edwardian Lady" by Elizabeth Holden. This book was originally taken to a small West Country firm called Webb and Bower, who published it in conjunction with Michael Joseph. The initial print run in June 1977 was 150,000 copies, including book club and American sales. By the end of 1979 it had gone through 19 reprintings, been translated into ten languages, and sold well over one and a half million copies. The financial flows are set out below as of December 1979:

UK Book Clubs (43,000 copies)	£2 million			
UK Booktrade (750,000 copies)	£5 million	shared by	(1)Production	£1 million
			(2)Distribution	£½ million
			(3)Booksellers	£2 million
			(4)M. Joseph	£1 million
			(5)Webb & Bower/ author's family	£½ million
American & Foreign (500,000 copies)	£4 million			
Spin-offs	£2 million			
Total Revenue	£13 million			

As the financial flows indicate, one of the most extraordinary things about this book is not merely that it is a hardback edition, but that it sells at a rather high price (£7.50 in 1980). Indeed, so successful is the hardback edition that no paperback edition is even on the cards; and all this for a book without a storyline.

Future generations will discover perhaps two million copies of this book mouldering on bookshelves or in attics, and may be given to wonder whether some kind of mania for nature struck their forefathers. Certainly, it is difficult to analyse the book's success in a wholly rational manner. Fortunately for publishers, however, hardback bestsellers generally come in more easily recognisable formats. Take, for example, a well-known author or personality, combine with a television prog- ramme or film, and stir with some heavy promotion and one ends up with, for example, David Attenborough's "Life On Earth" which sold 850,000 hardback copies in 1979, and is still going very strong in 1980, despite being much the highest priced hard- back bestseller at £8.95.

It may, of course, be argued that the majority of hardback bestsellers are non- fiction rather than fiction, with the latter taking off only after the paperback edition has been published. Where bestselling authors are involved the marketing of a book can be relatively complicated, taking in perhaps a British hardback edition, bookclub hardback, American hardback, British paperback, translations and film or TV adaptations. This last stage is increasingly critical if a book is to achieve a lasting position in the bestseller lists, Graham Greene's "The Human Factor" being a case in point, since the next sure-fire bestselling novel is soon ready to supplant it on the retailer's most prominent shelves.

The decline in the number of hardback fiction bestsellers is difficult to quantify. If we define a bestselling novel as one which sells 30,000 copies in hardback by the end of its first year in print, then Collins produced 32 bestsellers between 1952 and 1956 inclusive, and 22 between 1972 and 1976 inclusive. However, the significance of this decline is offset by the increasing reliance upon overseas sales and sales of subsidiary rights, the latter accounting in the case of, for example, Cape who publish a large quantity of new hardback quality fiction, for some 10 to 15% of turnover. A disturbing feature from the publisher's viewpoint, is that whereas traditionally he retained 50% of paperback rights, his share was reduced in January 1976 to 30%, and is currently even less for certain popular authors. As usual, this is a trend which originated in America, although it may prove to be partially self-defeating for authors since publishers will tend to grow increasingly reluctant to publish fiction in hardback format if probable losses in this area cannot be offset by gains elsewhere.

Under the circumstances, it is fortunate that certain publishers wear their hard- back fiction losses on their sleeves as a badge of cultural courage. Secker and Warburg make no secret of the fact that one half of their list loses money in its first year, although economic adversity may soon cause that proportion to decline, and publishers with seemingly philanthropic attitudes towards new authors do tend to be part of conglomerates which make profits from rather less highbrow titles. The need for the highbrow to be increasingly subsidised has led some members of the trade to forecast a future in which little fiction will be produced other than bestsellers with good prospects for the sale of subsidiary rights. As yet these forecasts have not been borne out in practice, and there does seem to be a problem inherent in this view of the world of fiction in that the number of instant best- sellers is somewhat limited at the best of times, with most authors needing to build up their readership over a long period of time. Hence an author's early novels need to be viewed as a form of apprenticeship, subsidised by the publisher in the hope and expectation that the status of bestselling master craftsman will ultimately be achieved.

THE PRICE COMMISSION REPORT ON BOOKS

Introduction

In the UK the Price Commission administered various forms of price control from
1973 to 1979. During its first six months of operation it produced five sector
reports under section II of the 1977 Act. In June 1978, after some delay, appeared
the sixth report on "prices, costs and margins in the publishing, printing and distribution of books, with particular reference to technical books".

The data provided in this Report are a valuable source of information about the industry under investigation in this book, and we have referred to its text and tables
in the preceding pages. Nevertheless, the Report must be treated with a degree of
scepticism for the reasons set out below.

The first difficulty with which one has to contend in the Report is that of defining
what is meant by a 'technical' book. As we have seen, the Business Monitor series
PQ489 distinguishes a category called 'technical and scientific', and this accounts
for some 17-18% of total book output, predominantly in hardback form. The Price
Commission preferred to define technical books more broadly as "books used in formal
education beyond the secondary stage", thereby including "scientific, technical,
academic, reference, medical and professional books", but excluding school textbooks.
Unfortunately, there is no mention in the Report of the proportion of total book
output which is accounted for on this definition. Furthermore, the Commission were
evasive when asked by the author for further information. Publishers do not normally
categorize their output in this way, so the process of distinguishing between technical and non-technical is necessarily somewhat arbitrary. A figure of 25% might,
however, be fairly near the mark.

Sampling Problems

A second, and related, problem arose by virtue of the manner in which the Commission
chose its sample of firms for investigation. In the case of publishers it included
all those with a turnover of more than £5 million per annum, together with 1 in 40
of smaller publishers. This yielded a sample of 72 publishers, of whom 64 submitted
usable responses. However, in the sections of the Report concerned with publishers
the Commission divided firms into 'large' (turnover in excess of £2.5 million) and
'small' (turnover less than £2.5 million), the former category containing 44 firms
and the latter containing 20. As there were approximately 30 firms with a turnover
of over £5 million, the sample of large firms must have included about a dozen
firms with a turnover between £2.5 and £5 million, or some 50% of all firms falling
into that category. It is worth bearing in mind, therefore, that firstly, the
sample of large publishers was clearly biased towards the very largest firms in the
industry whose performance was unlikely to be representative of the industry as a
whole, and that secondly, there were quite a number of firms in the £2.5 to £5
million turnover category whose output included a significant proportion of technical
books, some of whom must surely have been omitted from the Commission's sample.
This latter conclusion is borne out by the fact that the 29 large firms sampled
produced, on average, only 12% of total book sales in the form of technical books,
perhaps half of the average for all publishers using the Commission's definition,
as suggested above.

The sampling problem was compounded by the fact that the Report confused matters
with respect to technical books by introducing tables based upon different firm
samples, for example tables 4.3 and 4.4 refer to 29 firms, table 4.5 to 28 firms
and table 4.6 to 19 firms, all of which are significantly smaller than the original
large-firm sample of 44 firms. Despite this, the Report then went on to isolate
seven firms, selected from the 29 firm sample simply because they accounted for 84%

of technical book sales recorded by this group, the other 22 firms accounting for
the residual 16% between them. In this way the Report implied that the technical
book field was heavily concentrated in the hands of a very small number of firms,
which was clearly an overstatement of the situation in practice, given that there
were, according to the PA, about 90 technical book publishers, of whom some 15 were
major publishing houses.

This emphasis upon the performance of a few large firms was heightened in the Report
by the expedient of playing down the role of the 1630 small firms to the point of
insignificance. Small publishers merited a mere two brief paragraphs in the Report
and the associated table was based upon a 'representative' sample of only 6 firms.

Financial Results

The core of the Report is to be found in table 4.3 which shows that during 1976 and
1977 the contribution to overheads and profit made by technical books increased
noticeably as compared to that made by other books, and in the associated calculations of return on capital on an historic cost basis for the years 1974-76. These
calculations were derived from the replies to extensive questionnaires sent to the
firms sampled.

What the Report showed most clearly was that 1974 and 1975 were difficult years
for all types of publisher. But even in 1976 the Report concluded that returns
across the board were no more than adequate, and were only equivalent to those
which had been earned in 1973. This latter statement is, incidentally, open to
question because the Commission relied upon published accounts for its 1973 data,
whereas it made its own estimates for later years. The sting in the tail of the
Report came when the rates of return for the 7 technical book specialists were
compared to those of the other 21 large firms sampled. According to the Report
these 7 firms showed a rate of return close to the average in 1975, whereas they
averaged 29.9% in 1976 compared to 19.2% for the other 21, and this difference was
expected to continue through 1978. It is from these figures that the Report goes
directly to its conclusion that "publishers could reasonably exercise restraint in
raising prices of technical books for a considerable period".

But a further criticism which can be directed at the 7 firm sample used by the
Commission is that the latter apparently included 3 firms concerned exclusively
with publishing in a hardback format, and the identity of these somewhat unusual
publishers was kept and has remained secret. More significance can be attached
to their existence, however, than merely one's curiosity as to whether such firms
do indeed exist, because the Report noted in section 4.24 that the 8 large firms
which concentrated exclusively upon hardbacks fared much better than paperback
publishers. This inevitably meant that the high returns earned by the 7 technical
book specialists could possibly be accounted for by the fact that 3 of them were
apparently also hardback-only publishers. Unfortunately the Report failed to shed
any light on this hypothesis.

Indeed the Report really shed very little light upon the reasons why certain technical book specialists did better than others in 1976 and 1977, and upon why they
did better than firms with other specialisms. There were occasional references to
the hypotheses that risk is insignificant (section 4.33) and competition less strong
than in other specialisms (sections 8.3 to 8.6), but this is less than satisfactory.
In the case of technical book publishing the Commission, having allegedly discovered
a highly concentrated market associated with high returns, concluded that the former
caused the latter. But when one takes into consideration the fact that the technical
book market is much less concentrated than is suggested by data in the Report, this
relationship ceases to hold water. Besides which the Report several times remarked
upon the fact that the 7 specialists increased their sales substantially during

1976 and 1977. It was noted (section 8.5) that such an expansion of sales depends upon successful titles in a strong list. Yet a strong list surely is a mark of efficiency and skill, so the excellent results obtained by the seven specialists in 1976 may be deemed to have been their just reward rather than a monopoly profit. Furthermore, the export percentage in technical publishing is probably around 60%, rather higher than is the case for other specialisms. Thus the profits of these specialists are closely linked to their ability to sell abroad in competitive markets. Considered in this light, the Report's conclusions appeared to condemn the successful rather than to control the exercise of market power.

It was also interesting that the justification for stigmatising the seven specialists rested upon the fact that they did much better than the average in 1976 and 1977. At no stage did the Commission attempt to relate rates of return in publishing to those earned in other industries. This may, perhaps, have been just as well because the rates of return were all calculated on an historic cost basis, which is not all that illuminating during a period of rapid inflation. The PA asked independent auditors to convert most of the questionnaires submitted to the Commission on to a current cost accounting basis, which had the effect of reducing the average rate of return in 1976 to 7.5% and the rate of return earned by the seven specialists to 11%. If these calculations were correct then even the specialists did no better than successful firms in other industries, although it must be borne in mind that particular problems arise in publishing because some half of all capital employed is in the form of stocks which are difficult to revalue over time. But the Report generally told us little more, other than that profits in general were "adequate" without explaining what this meant.

In conclusion it must be said that the Commission appeared to be scratching around in order to find a justification for the time and expense of an investigation which really should never have taken place at all. For reasons explained above the Commission gave a distorted view of the competition faced by firms in the technical book market, and assumed, in my view without justification, that the relatively high profits earned by technical book publishers in 1976 and 1977 constituted a monopoly profit.*

---

*This section is a slightly modified version of an article which appeared in The Journal of Industrial Economics, XXVll, 295-299.

CHAPTER 3

The Net Book Agreement

INTRODUCTION

This chapter on the Net Book Agreement has been given a prominent place in the book partly because it introduces a wide range of matters which recur in the chapters which follow, and partly because in spite of the seemingly categoric Judgement in the Restrictive Practices Court the dispute over the desirability of the NBA has never been properly laid to rest. Members of the publishing industry, with rare exceptions such as Hughes (1977) and Norrie (1979), publically defend the NBA to the hilt although their private opinions may be somewhat different. Lined up against them are members of the academic profession, for the most part economists, who regard the NBA as an anachronism. But the debate has now been going on for so long that it is easy to lose sight of the issues originally set out in the Judgement of the Court. In this chapter we seek to survey everything associated with the NBA. It is, by the standards of this book, heavy going, and at the end of it all there are no clear-cut answers. Some readers may therefore prefer to look selectively at the paragraphs which follow, returning perhaps to read them in full on a subsequent occasion.

HISTORICAL RETROSPECT

The earliest attempt to organise the book trade occurred in 1812 when London booksellers attempted to form their own association in order to forestall an increasing tendency to underselling. Both this and a second attempt in 1828 were failures, and although a further attempt was made in 1848, this coincided with the Free Trade Movement and led to an arbitration conference in 1852 at which Lord Campbell ruled that publishers could neither prescribe retail prices nor refuse to supply booksellers who undercut them. Little progress was made during the ensuing four decades but Frederick Macmillan persevered in his opposition to underselling and in 1890 netted 16 books, the most significant of which was Alfred Marshall's Principles of Economics. In January 1895 the Associated Booksellers of Great Britain and Ireland was formed, followed exactly one year later by the formation of the Publishers' Association, and these two bodies agreed in 1897 that net books should not be sold at less than the published price. Agreement by the Society of Authors was not, however, forthcoming until 1899, and it was not, therefore, until January 1900 that the first Net Book Agreement came into operation.

The Net Book Agreement currently in force came into being in 1957, shortly after the

passing of the 1956 Restrictive Practices Act. This Act prohibited collective enforcement of restrictive practices but exempted individual enforcement. The Net
Book Agreement, being an example of the former, was investigated by the Restrictive
Practices Court, and a lengthy Judgement was delivered on 30th October 1962 which,
for reasons set out below, allowed the Agreement to stand. Although a Resale Prices
Act was passed in 1964 outlawing individual enforcement of resale price maintenance,
exemptions under the 1956 Act were allowed to stand unless a significant change in
trade practice could be proven to have taken place in the interim period. The NBA
was therefore allowed to retain its exemption by default, and its significance in
law lies primarily in the fact that only one other exemption has subsequently been
granted, that of medicaments in 1970, and that agreement is now for practical purposes unenforceable.

In the course of his Judgement Mr Justice Buckley uttered the now famous words
"Books Are Different", sentiments with which the publishing industry wholeheartedly
concurred. Unfortunately the economics profession just as wholeheartedly rejected
the Judgement as erroneous, and the controversy this engendered has never fully died
down. In the sections below we must therefore consider firstly whether the Judgement was appropriate in the light of the trade circumstances at the time, and more
importantly whether the NBA can still be justified in the light of current trade
practice.

THE AGREEMENT

The Net Book Agreement is binding upon those members of the Publishers' Association
who publish net books and concerns the conditions of sale relating to net books as
defined in the Appendix. Such books cannot, other than in exceptional circumstances,
be sold by booksellers at below the net prices fixed by the publishers. The Agreement is intended primarily to defend the interests of the so-called stockholding
booksellers who in general hold in stock more than 10,000 different titles. This
permits the public to purchase direct from stock and to browse through a collection
of related items in pursuit of a publication which precisely fits their needs. The
turnover of stock items tends to be high for general books in December, and for
academic books in September/October. Nevertheless a stockholding bookseller must
expect to hold a large proportion of his stock in the form of slow-moving items. He
must also (except in London) expect to subscribe, sight unseen, to many new books
before they are published. In 1962 it was not customary for a publisher to offer a
sale-or-return facility on such subscriptions so that the bookseller effectively
carried a significant part of the risk inherent in publishing books by unknown
authors.

In 1960 some 24,000 books were published, some 18,000 for the first time. Since
even a stockholding bookseller cannot be expected to hold more than a small proportion of these in stock a good deal of his time is taken up in tracing and ordering
books for customers. To be efficient in this respect the bookseller needs to have
a specialized knowledge. However, although the Net Book Agreement does not pro-
hibit a bookseller from charging for his services, customers react adversely to such
charges.

Booksellers buy from publishers at a discount off the net price. In 1962 the discount was $33\frac{1}{3}\%$ for most general books including fiction; 25% for most technical and
educational books; and $16\frac{1}{3}\%$ for more specialized books including special orders. The
rate of discount on export orders, which constituted approximately half of a typical
publisher's sales, varied between 40% and 50%. These rates of discount enabled few
booksellers to make more than very modest profits, and there was an appreciable
turnover of members of the profession.

THE JUDGEMENT

Summary

The Restrictive Practices Court accepted more or less in its entirety the case made out in support of the Agreement. It accepted that the termination of the Agreement would lead to (1) fewer and less well-equipped stockholding bookshops (2) more expensive books (3) fewer published titles, and that each of these consequences would arise in a sufficiently serious degree to make its avoidance a substantial advantage. The Court had certain reservations about possible trends in book prices were the Agreement to be terminated because it represented a state of affairs of which there was no experience or parallel at that time. Nevertheless the Court held that no real evidence had been presented to support the view that on the balance of probabilities retail prices generally would fall.

The Court also rejected claims by the Registrar under the balancing provision that any benefits arising from the Agreement would be negated by other associated detriments. It argued firstly that the Agreement did not reduce the incentive to publishers and booksellers to keep down costs because the competitive nature of the publishing industry forced publishers to be cost-efficient in order to survive, and because the small profit margin enjoyed by stockholding bookshops left them little latitude for inefficiency. Secondly the Court argued that the Agreement did not deprive booksellers of opportunities to dispose of stock at their discretion nor the public of opportunities to buy more cheaply because such a facility exists in the Standard Conditions of Sale item (ii) and in the existence of the National Book Sale. The Court also rejected the claim that prices were being maintained at artificially high levels, and that by protecting margins the Agreement compelled the public to pay more for books than would otherwise be the case. Finally the Court did not believe that the Agreement prevented libraries and similar purchasers from negotiating advantageous terms with their suppliers.

Detailed Provisions

It is desirable to consider certain of these points in more detail if we are to assess whether the Judgement still holds good. Those with hardy dispositions can of course, inspect the entire transcript of the case in Barker and Davies (1966). Before we begin, however, two general observations are in order. In the first place it must be remembered that a publisher has absolute freedom both to designate a book as either net or non-net, and to transfer it from one category to the other at any time. He also has absolute freedom to fix the net price at any level, and to sell a book to anyone whom he choses to supply at any price he so wishes. Thus the Net Book Agreement is not at all representative of the type of restrictive practice commonly investigated by the Court. Furthermore there are laid-down circumstances which permit a bookseller to sell a net book at less than the net price. Aside from Standard Condition item (ii) the main provision is for an annual two week National Book Sale during which any licensed bookseller may offer any book which he has not ordered during the previous twelve months at less than two thirds of its net price or at its buying-in cost to the bookseller, whichever is less.

In the second place there exists the Library Agreement, set up in 1929, which authorizes public libraries to obtain a library licence from the Publishers' Association. This licence entitles libraries to a ten per cent discount on purchases from designated booksellers. The Library Agreement was set up in order to prevent those libraries with large budgets from demanding such high discounts from booksellers that the latter could make little or no profit from the business once their costs were taken into account. It was widely accepted in the trade that the termination of the

Net Book Agreement would result in the concession of higher discounts to most libraries.

Now, as we have seen above, the Court accepted the view that the termination of the Net Book Agreement would lead to higher rather than lower prices. This was chiefly because firstly, if publishers could not rely upon stockholding booksellers to subscribe to, stock and display their books, they would have to be more cautious about their publishing strategy. Certain books would not be published at all, and those that were published would have smaller print runs, thus forcing up unit costs and hence prices. Also booksellers' margins would be forced up through, for example, a refusal by booksellers to stock a given publisher's books except on more advantageous terms.

The Registrar argued that the removal of a price restriction in the context of a competitive industry could lead only to price reductions rather than the reverse. The Court held, however, that the Agreement served not as an instrument for fixing minimum prices since the price of any individual book was determined independently, but as a device to preserve retail price stability. Furthermore publishers would still have to recommend retail prices in order to establish the discounted price at which they would sell to booksellers, and there was a tradition whereby book buyers expected to buy books at the prices printed on their covers. Thus price cutting would be selective rather than widespread, and would frequently manifest itself as a form of loss-leadership whereby a general store might offer bargain-price books in order to attract custom to the store. This would, in the Court's view, serve merely to transfer demand from one outlet to another rather than to generate additional sales, with the result that booksellers would be afraid to hold large stocks of any book which might be used elsewhere as a loss-leader subsequently forcing them to dispose of their holdings at a net loss. Furthermore there was no reason to assume that any particular type of book would lend itself to loss-leadership.

The Court also held that in the absence of the Net Book Agreement public libraries would either force higher discounts out of booksellers or would transfer their custom to specialized library suppliers, a factor which, when combined with selective price cutting, would drive many stockholding booksellers out of business. Those who remained in business would hold smaller and less varied stocks, and would be forced to do more special orders, which, because of the additional costs involved, would leave them with a negligible profit. In order to keep booksellers in existence publishers would be forced to concede larger discounts which would push up prices, as previously mentioned. Thus although selected price cutting would result from the termination of the Agreement, it would occur in the context of generally higher prices. Furthermore although libraries would obtain larger discounts, these discounts would be deducted from higher prices and the libraries would gain little or no advantage in the long run. Eventually a vicious circle would arise with higher prices leading to reduced demand; reduced demand to smaller print runs; smaller print runs to higher unit costs; and higher unit costs to higher prices.

The Court was not prepared to comment upon whether there was an excess supply of new books, a possibility denied by publishers. The Court felt that termination of the Agreement would lead to a reduction in the number of books published, the effects of which would be most severe in the higher reaches of literature. The Court felt strongly that this would deny to the public specific and substantial benefits.

The Court rejected the Registrar's contention that the Agreement served to preserve an antiquated system of book distribution. It held that there was nothing inherent in the Agreement to prevent innovation in methods either of book distribution or of book production. Indeed the competitive nature of the industry would ensure an adventurous approach in these respects.

Finally the Court rejected the Registrar's contention that it was against the public interest for the bookseller to be forced to retain the whole of his discount irrespective of the services he offered or of his need for the discount, since he was effectively prevented from sharing this discount with the customer even where, for example, a book was simply bought straight off the shelf. The Court held that the publishers fixed retail prices rather than discounts, and could if they so wished vary the discount to reflect the service provided by the retail outlet. However it did not appear to be the case in practice that retail outlets other than stock-holding booksellers were either willing or able to get by on smaller discounts.

REFLECTIONS ON THE JUDGEMENT

Introduction

At this stage in the analysis it is perhaps appropriate to remind ourselves that we do not, and indeed cannot, <u>know</u> what would be the long term implications of the overturning of the NBA. Like the Court in 1962 we must consider the balance of probabilities, and we must do so in the continued absence of precise quantitative evidence relating to, for example, the proportion of books which would end up being sold at reduced prices. The Court held that were such information to be required from publishers "it would be as hard, if not harder, for the Respondents to get through what has often been called the gateway of Section 21(1)(b) as we are told it is for a rich man to enter the Kingdom of Heaven." In a later section we will consider whether either the past history of the UK book trade or overseas experience in more recent years can shed any light on this matter. In the meantime we may note that the Publishers' Association remains firmly wedded to the view that all of the arguments presented by the PA before the Court remain as valid today as they did in 1962.

Discounts and Stockturn

In an early commentary on the Judgement Yamey (1963) pointed out that whereas the Court expected price cutting in the absence of the NBA to be only <u>occasional</u> and <u>selective,</u> it expected the consumers' interest to be affected in a <u>far-reaching</u> way. He felt that this lack of symmetry disguised the fact that the additional uncertainty engendered by selective price cutting would only affect stockholding practice to an insignificant degree, and could be compensated for by a slighty higher margin of discount on slow-moving stock. Since such stock would not itself be vulnerable to periodic price competition it would remain economically viable to produce. The question of the relationship between discounts and stockturn would certainly appear to be a fundamental issue. In 1962 the Registrars' economist argued that "the distributor should enjoy a larger margin on stock which is likely to be slow to move (and may not be sold at all) and a smaller one on stock which moves fast."

At the time trade practice was (as indeed it still is) based upon a diametrically opposed principle, namely that the risk was greatest in the case of a potential best-seller where the print-run was typically longer and the royalty typically higher as compared to an academic text. In the latter case the market was reasonably well-assured even in the absence of heavy bookshop exposure, whereas in the former case exposure and availability was all-important so that the bookseller had to be rewarded for ordering a large stock in case the book turned out to be a flop and the stock left unsold on the shelves. The publishers' economist argued that it was inappropriate to examine best-seller profitability after the event, since in the case of an individual title the risks were being run <u>before</u> sales took place. In his view the bookseller assessed the degree of risk at the <u>margin</u> when deciding how many of any given title to stock, and related this to the discount offered such that

an increased rate of discount on a particular book would make additional copies
desirable which it would have been too risky to order at a lower discount. In ac-
cepting these arguments the Court ruled that "rates have been evolved by ordinary
economic processes in the course of many years of business, and broadly represent
the margins which publishers find necessary to induce booksellers to stock and end-
eavour to sell their products." Rather interestingly this implies that the rate of
discount offered by a publisher on a given title is such as to render that title
economically viable in its own right, whereas publishers constantly argue that bestsellers subsidise the higher reaches of literature.

Now irrespective of the merits of the above arguments in 1962, this is clearly one
area where a significant change in trade practice has been taking place. Increasingly books are being offered to stockholding booksellers on a sale-or-return or
see-safe basis. Such a facility greatly reduces the risk inherent in subscribing
to a given type of book, and therefore enhances the original argument of the Registrar's economist that the discount be related to the rate of turnover. The fact
that the relationship between discounts and categories of book has shown no tendency
to move in the expected direction indicates the potential for, and indeed the logic
of, price competition among outlets selling prospective best-sellers were there
no NBA. An increasing proportion of such trade is anyway being serviced direct by
the publisher who may provide a rack which he stocks with his own books, and by
removing all titles which do not sell sufficiently quickly he effectively absorbs
the entire risk of the operation. It is frankly very hard to understand why a retailer should expect a high rate in these circumstances. A high discount should
constitute either a reward for exceptional risk to the retailer or for an exceptional level of service offered by the retailer. In the case of direct supply both
risk and service are negligible. This suggests that in the absence of the NBA the
stockholding bookseller who provides a proper service should simply be given a
higher rather than a lower rate of discount, thus allowing him to compete on price.

Trade thinking appears to be moving along different lines. In 1974 a report published by a joint working party of booksellers and publishers recommended "a standard minimum discount of 35 per cent (carriage paid) on all net books, academic and
technical no less than general." The rationale for this claim lay in the argument
that the costs of handling a book were broadly the same to a bookseller irrespective
of the type of book in question. This approach is fundamentally different from that
put forward in 1962 since it associates discounts with bookshop costs rather than
with the risks of holding stock. Its prospects for success are therefore limited
to those retailers with the necessary bulk-buying power. Nevertheless the rates
of discount quoted in the Judgement as varying from $16\frac{1}{3}\%$ to $33\frac{1}{3}\%$ have been gradually
edged upwards over the years, and it is evident that the bigger the discount the
greater the scope for price competition. Furthermore as discounts rise the most
efficient bookshops are placed in the happy position of being able to meet price
competition head-on where necessary. The effects on the less efficient will be
considered in a later section.

Book Clubs and Remainders

We have already refered above to the introduction of direct servicing of stocks
held at certain retail outlets such as supermarkets. However this represents only
one of the many instances of non-bookshop selling which have become commonplace
since 1962. In certain instances this has resulted from the widespread introduction
of paperbacks since most non-bookshop outlets are unwilling to stock high-priced
cloth-bound titles. The most significant factor, however, has probably been the
growth of book clubs which we will be considering in some detail elsewhere. Suffice
it to say that in 1962 the publishers viewed book clubs with some trepidation for
fear that they would take business away from stockholding bookshops. In the event,

however, the book club bandwagon gained momentum, and publishers even began to bring out simultaneous hardback and book club editions at substantially differing prices. This is symptomatic of a gradual erosion of the inter dependent relationship between publishers and stockholding bookshops and also of the belief among consumers that a book is only sold at its net price. The most recent indication of this trend has been the upsurge in remaindering. The increasing emphasis upon cash-flow discussed elsewhere has steered publishers towards a policy of rapid disposal of surplus stock to a degree which has made it economic for shops to open dedicated solely to the sale of remainders. Insofar as this generates a belief among customers that net prices are less than sacrosanct it may also be helping to undermine the NBA. Publishers often argue that the existence of the National Book Sale has not had this effect but bookshop sales never appear to offer anything like the range of titles available all year round at remainder shops.

THE NET BOOK AGREEMENT IN THE 1890's

At this juncture we can consider what lessons can be learned from the decade 1890 to 1900 in the UK during which no net book agreement was in force. It would appear that underselling was almost universal in the form of discounts off published prices, an outcome dismissed as improbable by the Court were the NBA abolished. Furthermore the discounts offered were uniform so that prices were very stable during the 1890's, whereas the Court condidered that they would be volatile in the absence of the NBA. Finally booksellers' gross margins were poor and the effect of netting books after 1900 was to raise prices rather than to lower them. In almost all respects, therefore, experience in the 1890's contradicts the outcomes foretold in the Judgement.

PRICE MAINTENANCE IN THE RECORD INDUSTRY

It may be argued that such retrospective comparisons are invalidated by the changed circumstances of the book trade between 1900 and 1962, and that other comparisons, such as with other industries where price maintenance was abolished in 1964, are more relevant. It has been suggested that the photographic trade provides a useful basis for comparison, but this appears unconvincing when one considers how dependent photographic dealers are upon a limited range of high-value items. The record industry would appear superficially to provide a valid basis for comparison because the systems for producing and marketing records and books are undoubtedly very similar as is demonstrated by Hill (1978). There is, however, currently one significant difference which is that there is normally no sale-or-return provision for record shops. Thus the current situation of the record industry closely parallels that of the book trade in 1962, but would prove an unreliable guide to the likely outcome of terminating the NBA at the present time.

OVERSEAS EXPERIENCE

Canada

The most valid basis for comparison must therefore be in the experience of other countries where r.p.m. on books has recently been abolished. In 1962 the Court heard about the abolition of r.p.m. on books in Canada, and was persuaded that the detrimental effects allegedly experienced there such as periodic cut-throat price competition leading to a reduction both in the number of bookshops and in the average size of stocks, would be replicated in the UK. In previous cases the Court had been reluctant to place much emphasis upon overseas experience, and there were those such as Yamey (1963) and Skeoch (1964) who felt that the Court should not have made an exception in this case. In view of this we are better advised to limit our discussion to more recent examples.

Australia

It has been alleged that the abolition of r.p.m. on books in Sweden in 1970 proved
highly detrimental to stockholding bookshops. However a more interesting debate
concerns the abolition of r.p.m. in Australia in 1972 where the decision rested upon
principles of economic theory rather than upon the predictions of members of the
book trade. As a result the conclusions of the Australian Tribunal were radically
different from those of the Court in predicting that prices would fall; that there
would be no reduction in the range of titles on offer; that booksellers' services
would be maintained; and that booksellers would continue to stock up on titles which
were likely to be the subject of price competition.

Nieuwenhuysen (1975) published a survey which in general supported the view that
"apart from isolated instances the predictions made by members of the book trade in
the tribunal case do not appear to have taken immediate effect". However the trends
discerned so soon after the abolition of r.p.m. on books might anyway have manifested themselves for other reasons, so one cannot place too much trust in the continued relevance of the book's findings. It has subsequently been argued by Zifcak
(1977, 1978) that in practice prices tended to rise rather than fall and that "good
traditional and culturally significant bookshops disappeared and new bookselling
outlets appeared .....under the same names...... with a different management approach"
This approach embodied reductions in stockholding, higher prices, less service, remainder selling and charges for placing special orders. However it is difficult to
comment upon these findings in the absence of a further comprehensive survey of the
trade.

France

In France book publishers traditionally supplied books with a recommended retail price
within margins set by the Government. But in the mid-1970's the discount chain
FNAC began selling books at below the recommended levels, a policy subsequently taken
up by some department stores. In July 1979 publishers were obliged to abandon recommended prices, thereby allowing bookshops to sell at any price they chose. Subsequently total book sales lagged behind inflation and only department stores with
an emphasis upon best-sellers profited from this new-found freedom. As a result
most stockholding booksellers voted for a return to recommended prices.

Conclusions

Reports of overseas experience tend to be ambiguous and inconclusive, often proving
more reliant on opinions than facts. Unfortunately no attempt has been made to test
scientifically what effect the abolition of r.p.m. on books has had over a period of
time and there is also the problem of variability of book industry practice from
country to country. Under the circumstances we appear to be left with a verdict of
not proven either way.

RECENT CRITICISM OF THE NET BOOK AGREEMENT

Pressure to abrogate the NBA could potentially arise from one of two sources. In
the first place there could be a declining belief in the need for the NBA within the
book trade itself. Symptomatic of this development was Norrie's thoroughly heretical
article in The Bookseller, referred to above, in the course of which he admits that

one does not have to sell at below net prices in order to offer a bargain to a bulk purchaser. He also pointed out that best-sellers often catch the trade by surprise, with the result that far from being caught with unsold, full-price stock were there no NBA, stockholding bookshops would often be able to sell as many copies as they could lay their hands on at as high a price as the market would bear. The second source of pressure could originate in the work of economists attempting to demonstrate that the economic principles expressed in the Judgement were analytically unsound. In a fairly recent paper Morris (1977) used calculus to demonstrate that (1) if the variable costs of publishing are constant or rising, the NBA will result in higher prices; (2) the NBA will result in less direct promotional activity per pounds worth of books sold; (3) the operation of the NBA will result in a higher relative level of service being provided; and (4) the abrogation of the NBA would not necessarily lead to a reduction in the number of outlets. His basic proposition therefore was that given the existence of the NBA it is in the interests of publishers to price at a higher level than they otherwise would choose, and in the interests of booksellers to offer a higher level of service than they otherwise would choose. Thus the majority of consumers are "faced with higher prices and a higher level of service than they desire. Only those buyers who use more than an average amount of the zero-priced services will be better off."

Acceptance of these propositions clearly undermines the three principal conclusions set out in the Judgement. It must however be recognised that what is true in theory is not necessarily true in practice. Let us therefore now turn to consider the three basic justifications for the NBA in the light of developments in the publishing industry since 1962.

THE NUMBER OF TITLES AND CONSUMER DETRIMENT

In the first place, would the abolition of the NBA result in fewer published titles to the substantial detriment of the consumer? As was shown by the quotation in the preface complaints about over-publication have been voiced for decades, yet in 1979 more books were published than in any previous year, and over 50% more than in 1962. Publishers appear to have no qualms about publishing books even where their prospects are severely constrained by the fact that they cover the same material for the same market as books already in existence. New technical books appear which are clearly inferior to existing texts, and plots in fiction books are rehashed ad infinitum.

Superficially such a publishing strategy would appear to be doomed to failure. Evidence exists, however, such as the continuing profitability of firms such as Mills and Boon, that duplication of proven formats may be as much the secret of success as of failure, although it probably depends upon the particular market in question. It is well known that the majority of loans from public libraries fall into categories such as romantic fiction, which suggests that the consumer would suffer some detriment were fewer titles in these categories to be published. Nevertheless in other areas of publishing the consumer surely gains so little from duplication that the rejection of near-substitutes would offer up a larger share of the market for such books as are published, thereby enabling print runs to be longer and unit production costs and prices to be lower. Thus overall consumers would benefit in these areas even though choice would be restricted since lower prices would be viewed by the majority as preferable to a larger number of near-substitute books.

If fewer books were published the reduction would not be in the categories mentioned above where demand is buoyant. The Judgement identified a potential reduction in the higher reaches of literature, itself a rather imprecise term. But in many cases there now exists alternative means of reaching a potential audience other than via the cloth-bound book so that the higher reaches of literature would hardly be decimated. Overall, therefore, I am inclined to believe that the Court was wrong in concluding that a "substantial" detriment would arise were fewer books to be published.

BOOK PRICES

In the second place, would books become more expensive to the substantial detriment of the consumer? Here one is obliged to follow the Court and consider the balance of probabilities. My own view is that there would be a combination of selective price-cutting in fast-turnover fiction and the occasional popular technical book, together with selective price-raising on slow-turnover books and on those which are in inelastic demand such as books catering to unusual hobbies. This would mean that on a straight head count by far the majority of book buyers would obtain their books at reduced prices. But what one makes of this depends upon ones measurement of consumer satisfaction. If one believes that the over-riding consideration is that the majority of buyers should cease to subsidise the minority then the consumer interest will be greatly served by the price changes described above. If on the other hand one believes that the consumer who buys regularly should be given more weight than the consumer whose purchases are irregular then a simple comparison of the number of consumers who occasionally buy fast-moving fiction with the number who regularly acquire quality fiction or technical books will not prove satisfactory.

Furthermore if one believes that every potential consumer should be entitled to expect a wide choice of books at reasonable prices however narrow the individual's interests then the abolition of the NBA would prove detrimental in that it would offer much the best choice and value to the lowest common denominator, namely the buyer of pulp fiction. I cannot see any obvious way to resolve these difficulties, although it is still worth pointing out that the Court believed that "substantial" detriment would occur as a result of relative price changes and once again this is difficult to reconcile with the arguments presented above.

STOCKHOLDING BOOKSHOPS

Finally, would termination of the NBA result in fewer and less-well equipped stockholding bookshops? One of the curiosities of the bookselling trade is that although it is none too profitable, and many shops go out of business each year, there is never any shortage of newcomers to the trade. This would suggest that termination of the NBA would not greatly affect the number of stockholding bookshops. The price competition which we have suggested would arise for high-turnover stock were there no NBA would obviously affect bookshop profitability. But by the same token bookshops would be able to charge a higher price for books in inelastic demand. Furthermore if publishers genuinely believe that the continued viability of the stockholding bookshop is a vital part of the whole publishing operation then they should alter their discount structure to achieve the desired end-result.

Irrespective of whether they do this the termination of the NBA would almost certainly induce most bookshops to rationalise their stock, eliminating perhaps those items whose slow stockturn could not be justified even at higher rates of discount. Thus bookshops would indeed be less well-equipped, but not necessarily to the point at which the consumer would suffer a substantial detriment. It must be remembered that a good bookshop stocking 30,000 titles is still only stocking 10 per cent of all titles in print, so that the other 90 per cent need to be ordered from publishers. Were a bookshop to discard 10 per cent of its titles in stock then this would affect only marginally the relationship between stocked and ordered items. Indeed discarding the 10 per cent slowest-moving items would prove even less significant from the point of view of the total number of books sold, and if a potential purchaser is particularly keen to obtain a book which is not held in stock why should he not be expected to order it, provided, of course, that he does not have to wait more than a few days.

Finally, it must be observed that one of the biggest drawbacks to the existing system for marketing quality books is that stockholding bookshops are distributed around the UK is an extremely unequal way. It may therefore be argued that any system which is designed to underpin this distribution is not in the interests of bookbuyers as a whole.

CONCLUSION

Thus, in conclusion, it seems to me that changes in the circumstances of the book trade since 1962 have had the effect of nullifying many of the arguments presented before the Court in favour of the NBA, even if we start from the questionable presumption that the Judgement was based upon sound economics. It therefore seems probable that, were the Net Book Agreement once again to come before the Restrictive Practices Court, the original Judgement would either be overturned or at best sustained on far narrower grounds than was the case in 1962. One must remember that although the Judgement seems to be highly categoric, the difficulties of assessing what would happen were the NBA to be terminated led the Court to acknowledge that "we are conscious that others might make a different assessment of what is likely." At the end of the day, therefore, one must conclude that the continuing justification for the NBA is not primarily economic. As is so often pointed out books have a special cultural, social and educational role. It may therefore be argued that this role is, and has always been, the over-riding factor, and that price maintenance for books needs no other justification.

APPENDIX: THE NET BOOK AGREEMENT 1957

We the undersigned several firms of publishers, being desirous that in so far as we publish books at net prices (as to which each publisher is free to make his own decisions), those net prices shall normally be the prices at which such books are sold to the public as hereinafter defined, and in order to avoid disorganization in the book trade and to ensure that the public may be informed of and able uniformly to take advantage of the conditions under which net books may be sold at less than the net prices, hereby agree to adopt and each of us does hereby adopt the following standard sale conditions for the net books published by us within the United Kingdom:

Standard Conditions of Sale of Net Books

(i)   Except as provided in clauses (ii) and (iv) hereof and except as we may otherwise direct net books shall not be sold or offered for sale or caused or permitted to be sold or offered for sale to the public at less than the net published prices.
(ii) A net book may be sold or offered for sale to the public at less than the net published price if
      (a) it has been held in stock by the bookseller for a period of more than twelve months from the date of the latest purchase by him of any copy thereof and
      (b) it has been offered to the publisher at cost price or at the proposed reduced price whichever shall be the lower and such offer has been refused by the publisher.
(iii) A net book may be sold or offered for sale to the public at less than the net

published price if it is second-hand and six months have elapsed since its date of publication.

(iv)   A net book may be sold at a discount to such libraries, book agents (including Service Unit libraries), quantity buyers and institutions as are from time to time authorised by the Council of The Publishers' Association of such amount and on such conditions as are laid down in the instrument of authorisation. Such amount and conditions shall not initially be less favourable than those prevailing at the time of this Agreement.

(v)   For the purposes of clause (i) hereof a book shall be considered as sold at less than the net published price if the bookseller
(a) offers or gives any consideration in cash to any purchaser except under license from the Council of The Publishers' Association or
(b) offers or gives any consideration in kind (e.g. card indexing, stamping, reinforced bindings, etc.) at less than the actual cost thereof to the bookseller.

(vi)   For the purposes of this Agreement and of these Standard Conditions: Net book shall mean a book, pamphlet, map or other similar printed matter published at a net price. Net price and net published price shall mean the price fixed from time to time by the publisher below which the net book shall not be sold to the public.
Public shall be deemed to include schools, libraries, institutions and other non-trading bodies.
Person shall include any company, firm, corporation, club, institution, organization, association or other body.

(vii) The above conditions shall apply to all sales executed in the United Kingdom and the Republic of Ireland whether effected by wholesaler or retailer when the publisher's immediate trade customer, whether wholesaler or retailer, or the wholesaler's immediate trade customer, is in the United Kingdom or the Republic of Ireland.

We the undersigned several firms of publishers further agree to appoint and each of us does hereby appoint the Council of The Publishers' Association to act as our agent in the collection of information concerning breaches of contract by persons selling or offering for sale net books, and in keeping each individual publisher informed of breaches in respect of such net books as are published by him, and we further hereby undertake and agree that we will each enforce our contractual rights and our rights under the Restrictive Trade Practices Act 1956 if called upon to do so by the Council of The Publishers' Association, and provided that we shall be indemnified by The Publishers' Association if so requested by us in respect of any costs incurred by us or by the Council of The Publishers' Association on our behalf.

CHAPTER 4

Innovation and Copyright

The closing years of the 1970's will probably be remembered in retrospect as the period during which deliberation about two major issues reached a crucial stage. The first of these issues is truly fundamental, namely whether publishers should persevere with publishing in book form or switch to alternative technology such as microform. We will therefore be examining in the paragraphs which follow both the economic viability of the system known as on-demand publishing, and at the wider controversy concerning the future of the printed word. The second issue also arose in the context of a new technology, in this case the photocopying machine, and re-volved around the protection of copyright. This issue has been doing the rounds for a great many years, and much has been made of the photocopier's potential to undermine the economic viability of book and journal production, but only in recent years has there been a formal investigation into the problem and into ways of coping with it. The issue of copyright can be approached from both a theoretical and prac-tical viewpoint, and both are incorporated into this chapter. What is particularly interesting about this issue is that some kind of solution is in sight, and one can-not say that about many other controversies in the publishing arena.

ON-DEMAND PUBLISHING

Introduction

During the first half of the coming decade we can safely predict the continuation of two trends with which we are already familiar. The first is a reduction in the real value of library budgets, and the second is a further narrowing of fields of study. As a result the potential market for specialised books will increasingly shrink towards the point of no return so far as the economics of conventional publishing are concerned. This then raises the question as to the most appropriate alternative method of disseminating information in published form. The most comm-only voiced solution is the system known as on-demand publishing, and it is the purpose of this section to examine the economic viability of this system.

In the conventional system copies of books are supplied direct from a pre-existing stock. However on-demand means that copies are supplied either singly or in small quantities, in response to individual orders, by means of photographic reproduction.

The original copy, and only one need be held, can be either in the form of a typescript or a microfiche. One advantage of this system is immediately apparent.
Whenever a book has sold well enough to exhaust its original print run, but not so
well as to suggest an economic reprint, it normally sinks without trace as the original copies are gradually worn out. However it may occasionally transpire that a
renewed demand can be identified which cannot now be met by the original publisher
unless, most unusually, he is prepared to offer a single order service reproduced
from a microfiche. It is understandable that conventional publishers are not in-
terested in this kind of service. But a publisher who specialises in this kind of
work, who gathers originals from a wide range of publishers, and who invests in the
latest reprographic equipment, may well be able to produce single copies of reasonable quality at a reasonable price. Indeed a growing number of concerns already
provide this kind of service. The investment required is small because the book
is already available in printed form, from which it can, if so desired, be directly
reproduced. Thus provided the original publisher accepts the quality and price of
the on-demand product as reasonable and that his reputation is thereby protected,
both parties are likely to gain from the arrangement.

Prospects

So far so good. But can we safely assume that because on-demand publishing often
provides an economic system for reprinting books it therefore provides an economic
system for original publication? There is no hard-and-fast answer to this question
which is discussed at length in Singleton (1979), Bailey (1975), Smith (1976) and
Nash (1976). On-demand publishing is obviously cheaper than conventional publishing.
The initial investment is lower; there are no warehousing costs; no interest charge
is generated by money tied up in stocks; no stocks are written off. However these
costs do not loom all that large when compared to other manufacturing costs of production. There is a tendency for the proponents of on-demand publishing to advocate
a system whereby the author types up his manuscript in a form fit for reproduction.
The publisher then sends out a few review copies and a list of available titles to
likely buyers, and waits for orders to roll in. But this is not altogether realistic.
Since many books with limited markets are already produced as camera-ready copy no
savings can be made as compared to conventional publishing unless the on-demand
publisher chooses to forgo his editorial function. In the second place any attempt
to do away with expensive advertising costs may be self-defeating because reviews
are often over a year out of date. In conventional publishing a book's highest
annual turnover often takes place prior to the publication of reviews because its
publishers are prepared to send out large numbers of inspection copies and to advertise in the press. These costs are avoidable, but if avoided quite a number
of potential sales are sure to be lost. It is also difficult to see what role the
stockholding bookseller can play in marketing on-demand books since no copies will
be available on his shelves and discounts can hardly be expected to match those of
conventional publishers.

A related question is whether on-demand publishing of original books will be acceptable either to potential authors or potential purchasers. It is clear that conventional publishing accords prestige to an author as well as a financial reward.
But this in turn makes his book desirable to the potential purchaser since it has
been passed as acceptable by referees and the publisher has risked sinking his own
money into the publication. Thus on-demand publishing must not merely be cheaper.
It must also overcome the ingrained conservatism of the intellectual community.

The prospects for on-demand publishing of original works do not therefore appear to
be all that promising. So long as authors remain hopeful that their work will be
published in conventional form it is difficult to conceive of an economically viable
on-demand system running parallel with the conventional system. Perhaps the current

'crisis' in publishing will change all that, although it will certainly take time
and it is as yet unclear as to what type of institution will be best suited to the
task of getting the system under way.

THE FUTURE OF THE PRINTED WORD

Introduction

As technology becomes increasingly sophisticated one is driven to consider whether
the written word in book form has had its day. The underlying hypothesis is that
man's ability to preserve and pass on information has depended for many centuries
past upon the written word. However the pool of available information has grown so
rapidly that it increasingly presents problems of information storage. Science has
responded to these problems through the invention of microform and the microchip,
and it is predicted that these will eventually take over completely and render the
book obsolete.

Economics of Microform

We are already familiar with microform whether it be fiche or film. The more commonly used microfiche is a sheet of film on which are recorded at 1/24th life size
the pages of a book or journal. Further reductions in size are known as ultrafiche
and superfiche. To read fiche one needs a machine called a reader which at present
is typically rather bulky and rather expensive. However it is probable that fiche
readers will become both cheaper and more portable within the near future. The
real problem is whether or not a portable reader will be a suitable product for the
high volume/low cost/low price/heavy sales sequence which has proved so successful
for electronic watches and calculators. In this respect there appears to be a
fundamental split between institutions and individuals. Microform has so far been
directed primarily at libraries where storage problems and budgetary constraints
have been most acute. Microform has proved especially suitable for reference works,
journals, newspapers and documents. Nevertheless it is unpopular with users for a
variety of reasons including the strain of reading from a vertically aligned screen.
As a result there is a demand for copies printed from the microform on to paper, a
process which destroys many of the economic benefits of microform. Equally there is
a considerable initial investment required by any institution going over to microform in a big way. It is this combination of user resistance and initial outlay
which makes the production of cheap and portable readers a commercially risky
operation.

There are several hundred microform publishers already operating in the USA compared
to only a handful in the UK, where slow acceptance of microform forced Blackwell
to sell its microfiche subsidiary in March 1979. Nevertheless microform is almost
certainly going to dominate the market for specialist reprints which are totally
uneconomic in printed form. Whether it will take over in other spheres is much
more doubtful. It can be argued that the only people familiar with microform at
present are at institutions whereas what is needed is to bring microform to the
attention of the general public, a process which requires the co-operation of booksellers. The price of such co-operation must be found in the form of high discounts
which make it worthwhile for a bookseller to invest in readers for customer use.
For the time being, however, microform publishers are unwilling to offer such discounts. It may be that they in turn are waiting for the introduction of cheap and
portable readers. If these are marketed then perhaps, but only perhaps, microform
will come into much wider usage. In their absence there is a negligible likelihood
of microform spreading beyond institutions.

Microchips

It may be argued that microform has anyway been rendered technologically absolete
by the extraordinarily rapid coming of age of the microchip. In his chapter entitled
'Death of the Printed Word' Evans (1979) has already published his prediction that
the printed book will be replaced by the electronic book. As the prediction of the
printed book's "slow but steady slide into oblivion" is due to come into effect in
the 1980's we must examine Evans' hypothesis with some care.

Evans believes that books and computers should be viewed primarily as devices for
storing information. However the computer has three major advantages over the book
in this respect. In the first place the information can be stored on silicon chips
which are so small that eventually it will be possible to store an entire library
in the same amount of space that is presently required by a single paperback. In
the second place the electronic book will be immeasurably cheaper than the printed
book. Finally the electronic book will be so small that the most economic method
of distribution will be direct from publisher to customer. Although bookshops will
therefore disappear publishers will survive, despite the very small margin of profit
per book, as a result of a massive increase in total sales stimulated by very low
prices.

Evans acknowledges that when viewed as a display unit the printed book is "marvell-
ously convenient and aesthetically gratifying." However he believes that small,
cheap and portable readers will be produced so as to make the electronic book convenient to read, and that these chip-readers will be made aesthetically satisfying
to look at and to touch.

In more controversial vein Evans then goes on to argue that the electronic book of
the 1980's "will no longer be passive, for it will be a sifter and interpreter as
well as a purveyor of information". He foresees the appearance of the "smart" en-
cyclopaedia which when programmed with certain key words will "do its own research"
and guide the user to the relevant sections of the book.

Not surprisingly Evans has come under attack for his views on the demise of the
printed book. But the attacks such as that launched by Fairlie and Corby (1979)
contain many arguments which serve primarily to obscure the basic issues raised
by Evans. In the first place we must ask ourselves whether the electronic book is
a practical proposition from a technological viewpoint. The answer to this question
must surely be a resounding yes. In the second place we must ask whether the book,
and the reader which is needed to scan it, can potentially be produced at a price
which will make customers seriously consider the purchase of electronic rather than
printed books. Here again I think the answer must be yes, although very large scale
production will be required. Thus the crucial question is the third and final one,
namely whether the reading public will take to the reader on the scale necessary
to make it an attractive buy. It is premature to answer this question with a categoric negative because the public have taken to electronic watches, calculators
and especially games without batting an eyelid. Nevertheless many reservations
inevitably remain and it will be many years before Evans' predicted slow and steady
slide can be identified with any certainty.

COPYRIGHT

Introduction

The issue of copyright presents formidable difficulties to the economist for a
number of reasons, of which two are of particular importance. In the first place
the accepted rationale for the existence of copyright has fluctuated from country

to country and from period to period, and has involved complex philosophical as well as economic ideas. Secondly we have virtually no statistical evidence of any link between the copying of copyright material and the economics of publishing books and articles. In the sections below we will firstly present a brief overview of the economic rationale for copyright, and subsequently analyse the debate between those who believe that all knowledge should be a free good to scholars and those who believe that a charge should always be levied for the reproduction of copyright material.

Ringer (1976) has reviewed the history of copyright. However the most thorough analysis of the rationale for copyright has come from Hurt and Schuchman (1966) who group the justifications advanced in favour of copyright under two headings. The first of these includes those justifications "which are based on the rights of the creator of the protected object or on the obligation of society toward him." The most obvious right in this context is the property right of the writer to the fruits of his creation. It can be argued that a publication is the result of intellectual labour, which, unlike physical labour, does not require the temporary loss of use of land or machinery for other purposes. Thus the award of a copyright cannot be said to deprive anyone else of something which they would have had in the absence of the writer's creative activity.

Secondly, there are those justifications "which are based on the promotion of the general well-being of society." It is widely recognised that the award of copyright is the most convenient way of meeting society's obligation to reward writers for their contribution to general welfare. No publisher would be willing to undertake the risk and cost of publishing a book which could be pirated without any form of redress since this would result in the private benefit to authors and publishers being disproportionately less than the public benefit to society. Hence copyright legislation is seen as a system for raising the rewards to authors and publishers and thereby encouraging the publication of books which would not otherwise have come into existence.

Historically the debate about copyright was concerned primarily with the piracy of whole editions. However for the past two decades the primary issue has been the spread of photocopying machines. On the whole, although piracy was, and indeed sometimes still is, commonplace in certain parts of the world, it was never regarded as the kind of problem which could potentially drive publishers to the wall. Photocopying, on the other hand, is seen as a much more severe threat, though not to the entire spectrum of publishing. Whereas it is possible to copy an entire book for less than its selling price the differences in quality and lifespan of the versions are such as to impose considerable constraints upon this practice. Thus the concern over photocopying is directed primarily at scholarly publications, and above all to journal articles.

The Right to Photocopy

In recent years a vociferous lobby has grown to support the right to photocopy without reservation. On the one hand this comprises those librarians who argue that since they cannot afford to maintain their purchases of books and periodicals, the best solution is a system of inter-library lending whereby each member library stands willing to supply to other institutions photocopies of anything which is held in stock. On the other hand there are those scholars who argue that conventional publishing is increasingly at odds with the needs of an ever more specialised academic community. Knowledge is viewed not as a marketable commodity but as a basic right. However two counteracting arguments can be put forward. In the first place the advocates of the free dissemination of knowledge are never dependent upon the proceeds from writing as a major source of income. Thus for them the benefit out-

weighs the cost. In the second place they appear to forget that for a photocopy
to be taken an original must already exist. Thus a vicious circle may be set in
motion whereby an increase in copying reduces the typical print run; which raises
unit cost and price; which fosters more copying; and which eventually causes
publication to cease.

This latter outcome can hardly be in anyone's interest. The problem, of course,
is to determine whether or not there is a close relationship between photocopying
and a reduction in the sales of original publications. That photocopying is widespread is not itself in question. In 1963 the British Lending Library Division
copied 13,307 articles from the 18,175 serials held in stock, whereas in 1974 it
copied 893,801 articles from 44,767 serials. These statistics provoked a debate
between Line and Wood (1975) and Van Tongeren (1976) which demonstrated little
other than that no unequivocal relationship between photocopying and journal sales
could be specified. Thus we can sum up the state of play by asserting that whereas
the majority view would clearly support the existence of such a relationship, we
do not know enough about it to help us devise an appropriate remedy.

Law of Copyright

It has been recognised for many years past that the matters discussed above needed
to be taken into account in a revised law of copyright. During the past three years
three more or less simultaneous efforts to update copyright law have reached varying degrees of fruition. In the UK the Whitford Committee was set up to consider
the law on copyright and designs. The Committee first met in February 1964 to
"consider and report whether any, and if so what, changes are desirable in the law
relating to copyright as provided by the Copyright Act 1956 and the Design Copyright Act 1968". The Committee produced its Report in early 1977. On the issue of
what is referred to in the Report as reprography the Committee was concerned in
particular with the question of fair dealing or fair use. Their starting point was
a joint statement issued in 1965 by the Publishers' Association and the Society of
Authors entitled Photocopying and the Law. In this they agreed that where, for the
purposes of research or private study, a single copy is made from a copyright work
of a single extract not exceeding 4,000 words or a series of extracts (none exceeding 3,000 words) to a total of 8,000 words, provided that in no case the total
amount copied exceeds 10 per cent of the whole work (poems, essays and other short
literary works to be regarded as whole works in themselves), then that copy would
be regarded by them as fair dealing. In essence this did not mean that these limits
had any backing in law, but that authors and publishers did not want to be bothered
with requests to copy unless the limits were exceeded.

In fixing these limits the publishers and authors were clearly acting in good faith.
Unfortunately, this faith was open to abuse. Under section 7 of the 1956 Copyright
Act anyone wanting to make a copy from library material has to sign a declaration
that the copy is for research or private study. But these terms are ambiguous and,
for example, allow in principle for every student in a large class to make a personal copy from the same original. Besides which there are no sanctions where
declarations are not completed. Librarians tend to turn a blind eye to copying.
In some cases they feel resentment at the practice of charging libraries much
higher journal subscription rates than individuals, and regard copying as a means
of redressing this imbalance. But this in turn annoys publishers who feel that
their guidelines already give libraries a good deal of latitude in allowing copies
to be taken, and that it is going too far to set up an inter-library lending scheme
the objective of which is to provide a systematic service involving the reproduction
of copyright works on demand.

The Report concluded, on the basis of submissions made to it, that the majority of people wanting photocopies were anxious not to harm the interests of authors and publishers. What they wanted was a method of obtaining copies in accordance with the law which was both relatively cheap and simple to operate. The Committee decided that the only way to meet this need was through the introduction of a system of blanket licensing. Under such a scheme individual authors and publishers would not be responsible for collecting their own royalties. Instead, payment at a standard rate would be collected by a central collecting agency or society which would undertake the task of distribution of the revenue to the individual copyright owners whose works were reproduced. From the user's point of view the blanket licence would cover all of his photocopying requirements, but its obvious drawback would be the need to pay a royalty for single copies which were previously supplied free. Nevertheless the Committee felt strongly that if a research worker "is content to pay for a photocopy the price paid we think in fairness ought to include not only the true cost of the photocopy but also a royalty element for the copyright owner. In the case of works available on the market it is scarcely "fair dealing" to get, even for private study, a cheap copy with no return to the author or publisher, more particularly when much of the cost of copying is borne by the ratepayers or taxpayers."

Revisions to US copyright law came into force in January 1978. The new law prohibited copying beyond the limits of fair use and also systematic library copying of copyrighted materials. Inter-library lending was permitted provided a library did not receive copies in such aggregate quantities (later agreed as a maximum of five) as to substitute for a subscription to or purchase of such work. The Australian Franki Report published in January 1977 also set out to fix certain limits for fair dealing, although it was more generous to users insofar as it reflected a view that a limited right of making multiple copies should be given to educational establishments*. Under the circumstances it is by no means surprising that the Whitford Report's switch away from the concept of fair dealing has not proved popular in all quarters, especially insofar as it penalizes the traditional taking of a single copy without payment of a royalty. Wall (1977) has produced a number of alternative schemes all of which preserve the sanctity of such fair dealing.

At the present time these problems remain unresolved, and no new copyright law is close at hand. However, the Publishers' Association and Whitford whose views they endorse represent a combination which will probably win the day, and the first piece of progress in respect of licensing has recently emerged with the publication of a report by the British Committee of Copyright Owners chaired by Lord Wolfenden. The Committee has drafted three licences to be offered to local authorities to cover copying in their institutions**, and these have been endorsed by the PA. The local authorities are likely to comply because in a recent test case the Music Publishers' Association successfully sued Wolverhampton Corporation with respect to unauthorised photocopying of music.

---

*The US legislation is reviewed in Whitstone (1977) and the Franki Report in Hall (1977)
**As reported in The Bookseller (April 19th, 1980)

CHAPTER 5

Printing

INTRODUCTION

In this section we will be concerned with general printing, which as we have seen
is commonly grouped with publishing for statistical purposes. The other main sectors
of the printing industry are newspapers and periodicals, packaging and stationery.
Because many firms operate in more than one sector it is difficult to separate out
the statistics with complete precision. However the British Printing Industries
Federation have assessed the relative importance of these sectors as follows:

TABLE 19 Sales and Employment in the Printing Industry

	Approximate Sales of Printing Companies in 1977 £ million	Percentage Sales of Manufacturing Industry	Number of Employees
General Printing	1350	1.13	161,000
Newspapers and Periodicals	240	0.20	13,000
Packaging	1280	1.07	46,000
Stationery	420	0.35	30,000
Total	3290	2.75	250,000

Source: BPIF estimates based on Business Monitor

The general printing sector incorporates not merely books but also reports, time-
tables, directories, greetings cards, and so forth. In 1977 large establishments

with more than 25 employees had sales of nearly £800 million with small establishments providing a further £400 million of sales. In addition large establishments
earned about £145 million from the provision of ancillary services such as typesetting, block making and binding.

SIZE OF FIRMS

The majority of all firms are small. The BPIF has produced a size breakdown of its
3,600 member firms in England, Scotland and Wales which appears as Table 20 below.

TABLE 20 The Size Distribution of Printing Firms

		Percentage of Firms
Under	25 employees	62
25 - 49	"	15
50 - 99	"	10
100 - 249	"	8
250 - 499	"	3
500 - 999	"	1
1000 or more	"	1
Total		100

Source: BPIF membership questionnaire 1977

Approximately 135 member firms are concerned primarily with book printing and
binding, and these employ about 23,000 employees. Since this constitutes about
9% of total employment as compared to $3\frac{1}{2}$% of total membership it is obvious that
these firms are on average relatively large, and in fact nearly one-half of them
employ over 250 employees.

SCALE OF PRODUCTION

Most firms are independently owned. However, a significant number of the larger
firms either form a part of a conglomerate operating within the publishing field,
or of a conglomerate with its primary interests in unrelated fields. Nevertheless,
even subsidiary firms are generally allowed to operate with a considerable degree
of autonomy both because a printer with a small share of the total printing market
can achieve all the significant economies of scale and because customers often prefer to establish personal links with printers in their close vicinity.

In their study of the economies of large-scale production Pratten, Dean and Silberston (1965) distinguished five sources of economies of scale in the printing industry,
namely the size of the print run; the use of high capacity machines; standardisation;
specialisation; and taking on more titles. That study is now out of date. But we
can adapt its findings by taking account of the technological changes which have

occurred during the past two decades.

Letterpress

The original printing process is known as letterpress. This process requires that
each letter or line of type be cast in lead in a matrix to form complete pages,
which are then inked and impressed on to sheets of paper. The process takes place
in three stages. First a keyboard is used to perforate a roll of paper with the
text; this roll then passes through a casting machine where air forced through the
perforations causes a matrix to move in to position to receive molten lead and to
form each letter; finally the type is printed on to paper. Letterpress machines
either print one side of the paper at a time or both sides simultaneously using
the 'perfector' process. If a high quality impression is required a flat-bed machine is used. Alternatively mass-production paperbacks can be produced with a
lower-quality impression but at much greater speeds using a rotary press. The cost
advantages of a rotary machine are to be found in its speed of operation and low
make-ready time, but these must be traded-off against the cost of making plates to
fit the machine and the higher cost of depreciation.

Offset Lithography

Letterpress is steadily being replaced by offset lithography. In this process a
page of type, cast as for letterpress, and of illustrations is initially pasted
together. The page is then photographed and the resultant image transferred on to
a plate which is inked. The image is finally transferred on to paper by offsetting
it on to an intermediate roller with which the paper comes into contact. Paper is
fed into the machine either in single sheets or in the form of a continuous reel
known as a web. As compared to letterpress the traditional offset process is therefore more complicated because it requires the additional operation of photographing
the typed page.

However, photocomposition is now typically used whereby characters are offered up
to a camera. The images are positioned by keyboard control, photographed and the
exposed film printed on to offset plates after corrections have been made. The
biggest advantage of photocomposition lies in the fact that the size of the characters can be altered within fairly wide limits during the photographic process, there·
by removing the need for the change in type matrix required by hot metal composition.
The flexibility introduced by the scissors and paste approach to preparing a page
for photocomposition is also a major virtue of this process.

Gravure

The third process in common usage is known as gravure, where the type is etched
into the printing surface. The greatest virtue of this process is that it is particularly well suited to high volume colour printing. However, its main drawback
is the time and expense involved in preparing the cylinders. The increased use of
electronics and laser engraving may reduce cylinder production costs in the future
but will do very little to close the gap in cost between gravure and offset litho
to which most such developments can also be applied. The minimum efficient scale
for gravure is currently around 250,000 copies.

In certain cases the particular requirements of a print run point inevitably to
the use of one process rather than another. However, the longer-run sheet-fed
offset jobs can often now be produced as economically using an eight-page or 'mini'
web offset press. Equally the improved quality of web offset work is making web

offset an increasingly viable alternative to gravure. Thus it is difficult to relate particular processes to the length of the print run which provides the most
obvious source of economies of scale in printing. The BPIF estimated in 1978 that
the use of offset litho as compared to letterpress was in the proportion 7:3.
According to the Price Commission Report large printers sampled in 1977 with a
turnover in excess of £2.5 million used web offsets for one-sixth of their output,
roughly the same proportion as for letterpress. Medium-sized printers with an
average turnover of £450,000 used offset litho for 80% of their output and letterpress for the other 20%. More recently the BPIF forecast* that the majority of
short run work during the early 1980's would involve the use of sheet-fed offset
litho presses, particularly in sizes up to A1, whereas there would be a move away
from larger sheet-fed presses to web presses for general colour work, particularly
for runs of 15,000 and over.

Specialisation and Standardisation

Since the size of the print run is determined by the publisher, and the use of
high-capacity machines is already well-advanced, attention is increasingly being
paid to the economies of scale arising from specialisation and standardisation.
The key saving lies in the elimination of make-ready costs which are typically
heavy because of the need to adjust machines for the vast range of paper sizes and
weights currently on the market. By concentrating on two standard weights and a
Metric Demy Octavo format Billings, for example, have been able to extend the limits
of the print runs which are economical on any given machine**. Thus whereas web
offsets are normally uneconomical for print runs below 15,000 copies because of
high operating and capital costs and excessive paper usage on start-up, this is
not applicable at Billings where standardisation means that machines are cheaper,
spoilage associated with re-webbing is eliminated, fewer staff are needed, and
make-ready time is greatly reduced. Savings also arise from the bulk purchase of
paper on reels and the use of binding machines modified to be capable of handling
web-folded sections.

A machine called the Cameron has recently been bought by Collins which is capable
of printing, assembling, folding and binding a book in a number of hours whilst
operating economically over a wide range of print runs. Each machine is capable
of an annual output of 12 million copies, but is vastly expensive and the print
quality is indifferent, so its use is unlikely to become widespread. There are,
in general, clear savings to be made where printing and binding are carried out in
close proximity. Although binding is increasingly becoming mechanised, the process
of transferring work between operations is highly labour intensive. Thus it comes
as no surprise to find from the Price Commission Report that all large firms sampled both printed and bound books, with 75% of aggregate turnover coming from books
both printed and bound by themselves. For the medium-sized printers sampled the
matching figure was only 50%. The need for separate binding facilities arises
because binding machines are slow-moving in relation to the speed at which printed
pages emerge from most printing presses.

---

*A full list of possible technological changes during the 1980's is set out in
British Printing Industries Federation (1979) pages 29 - 34
**See the report in The Bookseller (April 3rd, 1976)

EXPENDITURE ON PLANT AND MACHINERY

The 1970's were a decade of heavy investment in the printing industry. Primarily this represented a switchover from letterpress to offset litho machines. Some of the larger printers dispensed with letterpress entirely and invested in web offsets which cost up to £1 million apiece. The largest printers are now equipped with roughly five web offset machines and five sheet-fed litho presses, as well as four-colour printing capacity. Total expenditure on plant and machinery in general printing and publishing, the great bulk of which was accounted for in the former sector, was as follows:

Current Prices   1973 - £36.3m   1974 - £40.1m   1975 - £48.1m   1976 - £50.3m
1970 Prices   1973 - £31.9m   1974 - £23.8m   1975 - £22.9m   1976 - £19.8m

The data originate from the Census of Production and the 1970 prices were arrived at by deflating current prices according to the index of plant replacement prices prepared by the BPIF management accounting department. Although at current prices the sums invested have been considerable, real expenditure declined appreciably and the ratio of capital expenditure to value added both declined throughout and remained low in relation to manufacturing industry in general. Obviously this can be explained in part by the inclusion of general publishing in M.L.H. 489, and in part by the high ratio of capital cost to turnover in printing. According to the Price Commission Report a printer with a turnover of around £1 million needs to be equipped with machinery costing some £750,000. Thus a reasonably high rate of return on capital employed is a necessary condition for ongoing heavy investment, whereas as we shall see below this has been the exception rather than the rule.

CAPACITY

There is more or less continuous mismatch between demand and capacity in the printing industry. According to the Price Commission Report excess capacity in printing results primarily from cyclical forces and can be expected to reach critical dimensions when the economy is very depressed. Pressure on capacity is said to be even more variable in binding because printers who do their own binding try to maintain an even flow of work by parcelling out work surplus to capacity during busy periods, thereby creating big variations in capacity utilisation for independent binders. However one is inclined to believe that seasonal forces are at least as important. On the one hand the production of new books and reprints has continued to look remarkably buoyant despite the state of the economy, although one does have to take account of capacity available abroad for reasons stated below. On the other hand the peak demand periods for most major categories of work tend to coincide during the late summer and early autumn at a time when capacity is limited as a result of staff taking holidays. This tendency is accentuated by a number of other factors, notably the reduction in reprint manufacturing times due to the introduction of offset litho, since this tempts publishers to delay reprint orders until the last minute, and thereby save tying up capital in stock at high rates of interest. The Book Trade Capacity Committee estimated in 1974 that if demand were spread out evenly over the year manufacturing costs could be reduced by roughly 5 to 10%. Futhermore this would ensure that publishers received their stock in good time.

The obvious solution to this problem lies firstly in ensuring that publishers utilise an efficient stock control system which picks up well in advance those books likely to become out of stock at the critical time of year when demand for them is heaviest. Secondly, the solution requires that publishers be prepared to order reprints for delivery many months hence, which, whilst leaving the publishers' cash flow unaffected, enables printers to print during slack periods should they so choose even if a penalty is necessarily also exacted in the form of interest charges on capital tied up in stock.

A final point in this context is that a lot clearly depends upon the relationship between printers and publishers. Printer/publishers are the exception rather than the rule. According to the Price Commission Report publishers sampled, or their parent groups, carried out 20% of their own printing and binding. However four publishers specialising in paperbacks carried out only 4% of their own printing and binding. Most publishers have contracts with several printers. Too few and the publisher would be vulnerable to, for example, strike action at their printers; too many and it would become difficult to maintain a consistent quality and house style. Printers are often prepared to store paper on behalf of publishers despite the costs involved. Equally they are generally prepared to offer discounts for a high volume of work. Thus it is clearly advantageous to maintain good long-term relationships even though, as is suggested below, cheap overseas competition may be difficult to ignore in the short term. To some extent of course the choice of printer is determined purely by the need to obtain very long print runs in a short space of time or high quality colour plates, since in both cases the requisite machinery is short on the ground.

COMPETITION

It is difficult to calculate precise figures relating to the level of concentration in book printing and binding. We have referred to employment data in Table 19 above, and according to the Price Commission Report the five biggest firms in their sample accounted for roughly 24% of total book printing turnover. Although printers are widely dispersed within the UK they do not act as regional monopolies but take their work primarily from a limited number of publishers who may be located some distance away. It is generally agreed that concentration is at a level low enough to promote widespread competition especially at times of surplus capacity. On the whole it is true to say that competition from overseas, which does not show up in a concentration ratio, is potentially a more significant element in price determination than the level of concentration within the UK.

FINANCIAL PERFORMANCE

Table 21 below gives turnover, direct costs, overheads and net profit for eight printers sampled by the Price Commission with turnovers in excess of £2.5 millions. Of these, three were paperback printers whose relatively high paper costs may have biased upwards the proportion of costs accounted for by materials.

From 1974 to 1976 total direct costs increased faster than turnover, with 1977 much the same as 1976. No individual component of direct costs moved consistently up or down during the four year period, but the increase in direct costs was caused above all by the sharp increase in material costs between 1975 and 1977. As a result both the percentage contribution to overheads and profits and the net profit percentage declined noticeably from 1974 to 1976, although a modest recovery ensued in 1977.

Figures for the rate of return on capital employed measured on an historic cost basis for 1974 to 1976 are also given at the foot of the table. The Report went on to suggest that 1977 would show some improvement over 1976. Of the eight firms sampled one made a loss in 1976 whilst the others produced rates of return which fluctuated between the fairly narrow limits of 7.0% to 17.9%. The Report thus concluded that "The general picture is of an industry earning rather modest profits."

TABLE 21 Large Printer/Binders. Financial Results 1974 - 1977

Turnover	1974		1975		1976		1977	
	Books £36.1m	Total £43.3m	Books £38.0m	Total £46.0m	Books £40.9m	Total £49.1m	Books £47.9m	Total £58.1m
Direct Costs	%	%	%	%	%	%	%	%
Materials	22.3		21.6		24.9		26.4	
Labour	37.1		39.0		38.5		35.7	
Outwork	7.6		6.9		7.8		9.1	
Other	3.2		4.1		4.0		3.7	
	-		-		-		-	
Total	70.2	64.8	71.6	65.4	75.2	68.4	74.9	67.5
Contribution to Overheads and Profit	29.8	35.2	28.4	34.6	24.8	31.6	25.1	32.5
Overheads		25.4		23.7		24.6		24.1
		-		-		-		-
Net Profit Before Tax		9.8		10.9		7.0		8.4
Return on Capital Employed		14.1		17.3		11.8		-

Source: Price Commission Report

This conclusion is borne out by the BPIF's own calculations which allow in a rough and ready manner for the effects of inflation. As can be expected these real rates of return, which appear as Table 22 below, are considerably lower than those quoted in the Report.

Book printing and binding, as can be seen from these results, is not a particularly profitable sector of the printing industry. Whereas it is true that general printers are better able to pass on or absorb increases in the cost of paper and ink than are manufacturers of stationery or packaging, they are particularly subject to overseas competition and to problems associated with over-capacity. It is very difficult for book printers and binders to guarantee themselves a given rate of return. Prices quoted are generally based upon a costing system devised by the BPIF which allocates overheads and calculates labour costs on the basis of normal capacity utilisation. However, quotations may or may not be accepted, so there is

TABLE 22 Real Rates of Return on Capital Employed %

	March 1972	March 1973	Sept 1974	June 1975	June 1976	April 1977
All Participating Firms	8.9	10.0	9.5	9.3	4.0	6.1
Book Printing and Binding	9.2	4.6	6.1	3.9	0.8	0.3

Source: BPIF management ratios scheme

no guarantee that capacity actually utilised will be the same as that assessed as the basis for the costing system, and any shortfall obviously has a very serious effect on profitability.

COSTS AND PRICES

Statistics are available on two major cost items. In the first place the Department of Industry produces a wholesale price index covering printing and writing paper including boards. The annual percentage changes recorded by this index are as follows:

1974	29.7%
1975	13.8%
1976	16.5%
1977	- 0.5%
1978	13.7%

Prices almost exactly doubled in money terms during the five year period, although on an annual basis changes were highly variable. During 1977 and well into 1978 prices remained static after a period of very rapid advance. From late 1978 prices began once again to rise fairly sharply. However these changes affect overseas competitors as well even if to a lesser degree, and non-material costs are anyway a more significant component of direct costs. The competitive position of UK printers is therefore dependent primarily upon wage costs, productivity and the exchange rate. The BPIF produce an index of printing and binding costs, set out as Table 23 below, which excludes direct materials and outwork.

As can be seen from this table printers' non-material costs have not moved all that much out of line with the RPI. The two peak years were 1976 and 1979, although the intervening years saw some falling back in real costs, and this may therefore happen again in the future.

Complaints from publishers about printers' charges were most vociferous in 1974 and 1979. In a letter to The Bookseller (December 7th, 1974) a number of publishers led by Clive Bingley alleged that the consequences of rising material and non-material costs in printing were such as to lead to "price increases which the book publisher cannot survive." As we have seen above the increase in material costs recorded in 1974 was completely out of line with subsequent experience. Furthermore real wages rose only marginally between May 1973 and May 1975. In view of this the publishers' cries of outrage seem hard to justify in retrospect other than as a short-term ritual response to rising costs. Furthermore there is at least some evidence that printers absorbed some of the cost increases by

TABLE 23 Printers' Non-Material Costs

		Money	Real
August	1970	100.0	100.0
August	1971	108.6	98.4
April	1972	119.9	104.4
May	1973	130.0	102.8
July	1974	153.6	103.8
July	1975	198.8	106.4
July	1976	240.6	114.0
July	1977	267.4	107.8
July	1978	297.1	111.1
July	1979	356.8	115.4

Source: BPIF amended by author to allow for inflation

reducing their margins. On the one hand, according to the publishers' letter, "attempts by the employers to absorb significant proportions of wage rises awarded, appear to outsiders like us to have been minimal". On the other hand, a graph published in the New Scientist (May 10th, 1979) indicates that printers' charges have not been passed on in full at any time since 1970.

Cries of outrage about printers' charges were also voiced early in 1979 and 1980. Pay rises awarded to printing staff in 1979 were indeed substantial, although not seriously out of line with those ruling in comparable industries at the time. Nevertheless it was alleged by certain publishers' production directors that a 20% rise in printers' charges would cause book prices to rise by a similar margin. In fact such a causal relationship does not exist because if book prices do indeed rise in line with increases in publishers' material costs then either publishers' overheads have risen at the same rate or publishers' profitability has improved. In the event, of course, book prices rose by less than 10% in 1979, and it is therefore unfortunate that such misguided comments were used to obscure the real issues which involve not simply the domestic rate of wage inflation as such but its comparison with rates of wage inflation ruling in competing countries; the extent to which higher wage costs are reflected in higher productivity; and the variations in the exchange rate.

There can be no doubt that wage inflation in the UK both is, and for some years has been, high in relation to that prevailing elsewhere, although one obvious exception from the viewpoint of international competition in printing is Italy. Nevertheless absolute wage costs in the UK printing industry are, for example, only 40% of the average in the other European countries which take part in the Printers' International Comparisons Scheme. Unfortunately most of this advantage is offset by higher manning levels, as can be seen by reference to Table 24 below.

The UK percentage for wages and salaries to value added is lower than that recorded by other countries listed in the table, although it is tending to fall rather than to rise over time. Thus whereas wage differentials between the UK and its competitors are likely to narrow as a result of the UK's relatively high rate of wage

TABLE 24 International Comparisons in Printing

	UK	France	Sweden	Denmark	Norway	Holland
Wages and Salaries Per Employee (Swiss francs)	13,600	26,000	41,200	39,200	36,900	34,500
Added Value Per Employee (Swiss francs)	21,900	38,400	65,700	58,600	56,100	53,300
Wages and Salaries to Added Value %	62.1	67.7	62.7	66.9	65.8	64.7

Source: Printers' International Comparisons Scheme

inflation, UK printing firms retain for the present a competitive advantage which could be further exploited were equipment to be operated as efficiently as it is in competing countries. As we have seen above the necessary investment in modern machinery has already taken place, so the much higher foreign levels of productivity recorded in the table cannot in general be ascribed to superior equipment. This problem of low productivity is particularly acute when one considers the possibilities of printing in a country such as Hong Kong where productivity is higher and wage costs lower. Fortunately for UK printers these advantages are offset by loss of control resulting from great distance and by heavy shipment costs except, of course, where the final market is primarily Asia or Australasia.

Overall, therefore, in spite of their low productivity, UK printers should be able to compete provided the exchange rate is not too adverse. According to the Price Commission Report, between 1974 and 1976 their sample of publishers placed 84% of their printing and binding work in the UK. This figure varied by less than one per cent over the three year period, despite considerable movements in the rate both of inflation and of exchange, and it could therefore be regarded as remarkably stable even though it did disguise some modest shifts both towards and away from overseas printing by individual publishers. Publishers told the Commission that there needed to be a cost differential of around 10% before it became worthwhile to employ overseas printers. According to the BPIF at the end of 1979 such a differential appears when, for example, the pound/dollar exchange rate rises above approximately 2 dollars to the pound. As the relevant rate at that time was over 2 dollars it is not surprising that publishers were once again looking for printing capacity overseas.

The seriousness of the current situation is difficult to assess. Some publishers suggested in early 1980 that in terms of quantity, if not in number of titles, the proportion of UK publishers' books still being printed in the UK had fallen to between 70% and 75%, although the Publishers' Association maintained that the correct figure was over 80%. Unfortunately, on this occasion the portents are inauspicious since 1980 and indeed 1981 are likely to see sharp increases in printers' wage bills without the compensation of offsetting improvements in productivity, but combined with a fairly buoyant exchange rate. Since the exchange rate is beyond printers' control, the only solutions are either to hold down wages or to improve productivity. But with wages rising rapidly across the board in the UK the former alternative offers even less prospect of success than the latter, and one is thus

inevitably drawn to the conclusion that the printing industry is going to suffer
a fairly severe recession over the next year or two with some firms going out of
business.

CHAPTER 6

Marketing and Distribution

This chapter is unusually wide-ranging, encompassing as it does a discussion of the myriad problems inherent in the marketing and distribution of books. One is very hard-pressed to think of another industry which produces 40,000 new products every year and which stands ready to deliver any one of the 350,000 items held in stock. Little wonder then that the typical order placed by a retailer is small in value, and that the amount of paperwork appears disproportionate to the turnover involved. Of course things might well run more smoothly if there was an efficient wholesaling system, but such a system does not exist for the reasons set out in the section which follows. Equally things might well be improved by the introduction of new technology, yet the recently introduced teleordering system is already showing signs of imminent collapse.

The book industry is a substantial exporter, and its performance is unusually dep-endent upon all the factors which affect foreign trade. In this chapter we will be examining agreements to share out world trade in books, the associated controversy over closed markets, and the current economic problems faced by all exporters. Subsequently we will be returning to the home market to look firstly at the scale of and scope for book promotion in the UK. This leads on to a review of the Book of the Season scheme which is currently proving at least a partial success despite much initial criticism. Finally we turn to examine the role played by book clubs which are now an established part of the book marketing system in the UK despite the wide-spread fears expressed at their inception, and which are currently making a strong and successful bid to generate an increased membership.

WHOLESALING

Introduction

It has been clear for many years if not decades, that the UK lacks an efficient book distribution system. The essence of the problem is that there are too many orders of too little value transmitted between too many publishers and too many retail outlets for the distribution system to work speedily and efficiently. Hence the oft-voiced appeal for improved wholesaling services. All too often one is referred to the halcyon days of Simpkin Marshall. Between the Wars this wholesaler held stocks of all important publishers' lists sufficient to service single-copy and

small-value orders from booksellers. However publishers were unwilling to offer
the sort of discounts which would enable the company to trade profitably, and in
1955 the company was wound up. Subsequently publishers proved reluctant to set up
a single-copy distributor unless booksellers would accept very low discounts which,
not unnaturally, they refused to do. As a result publishers were obliged to service
small-value orders direct, leading to a prolonged and resentful debate about the
quality of delivery and the need for surcharges.

In the absence of a good national wholesaler publishers increasingly adopted the
strategy of setting up their own warehousing complexes some distance away from the
major conurbations. In so doing, however, they effectively destroyed any possibility of re-establishing a national wholesaler along the lines of Simpkin Marshall.
It is almost universally agreed that although national wholesalers stocking some
80,000 titles are sucessful in countries such as Germany, this is no longer the
practical solution given existing distribution channels in the UK. This is not, of
course, to argue that there is no role for wholesalers. Indeed a number of efficient
wholesalers currently operate on a more limited basis, amongst whom some prominent
examples are W.H. Smith, Bookwise, Bertrams, Hammicks and Gardners. These wholesalers concentrate on paperbacks. Hammicks stock some 4,500 hardbacks and 14,000
paperbacks and Bookwise some 3,000 hardbacks and 20,000 paperbacks. Somewhat exceptionally Gardeners stock some 12,500 hardbacks and 14,000 paperbacks. Attitudes
vary towards items not held in stock, which may or may not be ordered, and may or
may not be surcharged.

Discounts

The crucial issue, as ever, is discounts. From the bookseller's point of view he
has when buying direct from a publisher to trade-off a full discount combined with
a sometimes considerable delay in receiving the stock against a lower discount
combined with a speedier delivery from a wholesaler. Superficially the higher
discount would appear to be the over-riding factor. However a speedy delivery
means a faster stock-turn and therefore less capital tied up in stock, and many
bookshops therefore prefer to order from wholesalers. The most critical part of
the equation is ultimately the discount received from the publisher by the wholesaler. A minimum of 40% on hardbacks and 45% on paperbacks would appear to be the
order of the day, although most wholesalers would expect at least 5% more than the
minimum on most of their stock. Not all publishers regard these discounts with
enthusiasm arguing that the wholesaler is creaming off the most profitable part of
their trade. On the other hand it may be argued that if booksellers need to tie
up less capital in stocking these items they will be able to order more of the
slower-moving stock from publishers.

Stock

The performance of a wholesaler can be measured in terms of the range of titles
held in stock and of the speed of delivery. The figures given above indicate that
most major wholesalers currently stock some 20,000 titles. This figure is probably
too low for a really efficient operation given the existence of some 300,000 titles
in print, but is geared to the cost of stocking up, the fact that 20% of the titles
yield 80% of the turnover, and the need for a speedy delivery service. One way to
overcome the first limitation would be for publishers to deliver on consignment and
thus themselves cover the costs of tying up capital rather than the wholesaler.
Once again this is not an idea which publishers find appealing in the light of the
huge sums already tied up in their own warehousing complexes.

Delivery

That major wholesalers offer a speedy delivery service is confirmed by reference
to the annual BA delivery league table. Although only Bertrams and Bookwise are
included regularly these two wholesalers appear consistently among the top five, a
performance matched among publishers only by Allen and Unwin. However not all
major wholesalers offer a national service. Gardners, for example, operate on a
regional basis because of the difficulties of ensuring speedy delivery outside
their region. Most minor wholesalers supply on an even more limited scale and hold
very restricted stocks. A full analysis of wholesaling was carried out under the
aegis of the BA Trade Practice and Distribution Committee and was published as the
Hodges Report in January 1977. This Report* investigated 151 wholesalers of whom
53 were W.H. Smith depots, 30 were Menzies depots and 68 were independent. Not surprisingly the limited stock and concentration upon local delivery resulted in
speedy deliveries. Aside from this the other obvious advantages of a wholesaling
operation to booksellers were seen, for example, as a reduction of paperwork as a
result of dealing with a single supplier, fewer surcharges and the ability to
examine books prior to purchase. Nevertheless stock limitations prevent local
wholesaling from presenting a viable solution to distribution problems. Interestingly enough the questions put by the Hodges Committee to booksellers about their
ideal distribution system elicited more nil responses than preferences for any
particular system.

For its own part the BA accepted the Report's recommendation that the solution
should be a regional network consisting of wholesalers big enough to carry adequate
stocks but not so big as to require investment running to millions of pounds.
Clearly the major wholesalers mentioned above are the kind of operation which fit
into this picture, but others will be needed if this solution is to prove feasible.
A major advantage is seen by some as the opportunity to transfer a good deal of
business, and especially low-value orders, on to a cash-and-carry basis, which, if
combined with on consignment deliveries from publishers, would enable the wholesaler to conduct his business on a 5% margin.

The existing major wholesalers are clearly providing a valuable service. As yet
there are no signs of a truly regional network coming into being, and one remains
uncertain as to the proportion of trade which would actually take place on a cash-
and-carry basis. Even if such a network were to be set up it would still leave
largely untouched the basic problem of distributing 300,000 titles to large numbers
of outlets, given that each wholesaler will inevitably stock much the same sample
of 15 to 20,000 titles. Efficient wholesaling must therefore be viewed within the
wider context of the need to get publishers to shorten the time which it currently
takes them to get books into shops. This is a topic to which we will return in
the later chapter on bookselling.

TELEORDERING

It is customary to identify a close association between wholesaling and teleordering. The origins of this association lie in a visit paid by representatives of
the PA and BA to the book wholesalers Libri in Frankfurt in April 1976. In Germany
most bookshops record their orders on to a tape inside their Litos (Li(bri)
t(ele)o(rdering) s(ystem)) computer terminal. The wholesaler's computer is linked

---

*A full analysis of the Hodges Report is to be found in The Bookseller (January
29th, 1977 and February 5th, 1977).

to these terminals by phone and reads off the orders at any time of day or night.
Invoices are then printed out, and the books are looked out, packed and despatched.
The entire process takes roughly one hour and books are delivered to bookshops
within one or at most two days.

The bookseller is obliged to identify his orders using stock numbers obtained from
an ultrafiche catalogue supplied by Libri. This catalogue does not contain every
book a bookshop might want to order, but its 80,000 or so entries cover the great
majority of books which are likely to be needed on a regular basis. But one can
immediately detect a major problem in transferring this system to the UK, namely
the lack of any wholesalers operating on a scale similar to that of Libri. We have
already examined the reasons for this phenomenon. The important point to note,
however, is that it is impossible to duplicate the speed of the German distribution
system without duplicating the structure of that system.

So what benefits does teleordering provide in the UK context? It is argued that
the speeding up of orders between bookseller and publisher, using a clearing house
to assemble orders from booksellers and to transmit them to the appropriate publisher's warehouse, can save about two working days. Further savings may arise
within the warehouse. But this is still a far cry from the 48 hour service supplied in Germany, and the participating bookseller is obliged to buy and maintain
a computer terminal, code titles and key in to the terminal. The issue, therefore,
is whether this expenditure can be justified when set against the benefits of
speedier supply, fewer errors in supply, more accurate invoicing, and reductions
in staffing. In the light of the fact that speedier supply still means that the
great majority of books will take more than one calendar week to arrive at booksellers it is difficult to view this particular benefit as being of fundamental
importance. A good deal also depends upon the availability of an accurate and
comprehensive list of ISBNs on microfiche if all potential time savings are to be
realised.

The UK system is run by Software Sciences Teleordering Ltd. The company was incorporated in late 1978 and is owned jointly by Software Sciences Ltd (60%), J. Whitaker and Sons Ltd (20%) and W.H. Smith and Son Ltd (20%). In December 1978 the
PA and BA agreed to recommend the system to their members in return for certain
safeguards. The system came on stream in July 1979, and by the end of 1979 seventeen publishers and forty six bookshops had ordered terminals. Unfortunately this
was far fewer than had been anticipated. Many reasons were expressed to justify
refusal to join, but it was clear that there was a widespread reluctance to invest
in the system prior to it being proven a success, thereby creating a Catch 22
situation since it could not be proven a success until the majority of the large
publishers and booksellers were participants. In July 1980 there were only 73
terminals installed as against the predicted 250 to 300 and Software Sciences
declared a loss of £169,000 to October 1979 and an expected loss of £147,000 to
October 1980 excluding interest charges. As a result the company had to accept
that its £400,000 investment would not be recovered. It therefore declared its
intention to shut down the system unless increased support was immediately forthcoming. In order to make the system more attractive alterations were made in the
options open to publishers and in the charging structure.

The future of the system therefore hangs in the balance. In one sense the scheme
gives cause for concern because it draws attention away from the fundamental issue
which is the need to reform the distribution system. Until this system is put to
rights no amount of tinkering with the likes of teleordering is going to produce
results comparable with those already realised in Germany. On the other hand the
scheme does appear to have been a sucess in terms of its objectives, and it is an
even graver cause for concern that the possible demise of the system provides
further concrete evidence of the book industry's worst feature, namely the refusal

of the different sectors of the industry to recognise that what is good news for one sector is not by definition bad news for another. Thus the participation of much larger numbers of both publishers and booksellers would not merely ensure the success of the scheme but would provide that much-awaited glimmer of hope that co-operative ventures are not necessarily doomed to failure.

THE BRITISH MARKET AGREEMENT

For a period of almost forty years British publishers operated a system for divid-ing up world markets. Evolving from British Rights Agreement to British Common-wealth Rights Agreement, and thence via British Traditional Market Agreement to British Market Agreement, it was a system whereby British publishers agreed to-gether that they would not publish in the UK any book first published outside the bounds of their Traditional Market unless they were granted the exclusive rights to publish that book throughout that market. In effect the agreement was a means of dividing up the english-speaking world into two sectors, the USA and elsewhere, and British publishers guaranteed that if exclusive rights were granted by a US publisher then the British edition of an American book would not be marketed either in the USA or certain other countries. Equally a British publisher who granted to an American publisher the exclusive rights to publish a given book in the USA would normally require that the US edition would not also be marketed in the British Traditional Market.

The great benefit of the Agreement to British publishers was that it protected the export markets which were so crucial to the viability of UK publishing. Unfortun-ately the Agreement greatly offended the Australian book trade who were for the most part prevented from obtaining American books direct from the USA. Further-more, whereas an Australian publisher was not prevented from bidding for the rights to produce a non-US version of a book for the whole of the Traditional Market, he was prevented from bidding for the rights to publish an edition for the Australian market unless the US publisher considered that UK sales would be negligible. In many cases the sales in Australia of the UK edition of an American book were greater than its UK sales. Nevertheless Australian publishers could not obtain the rights to publish their own edition, and as imports of books entered Australia duty free the system appeared to prejudice seriously the potential growth of an indigenous publishing industry.

In view of the fact that the Market Agreement was entered into only by UK publish-ers one must ask why American publishers were willing to abide by its terms. In the first place the Agreement did not in any way prevent an American publisher from selling his own edition of a book directly to Australian booksellers provided a UK edition was not going to be produced. Secondly, the competitive nature of UK pub-lishing allowed US publishers to get a good price for the sale of rights for the Traditional Market as a whole. Finally, UK publishers had established distribution networks in the Traditional Market which could not be matched by US publishers. At a time when American editions were typically more expensive than UK editions of the same work these arrangements were not altogether unsatisfactory to the book trade in the Traditional Market despite the objections discussed above. However once US editions became competitive in price it became much harder to justify the Market Agreement. Hence in November 1974 the Anti-Trust Division of the American Department of Justice filed a law suit against 19 leading American publishers together with the US subsidiaries of OUP and Penguin Books which charged them with being "engaged in a combination and conspiracy in restraint of inter-state and foreign commerce" in violation of the Sherman Anti-Trust Act.

Once it became clear that the Justice Department were determined to take the de-fendants to Court if necessary, resistance rapidly crumbled, largely for fear of the potentially astronomical costs of defending existing policies. Thus in July 1976 UK publishers agreed to revoke the Traditional Market Agreement, and in November of that year the Consent Decree signed by all the defendants in the USA came into operation.

Once the Market Agreement was revoked it became possible for US books to enter Australia in one of three ways. Firstly the US publisher could supply Australia either direct or via the publisher's subsidiary or agent in Australia. Secondly a UK publisher could be sold the rights to the Australian Market. Finally the rights in Australia could be sold either to an independent Australian publisher or to the subsidiary of a UK or competing US publisher granting him permission either to produce a new edition or to sell the US edition under his own imprint. However, these alternatives were not tantamount to opening up the Australian market to several editions of the same book. Irrespective of whoever obtained the rights to sell a book in Australia those rights remained exclusive, and were protected by Australian copyright law.

CLOSED MARKETS

A UK publisher who has exclusive rights to publish a book in a country such as Australia can choose the method by which it is distributed to suit himself. After the Market Agreement was revoked publishers increasingly adopted the closed market system whereby Australian booksellers could no longer purchase directly from the publisher in the UK by means of an indent but had to purchase via a distribution centre in Australia in which the publisher would normally have a financial interest. Once a closed market was established it appeared that Section 37 of the Australian Copyright Act could be invoked to prevent booksellers obtaining a book other than through the closed market channel even if it could be obtained more cheaply elsewhere. Thus the closed market system appeared to offer publishers the opportunity to price their products with impunity and in the process derive a profit both in the UK and in Australia.

The existence of closed markets has been the subject of considerable controversy, especially in Australia*, although it remains unclear precisely how much of the Australian book trade is closed. The justification for closed markets lies primarily in the argument that UK publishers have established large stockholding complexes at their own expense which can service the needs of the geographically dispersed Australian book trade more efficiently, speedily and cheaply than the indent system. The fact that the bookseller receives a lower discount compared to indent purchases merely reflects the reduction in effort and risk to the bookseller which is associated with closed market distribution, especially if it is on a sale-or-return basis.

The counter arguments are that closed markets result in poor coverage of publishers' backlists; inadequate stocks of bestsellers; slow delivery; high prices; and low discounts and hence low profitability for Australian booksellers. The pricing issue is a particular cause for complaint in that it is alleged that the Australian bookseller's wholesale price is often more than UK retail price plus freight to Australia.

In response it is argued that although indenting is cheaper than supply via a local distributor, widespread indenting would undermine the economics of local distrib-

---

*See, for example, The Bookseller (October 1st, 1977), (October 22nd, 1977), (November 12th, 1977), (January 7th, 1978), (January 14th, 1978), (February 4th, 1978), (February 25th, 1978), (March 4th, 1978), (March 25th, 1978), and (May 19th, 1979).

ution to such a degree that even the efficient would go to the wall to the ultimate detriment of the Australian bookbuyer.

That feelings about closed markets can run high among the parties concerned was exemplified by the complaint lodged with the Examiner of Commercial Practices by the Booksellers' Association of New Zealand in January 1978 against Hodder and Stoughton's decision to close the New Zealand market. It is ultimately beyond the scope of this book to consider whether any individual closed market can be justified. What is clear, however, is that a market should only be closed where this results in a lower price and/or better service than would arise were a book supplied on indent. This suggests that publishers should maintain closed markets in places such as Australia primarily for fast-turnover stock which requires heavy local advertising and speedy delivery to the bookshop shelf. The decision as to whether or not to close a market must ultimately rest with the publisher concerned, and we must therefore turn to consider recent trends on the export front.

CURRENT EXPORT PROBLEMS

The demise of the Traditional Market Agreement inevitably raised the spectre of increased competition in export markets. Initially, however, there was no reason to expect US publishers to expand significantly into export markets because the size of their home market made such action largely unnecessary. Indeed if one considers exports to Australia one finds that whereas in 1976/77 UK publishers supplied 42% of Australian imports and US publishers 40%, in 1977/78 the respective figures were 48% and 33%. Furthermore, the demise of the Agreement appeared to stimulate an exodus of UK publishers to America. Whereas previously there had been considerable trade in rights and co-editions, there now grew up a considerable physical presence in addition to this trade. Thus by the end of 1978 some 20 UK publishers had taken over total or partial control of an American counterpart. Well known examples of this process were Macmillan's acquisition of St Martins Press and Penguin's acquisition of Viking. Those companies unwilling or unable to publish books produced entirely in the USA often acquired improved distribution facilities, perhaps by setting up a US subsidiary for this purpose. By the end of 1978 some 50 companies were distributing UK books in the USA, in many cases handling all the titles which had not previously been disposed of as a sale of rights.

Clearly the practice of a rights sale has always been the ideal way of dealing with a title which a US publisher is willing and able to market efficiently through his established distribution system. However, the demise of the Traditional Market followed hard upon the 1974 recession which was characterised by an increased unwillingness on the part of US publishers to buy British books. Furthermore when they did buy they demanded, and were given, unprofitably high discounts. In a sense, therefore, the Consent Decree had a positive as well as a negative aspect in that whereas it implied the loss of certain traditional markets it also woke up UK publishers to the potential of selling in the largest English-speaking market of all.

Unhappily this promising trend proved to be dependent upon an upturn in consumer demand and on advantageous exchange rate. The combination in 1979 of a deepening world-wide recession, a relatively high rate of inflation in the UK compared to the USA, and a significant improvement in the value of the pound compared to the dollar proved too much of a burden to bear. As a result, British publishers began to withdraw again from the USA with Granada leading the way closely followed by Hutchinson.

Obviously the same pressures affected other export markets such as Australia and Canada. In the latter case it became almost impossible to compete with US editions

of the same or similar books to those previously imported from the UK. Although
one is cautious about applying the term crisis to this situation, it is undeniable
that things can only improve provided either that demand picks up, the pound/dollar
exchange rate falls, or the UK inflation comes down to US levels. Indeed all three
conditions must probably be satisfied if the real value of exports is to be restored
to its former levels, and there are no prospects of that happening in the foreseeable
future.

TABLE 25 Exchange Rates: US dollars to the £

	1971	1972	1973	1974	1975	1976	1977	1978	1979	1980
Jan	2.42	2.59	2.38	2.27	2.38	2.03	1.71	1.95	1.99	2.26
Feb	2.42	2.61	2.49	2.30	2.43	2.02	1.71	1.94	2.02	2.29
Mar	2.42	2.62	2.48	2.39	2.40	1.91	1.72	1.86	2.07	2.21
Apr	2.42	2.61	2.49	2.42	2.35	1.84	1.72	1.83	2.07	2.22
May	2.42	2.61	2.57	2.40	2.31	1.76	1.72	1.83	2.07	2.30
Jun	2.42	2.44	2.58	2.39	2.18	1.78	1.72	1.86	2.17	
Jul	2.42	2.45	2.51	2.39	2.15	1.78	1.74	1.93	2.26	
Aug	2.45	2.45	2.46	2.32	2.11	1.78	1.74	1.94	2.25	
Sep	2.49	2.42	2.41	2.33	2.04	1.67	1.75	1.97	2.20	
Oct	2.49	2.34	2.44	2.34	2.08	1.59	1.84	2.09	2.15	
Nov	2.49	2.35	2.34	2.33	2.02	1.65	1.82	1.94	2.13	
Dec	2.55	2.35	2.32	2.35	2.02	1.70	1.92	2.04	2.20	

  The exchange rates in force since 1971 are set out in Table 25 above, and one can
see very clearly how the rate has risen sharply over the past eighteen months. It
is obvious that an increase of this kind is going to make life very difficult for
exporters. A clearer idea of the trade situation can be obtained by referring to
Table 26 below which contains statistics on the overall trade balance in books.
On the export side, despite some passing difficulties in 1974/5, the general trend
was buoyant up to 1978. The fall in the real value of exports in 1979 was, however,
much more severe than in any previous year. The real value of imports remained
static during the mid-1970's, but rose sharply in 1978 with a marginal decline in
1979. As a result the real trade balance in 1976 and 1977 broke all records, thanks
in good part to the advantageously low exchange rate. 1979, on the other hand, saw
a decline of unprecedented size, and continuance of this trend would be a matter of
grave concern.

TABLE 26 Overseas Trade Statistics. Books. £million

	EXPORTS			IMPORTS			TRADE BALANCE		
	Money Value	Real Value	Index Number	Money Value	Real Value	Index Number	Money Value	Real Value	Index Number
1970	46.3	46.3	100.0	20.8	20.8	100.0	25.5	25.5	100.0
1971	59.4	54.3	117.3	23.9	21.8	104.8	35.5	32.5	127.5
1972	69.2	59.0	127.4	27.4	23.4	112.5	41.8	35.6	139.6
1973	73.9	57.7	124.6	31.2	24.4	117.3	42.7	33.3	130.6
1974	84.0	57.1	123.3	42.5	28.9	138.9	41.5	28.2	110.6
1975	104.0	56.9	122.9	50.4	27.6	132.7	53.6	29.3	114.9
1976	136.1	63.7	137.6	58.1	27.2	130.8	78.0	36.5	143.1
1977	176.0	71.4	154.2	68.6	27.8	133.7	107.4	43.6	171.0
1978	206.5	77.4	167.2	88.1	33.0	158.7	118.4	44.4	174.1
1979	209.3	69.0	149.1	99.6	32.8	157.7	109.7	36.2	141.9

Source: Department of Trade. Overseas Trade Statistics of the UK

The figures in the above table do not tally with those produced in the Business Monitor because of differences in the data collection system. The above series in fact originate from H.M. Customs and Excise and are therefore the only ones which are gathered as books pass through ports of entry.

So far as the trade balance specifically with the US is concerned the situation has deteriorated noticeably as one would expect. In 1978 the US imported 232 million dollars worth of books compared to a total of 269 million dollars worth in 1979, an increase of 15.7%. However in 1978 the US exported 371 million dollars worth of books compared to a total of 439 million dollars worth in 1979, an increase of 18.5%. Within this latter total there was a 44% increase in exports to the UK which rose from 44 million dollars in 1978 to 64 million dollars in 1979. As a result the value of US exports is now very close to the UK total. Thus the pre-eminent position of the UK as an exporter of books does appear to be about to pass, probably for ever, to the USA and there is nothing short of a complete reversal of the above economic circumstances which can restore the UK publishing industry to its time-honoured position.

BOOK PROMOTION

Introduction

Book production is not very big business. According to the Price Commission large publishers spend only 4.5% of their turnover on advertising and promotion. However even this looks fairly munificent when one discovers that, according to Charter Survey figures, the average bookshop spends only 0.3% of its turnover on book pro-motion. Of course it can be argued that if a bookseller promotes specific books there is no guarantee that customers who read the advertisement will buy those

books from his shop. Thus it is normally expected that a publisher will promote
his own titles. However this raises the question of how much a publisher should
spend in relation to his turnover; what forms of promotion are most cost-effective;
whether books in general should ever be promoted; what role is to be played by
booksellers; and finally whether promotional efforts should be directed primarily
towards non-readers or towards lapsed readers.

The idea that books should be promoted collectively by both sides of the book trade
was first proposed by the National Book Council set up in 1925. On two subsequent
occasions, in 1928 and 1948, a book trade committee recommended the setting up of
some form of book promotion house. What actually transpired was the introduction
of the Book Tokens scheme in 1932; the National Book Fair in 1938; the Nottingham
Book Festival in 1954; the World Book Fair in 1964; and the National Book Week in
1972. Of these events only the first-named was of lasting significance, and a
book promotion house remained as elusive as ever. However in 1972 the PA and BA
jointly commissioned a Book Promotion House Feasibility Study which was published
in October 1974.

Book Promotion House Feasibility Study

The Study covered a good deal of ground without going into great detail. One particular concern was an evaluation of Book Promotion Houses already in existence
in other European countries. Of these two were studied in depth. The Danish organisation was found to be concerned primarily with producing and distributing book
lists, encompassed about 90 per cent of all booksellers, and was funded almost
entirely by booksellers. The Dutch organisation, on the other hand, was found to
be concerned primarily with expanding the market to the non-buyer or infrequent
buyer, had a large administrative staff, and was funded primarily by publishers.
A second major concern was an examination of co-operative promotion schemes in
other UK trades. The results of some research into buyer behaviour were also reported. This showed among other things that 65 per cent of consumers visit a bookshop once a quarter or less, and that most hardbacks bought between December and
March are intended as gifts, especially for children.

The Study considered that the buying habits of the public could be substantially
moulded by national advertising, and that by comparison with other leisure activities the amount of effective national promotion of books was miniscule. The pro-
ffered solution was the setting up of a Book Promotion House to administer major
national campaigns in order to create a greater demand for books and send more
people into bookshops. It was estimated that the sum of £1$\frac{1}{2}$ million would be needed to cover the costs of a three year period of national book promotion, and the
Study recommended that this should be funded by means of an obligatory levy on
publishers of $\frac{1}{2}$ per cent of their turnover (the same as in Holland) with booksellers
contributing a subscription to join the Book Promotion House.

The Study can be criticised on a number of grounds, quite apart from its tendency
to confuse book reading and book buying. In the first place it made no attempt to
explain why the public prefers to buy newspapers and magazines rather than books.
Presumably the fact that the best-selling women's magazines retail for 16 pence,
which is not much at any one time and indeed only comes to £8 over an entire year,
is something to do with it. Presumably the fact that magazine articles and stories
are short and are designed to appeal to a particular segment of the reading public
also has something to do with it. It is certainly curious that the Study made no
attempt to segment the book-buying market, since it is by no means obvious that a
campaign to promote books in general will have an equal impact upon all categories
of books.

In the second place the Study appeared to be confused about the role of libraries,

television, films and bookclubs. We have noted elsewhere that bookclub sales are
more likely to benefit than to harm bookshop sales. We have also explored the
close relationship between publishers and libraries and pointed out the fallacy of
the argument that a library loan is a book sale lost. Equally it is easy to prove
by reference to bestseller lists that successful books are often linked to successful TV programmes or personalities. Once again one detects the book trade's tendency to view all new developments as a threat rather than as an opportunity.

In one respect the Study was unquestionably optimistic, and that was in the expressed belief that the generic promotion of books could be both possible, cheap
and cost-effective. But the sum of £1½ million (at 1974 prices) spread over three
years doesn't buy much peak television time. Equally the fact that tea or eggs
can be promoted generically doesn't mean that the same is true for books. It can
be argued that books are individually different to a degree which is in no way
matched by individual brands of tea or eggs. A limited attempt to test the Study's
hypothesis was introduced in the Yorkshire TV region in December 1976 when certain
publishers and booksellers bought 18 spots of 15 seconds duration on Yorkshire TV.
Specific names of publishers and booksellers were included in the spots so it was
not a true test of generic promotion. Equally no proper tests were conducted to
determine whether the campaign had been cost-effective. However there is no doubt
that the participants felt that the campaign had been worthwhile.

The main difficulty in introducing truly generic promotion is overcoming publisher
resistance. Corgi, Mitchell Beazley and Octopus all advertise fairly heavily but
see no benefits to themselves from generic promotion. Octopus, the heaviest ad-
vertiser of all, believe that if other publishers advertised to the same extent
the book trade would flourish. Record companies such as K-Tel certainly appear to
prosper on the principle of massive TV promotion of individual records. Another
record company Topaz have had some success applying the same principle to books but
their example has not elicited much enthusiasm among book publishers to follow suit.
A recent convert to TV promotion is Mills and Boon who promote their romantic
fiction in general rather than individual titles. Other publishers, it is true,
rarely base their reputation on such a well-defined segment of the market for books,
but this again points up the illogicality of embarking upon generic promotion before one has decided whether there is a market for books in general.

In an article critical of the Study Hepburn (1975) suggests that there are nine
different book markets, namely schools; college students; medical, legal, and professional; domestic; recreational; children; present givers; and religious. One
can quibble about the list and there are admitted overlaps. Nevertheless he makes
the important point that much book buying is done by experts such as librarians
and teachers with whom the publisher has long-established lines of communication.
Clearly generic promotion is going to leave these markets almost entirely untouched.
Hepburn therefore believes that the domestic market and present givers are the
appropriate targets for a national campaign to get the public to buy more books.

Aims of Book Promotion

This raises the interesting question as to whether book promotion should be directed
towards those who already buy books or towards those who do not. It can reasonably
be argued that the time to start people off on the reading habit is when they are
at school. If they do not read when they leave school it is unlikely that any kind
of book promotion will stimulate the habit in later years. The most important
distinction may therefore be between those people who read regularly and who can
perhaps be stimulated to read even more, and those who read books only rarely because there are other leisure pursuits, doubtless including magazine reading, which
they prefer. The ideal way to preach to the converted is via book reviews, which

have the extremely desirable quality of being almost costless to the publisher. Thus the obvious category of reader towards whom promotion should be directed contains people who read infrequently. These people almost certainly read either newspapers or magazines and watch television, and are therefore best approached by publishers via these media. Publishers often seem over-complacent about book reviews in that they appear to believe that such reviews are a substitute for advertising and reach the bulk of the reading public. However the line of argument pursued above would suggest that this view is mistaken. The reviews cater predominantly for the regular reader whereas accompanying advertisements are needed to promote books to the occasional reader. Interestingly enough this fact is recognised by some booksellers who advertise in local newspapers such as the Hampstead and Highgate Express.

Role of Bookseller

This brings us on to the final strand in the argument which is the role of the bookseller. By and large booksellers concentrate on point-of-sale material. It is hardly surprising, therefore, that they typically allocate such a miniscule part of their turnover to book promotion. It may well be argued that if publishers promote their wares more vigorously this is all that should be necessary. However as things stand at present a more active policy may be desirable whether it be advertisements in local newspapers and local radio, or contributions to TV campaigns. The most interesting question is whether or not bookshops should move into High Street locations. In many cases they have moved in the opposite direction, driven away, so it is claimed, by their inability to get better terms from publishers than shops in lower rental locations.

Now it is obvious that much more consumer expenditure passes over High Street counters than over the counters of outlying shopping precincts. Indeed those bookshops which remain in central locations do have untypically high turnovers. The problem is that profitability is often very poor. It is interesting to note that record retailers stick resolutely to central locations. One of the main reasons for this difference must therefore be the immense amount of money spent promoting records. Another reason must be the inadequacy of bookshop margins in central locations, compared to margins in other trades which compete for the same outlets. It is hard to understand why publishers fail to give improved terms to High Street bookshops. If such locations boost turnover significantly, this obviously means bigger and more regular orders for publishers, and it must, therefore, be in the interests of publishers who benefit from this to share the benefit with the bookseller. A system of discounts which varies according to the size of orders placed with publishers would be one way to resolve this problem. If there is one lesson which the book trade should have learned by now it is that the public does not buy products which are not brought regularly to its attention.

BOOK OF THE SEASON

The idea of promoting individual books originated in Holland where a quarterly Book of the Month scheme was instituted in order to attract customers into bookshops through widespread and persistent publicity. In April 1978 a similar scheme was agreed for New Zealand, and this was almost immediately followed by the acceptance of a thrice-yearly Book of the Season scheme for the UK to be run by the Booksellers Association Service House Ltd (BASH) set up in 1977. The book chosen to set the scheme in motion was W. Vaughan-Thomas' The Countryside Companion published jointly by Webb and Bower, and Hutchinson. An offer price of £4.95 was decided upon as compared to the subsequent normal edition price of £7.95.

A brochure about the book was circulated to booksellers who were required to subscribe, sight unseen, for a minimum number of copies. This was in order for BASH
to be able to contract with the publishers for a specific number of copies. This
meant, however, that bookshops would only be able to receive the subscribed copies
with no opportunity to top up if demand was under-estimated. In order to meet
promotion and administration costs the customary 65%/35% price split between the
publisher and booksellers was altered to 55%/25%, each party contributing 10% to
cover these costs. It was emphasised that the selected book was to be sold by all
booksellers at the same net price and without prejudice to their customary discounts
on normal sales.

The reaction of many booksellers was less than euphoric. It was argued that the
effect of the scheme was to transfer all risk from publishers to booksellers. On
the one hand the publishers were guaranteed pre-publication subscriptions, cash
paid with orders. On the other hand booksellers had to pay in advance a minimum
subscription of £50; could not inspect the book; could not return unsold copies;
could obtain no extra copies; and received only a 25% discount. It was pointed out
in reply that the object of the scheme was not to make excessive profits either for
BASH or for the publishers, but to create new readers who would have to enter the
subscribing bookshops if they wanted to buy the book.

Despite initial reservations most large booksellers eventually decided to join the
scheme, possibly swayed by the reasoning that if a similar scheme was successful
in Holland it could well also work in the UK. The eventual print run was 55,000
copies, of which 12,500 were taken by W.H.Smith, and the book appeared in bookshops at the beginning of November 1979. The scheme was more successful in the
out-turn than most participants had expected with many selling out by Christmas,
although there was some dispute about whether the sales were stimulated primarily
by the unusually low price or by the unusually good publicity.

Just how successful the first scheme was is difficult to assess because it is not
sufficient merely to count the number of copies sold or the speed with which they
are sold if the primary object of the exercise is to get new customers into bookshops on a regular basis. Nevertheless the sales count for the second Book of the
Season, Godfrey Talbot's The Country Life Book of the Royal Family was a marked
improvement on the first. BASH purchased 97,500 of this book from Hamlyn who offered BASH a 50% discount off the special offer price of £7.95, as compared to an
eventual trade price of £10. BASH appeared to have done well to get copies for £4
apiece, but an equivalent book club order would have been sold at around one-fifth
of trade price, in this case £2. Thus whereas the publishers had to deliver to
bookshops rather than in bulk to a book club, the extra £2 per copy on the BASH
deal left them well in pocket. In addition to the publisher's 50% the residual 15%
of their customary 65% share went towards the promotional budget, 5% more than on
the first occasion. This meant that booksellers needed to forgo only 5% of their
customary 35% share, leaving them 5% better off than on the previous occasion,
although the somewhat onerous conditions of sale remained unchanged.

Presumably the improved discount explained in part the much larger subscription to
the second title. W.H.Smith trebled their order to 35,000 and Boots took 6,000,
although the number of participants remained unchanged overall at some 750 orders
for 1200 shops. Another contributory factor would appear to have been the topic
itself, thereby stimulating criticism to the effect that the book would have been
a bestseller anyway at its full trade price. Quite probably this was true, even
though less would have been spent on promotion. The higher price and larger edition
of the second special offer meant that a six-figure sum could be spent on its promotion compared to the £36,000 spent on promoting the first offer. In addition a
proper attempt could be made to assess the efficacy of the promotion using reply-
paid postcards inserted in the book, the result of which has yet to be declared.

BOOK CLUBS

Introduction

In many respects the changed economic and social circumstances which brought into
being the commercial lending libraries also laid the foundation for the subsequent
development of book clubs whose main period of growth coincided with the free public lending library service.

Most importantly both depended upon a desire by the public to obtain books other
than at their full published price and upon the accessibility of that public to
centralised sources of supply. The key to book club viability is to be found in
their economies of scale. Provided sufficient members are willing to purchase a
specific book it can be produced at a low unit cost and hence can be sold profitably even at a substantial discount off net price. Thus to be successful a book
club must be able to identify subject areas which will interest large numbers of
potential members and be able to convert that interest into purchase decisions
through the selection and advertisement of suitable books.

Clearly a book club cannot afford to offer too great a range of choice. What is
offered must cater to the common denominators among the actual and potential readership. In this sense therefore, a book club's philosophy is directly opposed to
that of a public lending library which sets out to cater to minority interests even
in the face of budgetary constraints. It can be seen in retrospect that the development of the book club was historically inevitable and could in effect be regarded as the second coming of the commercial lending library.

History of Book Clubs

The idea of the book club probably originated in Germany although it flowered
primarily in the USA during the great depression at a time when there were few
bookshops in existence. Nevertheless, the American book trade was initially host-
ile to the growth of book clubs, a phenomenon paralleled in Britain during the
same period. The original British book clubs were the Reader's Union, the Book
Society and the Reprint Society.

At first the Publishers' Association proved successful in imposing severe restrict-
ions upon book club operations culminating in a ban on the publication of special
editions of works of fiction until one year had passed from the date of original
publication.

During the War years and into the 1950's, the restricted availability of raw materials proved more irksome than the PA rules. Membership of both old-established
and new clubs grew satisfactorily. Odham's Companion Book Club gained some 450,000
members and membership of clubs overall eventually topped the million mark. But
bad times were to come. Perhaps it was television, perhaps a switch from hardback
to paperback, perhaps something altogether different. In any event club membership declined rapidly and changes of ownership began to take place. In particular
W.H. Smith and Doubleday combined to set up Book Club Associates which took over
the Reprint Society.

The most crucial decision was that taken in February 1968 which allowed simultaneous publication of new books in original and book club editions together with a
35% book club discount for fiction and 25% for non-fiction. This led to the setting
up of the Literary Guild as a subsidiary of BCA. Later came the Mystery Guild and
the New Fiction Society, although the majority of book clubs preferred to stick to
reprints. These grew in number during the 1970's to some 40 or so including groups

owned by Foyles, Odham's, BPC, David and Charles and Heron Books. They prospered partly as a result of a gradual relaxation of the rules governing such clubs. Larger discounts were made available; more books could be included in the list of introductory offers; and a member need not commit himself to purchase more than 3 books per year.

It is interesting to note that the simultaneous clubs, dominated in practice by the Literary Guild, did not grow purely at the expense of reprint clubs. The 1968 decision, needless to say, had been controversial. It was argued (in declining order of accuracy), that the changed rules would stimulate special interest clubs, expand overall club membership without affecting existing clubs, leave bookshops unaffected, and obviate the need for special introductory offers. In opposition it was claimed that bookshops would be adversely affected partly because the considerable advertising undertaken by clubs would not rub off on books not specifically mentioned, and also that if clubs proved successful they would be able to improve the terms on which they bought from publishers to the detriment of the latter. In the event the decision proved to be correct if success is to be measured in terms of club membership. The Literary Guild currently has over 350,000 members and BCA over 600,000. Total membership of all book clubs easily tops the one million mark and total turnover exceeds £20 million.

Future Prospects

In view of the fact that a large proportion of members resign their membership each year, book clubs need to acquire increasingly more new members simply to stand still. It might appear, therefore, to be the case that the prospects for future growth are very limited. This view is not, however, shared by Bertelsmann, the dominant German book club group, which moved into the UK in 1977 with a new club called the Leisure Circle. Unlike existing clubs, the Leisure Circle recruits members by door-to-door selling. Furthermore, it seeks to recruit members from outside the book-buying public. The object of personal selling is to tie-in publications more closely to the desires of potential members, and to maintain membership over longer periods of time. Bertelsmann, with a current membership of over 150,000, of whom 80% are women, believe that they can recruit one million members, allowing them both to make their choices available in bookshops, and eventually to set up their own wholly-owned retail outlets just as they already do in Germany. They believe that co-operative ventures with bookshops, which will both service existing members and recruit new ones, will boost the latters' turnover by some 15%. For the moment, it is too early to gauge whether Bertelsmann will be successful, but what is clear is that they have blown a wind of change into a market which was showing signs of becoming static.

It is extremely difficult to gauge the overall impact of book clubs. It is undeniable that the bulk of their turnover is an addition to, rather than a subtraction from, bookshop sales. The initial hostility of the book trade hierarchy can be put down to the trade's deep-rooted conservatism and most publishers now look to the sale of rights to book clubs as a useful, though by no means excessive, boost to their profitability. In all probability, book clubs have also benefited book shops. Their advertising is very heavy in comparison with that of publishers and some book club members can be expected to acquire the reading habit. Many club members anyway doubtless join simply because they do not have easy access to a good stockholding bookshop. In the longer term some bookshops should also benefit from co-operative agreements with Bertelsmann. Whether the latter will be able to stimulate a large new market is as yet unclear. Certainly book club membership is much more widespread in America and Europe, but these continents do not possess a public lending library service on the British scale.

CHAPTER 7

Bookselling

INTRODUCTION

The critical element in the business of selling books is easily identified. It is
a product range of several hundred thousand individual books increasing at the rate
of some forty thousand new items each year, and supplied by some five thousand publishers of widely differing sizes. Obviously no bookshop can hope to stock more
than a reasonable proportion of all titles in print, and the typical bookshop stocks
no more than twenty thousand titles, roughly 5 per cent of the total. In many cases
a customer merely seeks a book in a particular subject area, and is satisfied provided he has a reasonable choice of suitable titles. But other customers either
have such specialised interests that no suitable stock exists from which to choose,
or seek a specific title which is not held in stock.

If a book is not held in stock a customer will either walk out or place an order.
The placing of orders is particularly critical since, for better or for worse, a
customer expects both to receive books quickly and for the order service to be free.
For this reason we will turn in subsequent sections to a detailed consideration of
problems of speedy distribution and also of special order changes.

Obviously, the real art of bookselling lies in the ability to hold a stock which
closely matches up to the requirements of potential customers, since this minimises
money tied up in stock, increases stock turnover and reduces the need for single
copy orders. To make life easier, in certain cases, bookshops specialise in the
holding of certain types of books, such as academic or theological, in the belief
that this will attract customers with specialised interests in these areas. In
other cases, such as country bookshops, the clientele is largely well-established
and makes known its particular interests to the bookseller. On the other hand High
Street bookshops are heavily dependent upon passing trade and must be extremely
sensitive to, for example, the birth and death of fashions and crazes which may
have a limited life. Thus it is clear that there are no hard and fast rules about
optimal book stocking policy, and as the letter pages of <u>The Bookseller</u> constantly
indicate, a category of books which provides one bookseller with his main source
of income may be of little consequence to a bookseller elsewhere.

STRUCTURE AND COMPETITION

Altogether there are roughly 36,000 outlets which sell books, over half of them

being newsagents. Of the remainder, 3,200 are members of the Booksellers Association, but many shops join the BA simply in order to obtain the right to sell, as
against to exchange, book tokens. Thus the number of real, or stockholding, booksellers almost certainly totals fewer than one thousand, of which perhaps 90% are
members of the BA. Amongst these the core group of stockholding bookshops is the
Charter Group. This Group, established in 1964 and whose financial affairs are
analysed in detail below, comprises some 340 businesses owning 400 shops. The
Group came into existence in order to promote the mutual self-interest of publishers
and stockholding bookshops. From the publishers' point of view the significant
factor was that some 80% of their home trade was being transacted through 20% of
their retail outlets. It therefore appeared worthwhile to ensure that such outlets
were maximising the turnover derived from major publishers' lists by offering
improved discounts in return for a guarantee that the Charter bookseller would
bring his shop up to a laid-down standard, train his staff, and maintain a proper
bibliographical service. In addition to an improved discount the bookseller also
hoped to obtain such benefits as reduced service charges and the see-safe system
whereby books which do not sell are replaced by others of equal value without
penalty.

Compared to most other European countries, the UK boasts a relatively small number
of stockholding bookshops, whether Charter or not, per head of population. This
may be due, in part, to the widespread public library system. This latter point
does not, however, explain the uneven geographical spread of good bookshops which
tend to cluster in middle class areas, although the BA feels that coverage is
adequate. Aside from W.H. Smith, which had 320 shops and 13.5% of the market in
the late 1970's, and which also owns Bowes and Bowes a chain of bookshops mostly
in university towns, no other group has as much as 5% of the market. Like John
Menzies, the second largest group, W.H. Smith deals primarily in general non-fiction
which comprises perhaps only one quarter of a typical large bookshop's turnover.
The success of these books is therefore heavily dependent upon the prominence which
they receive in displays in W.H. Smith bookshops. On the other hand W.H. Smith
largely ignores technical books which typically contribute one third of the turnover of other large bookshops, including Bowes and Bowes. It may be argued that
competition is only meaningful on a local basis, because books of general interest
are sold everywhere at identical net prices which removes any incentive to shop
around, although the fact that one can pick up an absolutely identical product
anywhere on ones travels militates against this somewhat. Thus competition is only
likely to be fierce if there are a number of large stockholding bookshops in close
proximity, and this is very much the exception rather than the rule.

It is only to be expected, therefore, that large established bookshops are but
little affected by competition over time. According to the Price Commission Report
large bookshops sampled (1977 annual turnover in excess of £200,000) had been
trading for an average of 71 years with only three of the twenty sampled being less
than 10 years old. On the other hand there is considerable change at the smaller
end of the size spectrum for reasons set out in the financial analysis below, and
of the small bookshops sampled in the Report one half had been in business for less
than 10 years and one quarter for less than 5 years. Clearly, therefore, entry
into bookselling is easy. On the other hand exit is also fairly commonplace.

DISCOUNTS

The subject of discounts has always been, and will doubtless always continue to be,
highly controversial. It would be a great help for analytical purposes if publishers were to agree to a common schedule of discounts. Unfortunately, this
appears to offend their finer sensibilities, and one has only to scan the directory
which sets out publishers' terms to realise that no two are precisely alike.

Based upon their sample of 20 large booksellers and 54 small booksellers, the Price
Commission calculated the following schedule of average discounts:

TABLE 27 Average Discounts Allowed to Booksellers

	Large Bookshops %	Small Bookshops %
Non-Net Books	18.8	22.0
Net Books		
Paperbacks	37.1	33.2
Technical Hardbacks	27.6	25.2
Other Hardbacks	34.9	33.2

Source: Price Commission Report

These discounts can be compared with the Book Trade Working Party recommendation
that a standard discount of 35% should be given for non-technical net books, a
target which is already matched on average in certain categories but not in others.
Care must be taken not to treat these figures as the average gross margin of profit
for a bookseller. A Charter bookseller would expect an additional 2 or 3% margin
as a reward for meeting the terms of membership, and variations in terms are to be
expected in line with variations in the value of orders. Furthermore some stock
will either have to be disposed of as remainders or put into the annual book sale,
and there is inevitably some stock wastage and theft. The Report estimated wastage
and theft, both internal and external, at 8% of turnover for large booksellers and
5% for small booksellers.

        FINANCIAL ANALYSIS

The most recent financial survey of booksellers who are members of the Charter
Group is for 1978 - 79. This was the third survey conducted by the Manchester
Business School with the aid of their computers, and it contained, in comparison
with book trade statistics generally, a positive wealth of information. Almost
inevitably these statistics are already somewhat out of date, and there are some
problems of comparability from year to year. The paragraphs below therefore are
an attempt to utilise the survey selectively in order to throw as much light as
possible upon the economics of bookselling without getting too bogged down in the
detailed analysis of individual categories in individual years.

The most valuable statistics are those which identify a consistently defined picture
over a period of years. Table 28 below presents some of the overall results which
span the period 1972 to 1978, the former year being chosen because of a near doub-
ling in the size of the sample completing questionnaires. Within this table we can
detect a number of trends. We can see first of all that stockholding bookshops
have become more dependent upon retail sales in recent years. This is counter-
balanced by a decline in institutional business, partly for the reasons discussed
elsewhere. On the other hand there has been no significant tendency for such shops
to switch into non-book goods. Gross profit margins have gradually improved as a
result of pressure upon publishers for improved discounts. During the mid-1970's
this resulted in a reasonably consistent level of net trading profit since expenses
were rising at much the same rate as gross margins. From 1976 onwards, however,
expenses shot up much faster than gross profit, causing net trading profit to fall

TABLE 28 Overall Results 1972 - 1978

	1972	1973	1974	1975	1976	1977	1978
Completed Questionnaires	352	353	376	355	355	342	343**
% Sales : Retail	50.5	51.2	51.2	53.0	54.7	56.4	53.9
Library	9.4	9.6	8.9	9.3	9.3	8.0	9.4
Book Agents	0.6	0.4	0.4	0.5	0.9	0.4	0.3
Schools	9.4	9.6	9.1	6.1	6.7	5.4	5.5
Other Goods	30.1	29.2	30.4	31.1	28.4	29.8	30.9
Gross Profit*	26.3	26.6	26.7	27.8	27.9	28.1	28.9
Total Expenses*	21.6	21.7	22.3	23.5	24.6	25.0	25.8
a) Wages/Salaries*	12.7	12.9	13.3	14.1	14.7	15.2	15.1
b) Rent/Rates*	2.9	2.7	2.7	2.9	3.5	3.5	3.6
c) Other Working Expenses*	6.0	6.1	6.3	6.5	6.4	6.3	7.1
Net (Trading) Profit*	4.7	4.9	4.4	4.3	3.3	3.1	3.1
Stockturn per annum	4.7	4.9	4.2	4.0	4.2	4.1	3.9
Sales per person employed (£000)	9.0	10.2	11.6	13.7	14.4	19.3	22.9
Sales per sq. ft floor space(£)	41.9	45.7	52.8	58.0	71.1	82.1	87.0
% Write Down of Book Stock	--	--	--	--	39.5	39.7	39.5

* All expressed as % of total sales
** 343 questionnaires representing 389 shops

Source: 1978 - 79 Charter Economic Survey

sharply. This in turn was caused by a substantial increase both in wage costs and in rents and rates.

Stockturn in the mid-1970's was consistently indifferent, although 1972 and 1973 were historically the exception rather than the rule. From 1972 to 1975 there appeared to be a close relationship between stockturn and net trading profit, but here again this occurred during neither the preceding nor ensuing periods. What is, perhaps, significant is the implication that the only way to offset the recent upsurge in expenses is to improve the stockturn dramatically. The figures for sales per person employed and sales per square foot of floor space look auspicious, but are not adjusted for inflation. When so adjusted both figures prove to be constant in real terms in 1977 as compared to 1975, with the former showing a real improvement in 1978 and the latter a real decline.

The Charter survey then goes on to analyse 194 businesses which had experienced

little physical change between 1977 - 1978 and 1978 - 1979 and which could therefore be compared on a consistent basis. Not surprisingly this sample performed
rather better than the overall sample as the businesses were well-established with
better margins and lower expenses than businesses not included. The overall sample
is subsequently divided into five categories according to value of book sales as
follows:

Category	Book Sales
Small	£50,000 and below
Small/Medium	£50,001 - £89,000
Medium	£89,001 - £148,000
Large/Medium	£148,001- £313,000
Large	£313,000 and over

Application of these categories to the composition of sales in 1977 - 78 and 1978
- 79 reveals that the smallest two categories were more dependent than the others
upon retail sales. Conversely the largest two categories were more dependent than
the others upon library sales, as indeed one would expect. Somewhat curiously,
however, only the medium-sized firms did a disproportionate amount of business in
the form of school-book sales. Unfortunately no explanation for differences in
composition is provided.

Of particular interest is the table of net profit as a percentage of sales divided
according to type of specialisation; by size of book sales; by region; and by type
of centre. Some of the samples used in each category are rather small, but it is
possible to overcome this deficiency to some degree by setting out the figures
for the four years for which data are available. This appears as Table 29 below.

If we examine the individual categories we discover that:

(a) The only specialism currently running ahead of the field is technical and
scientific, whereas the profit performance of paperbacks is in severe decline.
Secondly the profitability of bookshops which are heavily dependent upon sales of
books is generally and increasingly inferior to that of bookshops selling a lot
of other goods. However, the range of values in the original samples precluded
a significant relationship between specialisation and profitability in 1978 - 79.

(b) The tendency for specialist bookshops to do better than general bookshops is
attributable principally to differences in size, the former being typically larger
than the latter. However, it is a statistically significant aspect of size that
the smaller the turnover the greater the probability of making a loss. In 1978
- 1979 38.4% of all small bookshops ran at a loss whereas the equivalent figure
for medium and large categories only varied between 13.8% and 21.6%. It is not
possible to generalise about these other categories, however, as in 1976 - 77
there was a marked inverse relationship between the percentage of loss-makers
and the size of shops. The fact that 25.1% of all bookshops made a loss in 1978
- 1979, the comparable figure for 1977 - 78 being 24.3% and for 1976 - 77 being
20.4%, certainly gives one cause to wonder why so many bookshops are unprofitable.
One potentially useful piece of information is unfortunately not to hand, namely
the effect of stock appreciation provisions as laid down in the various Finance
Acts since 1974. With so much capital tied up in stock bookshops should be able
to put these provisions to good use. One further factor is that the loss-makers
have a disproportionate effect upon the average net profit. Hence whereas the
average net profit for large shops in 1978 - 79 was 4.8%, some 48% of these shops
earned at least 5%.

TABLE 29 Net Profit as a % of Total Sales

	1975 - 76	1976 - 77	1977 - 78	1978 - 79
A) By Type of Specialisation				
Technical and Scientific	3.1	4.9	4.8	5.6*
Theological	3.7	4.3	3.6	3.0*
Paperback	6.4	5.0	3.0	1.3*
Books 95% of sales	2.5	2.9	2.2	2.4
Books 75 - 94% of sales	3.0	2.9	2.3	2.5
Books 50 - 74% of sales	3.3	1.9	4.2	4.5*
Books less than 50% of sales	3.9	3.6	4.6	4.2
B) By Size of Book Sales				
Large	3.8	4.6	3.8	4.8
Large/Medium	3.7	4.2	4.4	4.1
Medium	5.5	4.9	4.1	3.6
Small/Medium	3.0	3.1	4.0	2.0
Small	0.1	-0.7	-0.9	1.3
C) By Region				
North	4.0	4.7	3.8	3.5
South-west	3.4	4.3	3.4	3.3
Scotland and Wales	5.1	3.9	3.6	2.2
Midlands	2.6	2.7	2.4	2.5
South	3.0	2.6	2.9	3.3
London	2.0	2.1	3.5	3.4
D) By Type of Centre				
Central London	2.9	3.6	4.6	5.4*
Major city centres	5.8	5.3	4.5	3.3
Weekly centres	2.8	3.0	3.7	5.0
Small Towns	3.4	3.8	-0.3	1.9
Suburban London	1.4	0.2	1.3	1.8

* Small samples registered in 1978 - 79

Source: Charter Economic Surveys

(c) It is interesting to observe that bookshops are more profitable in the north than in the south. Presumably this reflects variations in overheads and in wages and salaries. However, the differences have largely disappeared over the past two years.

(d) Larger conurbations generally provide advantageous locations for bookshops because such shops tend to be larger and more specialised. The place not to be located, however, is suburban London.

The Charter survey turns next to consider performance by specialisation. Technical bookshops obtain a gross profit margin of little more than 25%, which is lower than all other categories because of the relatively low discounts on academic books. However net profitability is consistently good firstly because city centre locations are not needed so overheads are low, and secondly because a large quantity of inst-itutional business can be handled very cheaply by utilising existing labour during slack periods. As a result sales per person employed and sales per square foot of floor space are higher in most years than for any other category. The fly in the ointment, however, is a rather poor stockturn of consistently less than 4 times per annum.

The stockturn for theological bookshops is understandably even worse. However, they make a reasonable net trading profit on average because their gross profit margins are good at around 30%. Much more surprising is the fact that both these categories show a higher stockturn than paperback specialists, although the sample size for the latter is too small for complete confidence to be placed in this finding. The latters' gross profit, at just over 30% is also rather lower than one would expect, and this factor combined with high wages and high rents and rates resulting from city centre locations, has a depressing effect upon net profitab-ility.

It is difficult to draw useful comparisons with non-specialist bookshops because they are so varied in character. They do, however, appear to have an average stockturn noticeably higher than for specialist shops. Additional analysis of general bookshops in the surveys indicates that the ideal general bookshop prod-uces roughly 75% of its turnover from the sale of books and that roughly 80% of these book sales should originate from retail customers. To achieve an acceptable level of profitability a general bookshop appears to need a turnover of at least £80,000 at 1978 prices. The most conspicuous lessons to be learned from the surveys, therefore, are the straightforward ones that under-capitalisation which prevents a bookshop from attaining a turnover of the size indicated above within a year or two of its establishment increases the odds of becoming insolvent to roughly fifty-fifty, and that there is clear evidence of economies of scale in book retailing which is what one would expect from a business in which there is a considerable element of self-service.

SMALL ORDER SURCHARGES

One could probably devote a large part of this book purely to recounting the charges of unfair conduct brought by booksellers and publishers against each other. The avid reader of The Bookseller's letter pages will already be addicted to the weekly cries of outrage about such topics as publishers' errors, but most of these do not merit further analysis. One or two issues are, however, of especial im-portance and worthy of comment in their own right. The first of these is the issue of small order surcharges.

That the book trade has a single-copy problem is far from surprising. With over forty thousand new titles being churned out each year no bookshop can be expected to have in stock every title which would-be customers have read or heard about at any given point in time. Acquiring a single copy is, however, an expensive business, both administratively and more especially in terms of postage. Unfor-tunately publishers price books on the basis that each book will be sent off to the bookseller as part of a bulk order, a factor which much reduces the distrib-ution cost borne by each individual book. Thus when publishers receive single

copy orders they tend to respond by transferring the unbudgeted cost of servicing
the order on to the bookseller, either by reducing the discount allowed or by imposing a surcharge. In principle such surcharges can be passed on to the customer,
but in practice this rarely occurs because customers are unwilling to pay more than
the printed price and often prefer to look elsewhere for the title rather than
incur a surcharge.

The problem is not necessarily serious where both large publishers and large booksellers are involved, since the bookseller can always delay sending off an order
to the publisher until it consists of several items. But where a bookseller does
only sporadic business with a publisher, and more especially where the publisher
is so small as to be unknown to the average bookshop, the problem can become acute,
especially where the bookseller needs to search for details about the publisher.
Unfortunately most publishers remain unrepentant about their policy of passing on
the additional costs incurred by special orders. They argue that the only alternative is to budget for such costs by raising the price of their books which will
price some of them out of the market. Booksellers, on the other hand, believe
that this attitude is self-defeating because it induces them to discourage single
copy orders to the detriment of both publisher and bookseller.

There are a number of possible solutions to this problem. In the first place the
existence of a single copy problem could be acknowledged by publishers and budget-
ed for by raising net prices, although this also raises the objection that it
penalises all book buyers when the problem is often created by reluctance on the
part of a customer to look for and buy from stock a book equally suitable for his
purpose to that which he wishes to order. Alternatively the bookseller could put
up notices to the effect that ordering books is a costly business which must be
paid for in the form of a service charge levied upon the customers. Obviously this
would discourage some sales, but it would at least ensure that those which are
placed are as profitable for the bookseller as purchases out of stock. Wherever
possible orders should be grouped together, and although this will inevitably
delay delivery it will often make little material difference because delivery is
already so slow. Finally, cutomers could be given the choice between paying a
service charge or waiting until the bookseller has accumulated several orders for
the publisher in question, which will, if nothing else, bring home to customers
the nature of the problem.

Clearly none of these solutions is ideal. It would help a great deal if there
was at least a coherent and uniform policy across the whole industry. A standard
charge agreed by all publishers and booksellers would have a lot to commend it as
it would transfer the cost of single orders on to the customer and make it plain
to him that it was not being levied at the whim of the individual bookseller.
Alternatively all books could be dual-priced ex-stock and special order. At the
end of the day anything would be better than the present confusion of practice
which is almost guaranteed to alienate at least one of the three parties concerned
with a single copy order.

    DELIVERY

A seemingly perpetual area of contention between publishers and booksellers is
that of delivery periods. Indeed so contentious is it that for over ten years the
BA has supplied itself with ammunition with which to shoot down publishers in the
form of the annual publishers' delivery league table. The most recent delivery
survey was conducted during September and October 1979 with ten booksellers monitoring deliveries from 75 publishers and 4 wholesalers. In all previous years
the survey was conducted during the Spring. The 1979 Autumn survey was intended
as a test of delivery performance during a busy time of year, but there was as a
consequence a marked reluctance to take part, and not all of the participating

booksellers were able to complete the course. The BA nevertheless continued to
believe that the small sample analysed gave a reasonably accurate representation
of the overall picture.

A further innovation introduced in 1979 was to measure a publisher's performance
by the number of working days elapsed between receipt of an order by a publisher
and delivery of that order to the bookshop in question. In previous years the
starting date was that on which the bookseller sent the order, and this meant that
1979 league positions are not directly comparable with those of earlier years.
With these provisos in mind we can now inspect the overall picture as it appears
in Table 30 below.

TABLE 30 Average Time Lapse of Delivery

Time Lapse From	Working Days*			
	1976	1977	1978	1979
Date order sent to receipt of order	-	-	2.8	3.1
Receipt of order to despatch by publisher (in-house time)	4.4	4.4	4.9	6.4
Despatch by publisher to receipt in bookshop	3.6	3.4	3.6	4.1
Total: Date order sent to receipt of parcel	-	-	11.3	13.6

*Excluding Saturdays, Sundays and bank holidays

Source: BA Publishers Delivery League Table 1979

Because circumstances were somewhat more adverse than usual in 1979 the deterioration in overall delivery performance must be treated with care. Nevertheless,
there is certainly no reason to believe that things are getting better. The key
problem appears to be the publishers' in-house time although the average in 1979
was pulled down by some remarkably poor performances by publishers languishing at
the foot of the league table. The worsening position elsewhere in the table was
due, in part, to a deterioration in the performance of the Post Office, over which
the trade has no control.

Although a limited amount of information about the effects of teleordering was
available in the survey, it was not statistically significant and we will have to
wait for the 1980 survey before anything useful can be said in this respect. On
the issue of availability of titles, the percentage of lines not supplied was as
follows:

        1976 - 15%;   1977 - 9%;   1978 - 11%;   1979 - 8%:

Although no deterioration was recorded over the period it is still regrettable
that roughly ten per cent of orders could not be satisfied. Perhaps the most
surprising figure thrown up by the survey in the light of booksellers' constant
complaints is the percentage of lines supplied in error which was as follows:

        1976 - 1%;   1977 - 0%;   1978 - 1%;   1979 - 0%:

Since the names of participating booksellers were known to publishers it is, however, just possible that these percentages were untypical of general experience.

The 1979 league table confirmed one irrefutable conclusion, namely that wholesalers who have the books in stock can satisfy orders much faster than all but a very few publishers can supply them from their warehouses. The top three positions in the 1979 table were filled by Gardners, Bertrams and Hammicks respectively. The only surprise here being that Bookwise filled 9th place as against 1st place in 1978 and 3rd place in 1977. The only publisher able to perform consistently as well as wholesalers, taking into account lines not supplied, was Allen and Unwin. It may of course be argued that with Gardners failing to supply 35% and Hammicks 26% of lines ordered in 1979 that their service was rather limited. Nevertheless the comments made elsewhere about wholesaling still hold good, and with more large-scale wholesalers, and improved co-operation between publishers and wholesalers, service to booksellers can surely be improved in future. The widespread introduction of teleordering together with a reduction of in-house time to no more than 3 working days should help bring down delivery times to more realistic levels.

SCHOOL BOOKS

The supply of books to schools involves some 120 local education authorities, 110 educational contractors and school suppliers, and 40,000 schools. According to the Publishers' Association some 25,000 books fall into the category of school textbooks. Department of Industry figures show that in recent years school textbooks have accounted for 16 or 17% of total hardback and paperback turnover, although a sizeable proportion of this has arisen from export sales. Throughout the period 1971-1978 home sales of school textbooks measured at 1971 prices fluctuated only between an upper limit of 20 million pounds and a lower limit of 18 million pounds.

LEAs normally select school book suppliers on the basis of a public tender which may either be for books alone or for all school needs. Contractors offer a price for fulfilling the tender and in many cases LEAs are obliged to accept the lowest price. Most school books are non-net, so the contractor must specify the discount which he will offer to the LEA after calculating what he himself can expect to receive from the publishers who supply him. The supply of school books is a competitive market. Typically a publisher offers anything from 17 to 21% on average by way of discount to a school book supplier. The Price Commission found the overall average discount in 1976 to be $17\frac{1}{2}$%.

Specialist educational contractors, some of whom operate nationally, tender both for composite contracts and for the supply of school books alone. In the latter case they may face competition from booksellers who may be locally situated or on an approved national panel. LEAs may award contracts either to a single supplier; to a number of suppliers who are each awarded a specified share of the contract; to a number of suppliers amongst whom schools are at liberty to distribute their orders; or they may allow schools to purchase from whomsoever they like, although often only within certain laid-down limits. A small number of LEAs, in particular the Inner London, bypass both contractors and bookshops and deal directly with publishers. This is not altogether popular because it deprives local bookshops of a potential source of income.

Data on local education authority expenditure on libraries and textbooks in England and Wales published by the DES reveal a slow upward trend in money terms during the 1970's. Translated into real terms the trend is almost solidly downwards. Concern about this trend resulted in the setting up of the National Book League Wor￼ng Party on the use of books in schools. In May 1979 the Working Party publi￼ Report which dealt both with the best ways to provide books for schools ￼ financing their provision. The Report revealed that in 1977-78 the ave￼

capita expenditure on books in primary schools was £3.69 and in secondary schools
£6.20. This latter figure was a reduction in both money and real terms as compared
to the previous year. In 1977-78 only 0.9% of total education expenditure was
allocated for the provision of school books, a very low figure by international
standards. Because the quality of school books had deteriorated as publishers
sought to hold down prices, books bought in 1977-78 could not be expected to last
more than two or three years on average. Thus with an average per capita allowance
sufficient to buy four books each year this meant that there were only roughly 10
or 12 books available per student year of 1200 hours.

The Report regarded provision on this scale to be wholly inadequate. Naturally
some LEAs spend much more than others. Of the 116 LEAs sampled by the Working Party
in 1977-78 only 4 spent more than £7 per head on books for primary schools whereas
3 actually spent less than £1 per head, and only 5 spent more than £12 per head on
books for secondary schools whereas 4 actually spent less than £1 per head. The
first figure of each pair, regarded by the National Book League as a 'reasonable
allowance', has been raised for 1979-80 to a figure of £7.23 per primary school
child and £12.05 per secondary school child. However, projected LEA spending for
1979-80 yields much lower estimated expenditure of £4.42 per primary school child
and £7.44 per secondary school child. Nevertheless even these figures may turn
out to be over-optimistic in the light of certain LEAs' avowed intention to slash
school book spending this year.

Although there is always room to quibble about the definition of 'a reasonable
level of expenditure', current projected expenditure must surely be regarded as
unreasonable even if judged by historical standards alone. It is slightly alarming
that attempts to hold down prices have resulted in a shortening of average book
life, although such a relationship is hardly surprising, since it is by no means
obvious that fewer longer-lasting books are an inferior alternative to more shorter-
lived books. However the real misfortune is that such a choice has to be made in
the first place, and one can only hope that the downward trend in real expenditure
will be reversed in the near future even if it is too late to prevent it making a
contribution to the current crisis in publishing generally.

LIBRARIES

Introduction

In the UK there are approximately 14,500 public library service points which issue
around 600 million loans per year. It is widely alleged that whereas in 1920 one
book was borrowed for every ten bought, in 1965 ten books were borrowed for every
one bought. By international standards, this ratio is very high. In West Germany,
for example, more books are bought than are borrowed, and in the USA the categories
are roughly equal. Thus the public library system has a special role to play in
the UK with respect to access to the written word.

In general, public libraries do not buy direct from publishers. Instead they allocate
their purchases amongst a number of stockholding bookshops and specialist library
suppliers who give licensed libraries a 10 per cent discount off net prices. Many
libraries consider this to be inadequate given the bulk orders which they place,
but they are constrained by the Library Agreement. Traditionally library purchases
are of hardback editions because they are more durable, but libraries are more and
more buying paperback editions both in order to save money and also because planning
for a short shelf-life is appropriate for those books which are likely to have a
short-lived popular appeal. Paperbacks are sometimes strengthened by the supplier
by plasticising the covers or by fitting plastic jackets. The Library License
requires that libraries be charged for such services, although in practice charges
are often not submitted as a method of indirectly raising the discount.

Local Authority Libraries

The great majority of all library books are purchased by local authorities. In
recent years, their recurrent spending on libraries has declined in real terms from
£188 million in 1975-76 to £187 million in 1978-79. Equally capital spending has
plummeted from £32 million in 1973-74 to £20 million in 1975-76 and to £11 million
in 1978-79. As a result spending on libraries as a proportion of all local government spending has fallen steadily throughout the past decade to a current all-time
low of less than 1.5%. However even this disguises the full impact of such cuts
upon book budgets as is shown in Table 31 below.

TABLE 31   Expenditure by Public Library Authorities - England and
           Wales %

	1967 - 68	1972 - 73	1975 - 76	1977 - 78
Other Expenditure	28.9	29.2	30.5	30.2
Expenditure on Books	23.3	21.5	17.0	17.1
Expenditure on Staff	47.8	49.3	52.5	52.7
Total	100.0	100.0	100.0	100.0

Compared to expenditure on staff, expenditure on books fell from a ratio of 1 to 2
in 1967-68 to a ratio of 1 to 3 in 1977-78. Although this ratio now appears to
have stabilised, the number of books added to stock each year continues to fall.
In 1976-77 10.6 million books were added to stock compared to 11.95 million in
1975-76 despite an increase in the proportion of books bought in paperback format.
By way of comparison the number of non-manual staff employed fell during the same
period by 2% whereas the number of professional posts fell by 1.5%.

The fact that expenditure cuts tend to fall disproportionately upon book funds
parallels American experience during the early 1930's. In the USA book funds dropped to 54% of the 1930 base by 1933, whereas salaries dropped only to 89% of the
1930 base. It is of interest that demand for loans rose rapidly at that time, because this is also happening in the UK as unemployment becomes more widespread.
This obviously makes it more difficult to cut staffing expenditure. Furthermore
the trend these days is to provide more labour-intensive services in libraries.
Thus it is invariably the easiest option simply to reduce the book budget when the
alternatives are cuts in salaries, overheads, periodical subscriptions or binding.

What it all boils down to at the end of the day is that the provision of an efficient
and comprehensive service, which is interpreted by the Department of Education and
Science to mean the addition each year of 250 books per 1000 population, is still
a long way from realisation since the current provision is less than half of that
figure. Furthermore, a lot depends upon where one lives. According to CIPFA,
people living in cities are generally better served than those living in the counties. However there are notable exceptions such as Coventry which has only 1.2
books per person in total. Furthermore, although London boroughs are generally
well-stocked, commuters borrow so many books that residents often feel disadvant-
aged. Amongst the counties the southern are generally worse-stocked than the
northern. Berkshire at 1.47 books per person in 1977/78, and Buckinghamshire, at

1.5 books per person, were notably bad, a fact emphasised by their 1977-78 provision
of new books at 40p per person and 33p per person respectively.

University Library Expenditure

The other major category of library expenditure is that undertaken by the universities which spent £7 million on books in 1976-77. University library expenditure
is regularly surveyed by the National Book League, the most recent survey covering
the six year period 1971 to 1977. This survey reveals that between 1971 and 1977
expenditure on books at constant 1971 prices fell from an average of £14.48 per
student to £12.51 per student, a reduction of over 13%. However, real expenditure
rose during the first half of this period, so that the decline during the latter
half was in practice quite severe. In part this decline reflected a tendency for
university libraries to switch from the purchase of books to the purchase of journals.
Gross expenditure on journals in 1976-77 amounted to £6½ million and between 1971
and 1977 real expenditure on journals rose from £9.65 per student to £11.83 per
student. Taking both books and journals together, therefore, the increase in real
expenditure was negligible, rising from £24.13 to £24.33 per student.

The significance of the decline in book expenditure during the mid-1970's is most
readily shown by calculating the proportion of all universities whose real book
expenditure fell during a given year. The relevant figures are 75% in 1974-75,
59% in 1975-76, and 63% in 1976-77. Although no figures are available for subsequent years there is every reason to expect these proportions to continue. For two
universities this reduction in real expenditure occurred during each of the six
years surveyed, and for more than a quarter of all universities this reduction
occurred in each successive year from 1973-74 onwards.

A final point to note is that there was no major switch during the period surveyed
from expenditure upon books and journals to expenditure upon wages and salaries,
other than in 1974-75. This is shown in Table 32 below.

TABLE 32   Percentage of UK Library Expenditure by Category 1971 - 1977

	1971-72	1972-73	1973-74	1974-75	1975-76	1976-77
Books	23.40	23.44	22.68	19.71	19.48	19.32
Journals	15.59	16.05	17.08	16.80	17.00	18.28
Wages and Salaries	51.60	51.72	50.72	54.68	54.05	53.23

Libraries, Bookshops and the NBA

By and large publishers are very reticent about the significance of library sales
for print runs and prices. It would in any case be extremely difficult to generalise because, for example, whereas academic monographs are directed primarily
towards the library market, paperback fiction is dependent upon library sales to a
far lesser degree. We are, however, in a position to comment upon the significance
of library sales for stockholding bookshops, currently a highly contentious issue
because of the alleged widespread infringement of the Net Book Agreement.

The Charter Economic Survey for 1977-78 reveals that Charter booksellers obtained 8% of their total turnover from library sales and a further 5.4% from sales of school books. These percentages were roughly the same as those for 1970, but comparatively low in relation to the mid-1970's. Library and institutional business thus represented nearly 20% of the average Charter bookseller's turnover derived from sale of books, and a much higher proportion for those bookshops selling only books. It is extremely difficult to estimate how many stockholding bookshops would go out of business if they were to lose their library and institutional trade, but a figure of 20 to 25% has been suggested. The main reason why library business can have this apparently extreme effect upon viability is that library business can be transacted during those times of day when retail sales are sluggish without necessitating any increase in wage costs.

Under the terms of the NBA a library with a licence is entitled to a 10% discount from the supplier. On average a bookseller may himself receive some $17\frac{1}{2}$% discount on non-net books which comprise a large proportion of sales to school libraries. Allowing for overheads, therefore, and the libraries' discount, the margin of profit is fairly small. Furthermore servicing costs of library orders can be disproportionately high where such orders consist of large numbers of single copies, and profit margins consequently non-existent. By way of compensation the bookseller also expects to receive library orders for net books where his discount is considerably higher, thus allowing him to show a decent profit even after the libraries have taken their share.

Thus, in principle, the system works satisfactorily. In practice, however, a number of drawbacks arise. In the first place, although a library must be "public" in order to obtain a library licence, many licences are issued to libraries whose qualifications for the term "public" are at best doubtful, and more importantly licences are issued to academic libraries in the public sector. Furthermore discounts on academic books rarely exceed 30% on average, and such books require a good deal of servicing both because so many orders are for single copies and because such books are often difficult to trace. Thus the overheads are high and the profits are very low.

At the end of the day, therefore, a large part of a bookshop's library trade is barely worth the effort. But so long as the bookseller can make a good profit on net books to non-academic libraries all is not lost and this profit is protected by the terms of the NBA which limit the library discount to a maximum of 10%. However it is now a matter of public complaint that bookshops are having to concede additional discounts in order to retain library business, and that the Publishers' Association is refusing to take any action to enforce the Agreement. Such a situation is unacceptable, both because it unfairly undermines the profitability of bookshops and also because it undermines the Net Book Agreement, in defence of which it was argued that its abrogation would result in libraries demanding and receiving higher discounts!

Should Library Services Be Provided Free of Charge?

The principle of free access to public library services was established under the first Public Libraries Act in 1850, and was upheld in a series of subsequent reports such as those by Adams in 1915, Kenyon in 1927, and Roberts in 1957. Although they were originally in competition with the commercial lending libraries, the public libraries have achieved such a total ascendency during the post-war years that the very idea of paying for the loan of a library book now strikes a discordant note. Nevertheless the unhappy financial condition of the public library service inevitably leads one to wonder whether a solution might be found in a system of fees for the provision of certain library services.

This solution understandably appals the Library Association whose defence of a free service asserts that it is needed, inter alia, in order to maintain a civilised and democratic society; to promote education and encourage literacy; to attract children to the world of books; to encourage the positive use of leisure; and to help the economy through the information services provided to local industry, commerce and business. The Association believe that the introduction of charges would discourage intellectual curiosity; result in an excessive dependence on the income from such charges and hence lead to the provision exclusively of high-turnover stock; undermine the complex network of inter-library co-operation; and exacerbate the already serious problems of the publishing industry.* The Association also foresee considerable administrative difficulties, especially in relation to the need to ensure some kind of uniformity among the large number of authorities responsible for library provision. In addition they consider that the income net of administrative expenses which a system of modest charges will generate will be an insignificant proportion of a library's total income. But this in turn will generate pressure for higher charges resulting in a vicious circle of higher charges leading to reduced use leading to higher charges and so on until the service either is destroyed or becomes an elitist facility for the affluent.

One must not lose sight of the fact that the public library service is funded out of tax revenue. Hence it is something of a misnomer to say that the services are free. In effect the first so many borrowed books from a library are paid for by a household's own contribution towards the costs of the service. An element of subsidy therefore exists insofar as non-borrowing households end up subsidising those which borrow heavily. Thus, given the social objectives of the public lending library system, it would be highly regressive if, in practice, libraries largely ended up circulating romantic fiction among the affluent middle classes.

It is the widespread belief that this is precisely what does happen which inspires adverse comments about poor ratepayers subsidising the leisure activities of the middle classes which they are perfectly capable of paying for in full, but one must examine this assertion with care. In March 1976 the English counties as a whole held 9.3% of their stock as reference books; 33% as adult fiction for loan; 40.4% as adult non-fiction for loan; and 17.3% as childrens' books. However DES (1977) using a four county sample calculated that each adult fiction book on open shelves was borrowed 9.5 times per year; each adult non-fiction book 5.4 times per year and each childrens' book 6.5 times per year. Thus by far the largest total number of loans are in the adult fiction category which satisfies comparatively few of the objectives set out by the Library Association. Whilst one should beware of reading too much into simple evidence of this kind, it does suggest strongly that something should be done to ensure that any cutbacks in library provision should be directed as far as is possible towards the provision of adult fiction. The obvious objection to pricing as a solution to a shortage of funds is that whereas the middle classes will probably be happy to pay a nominal charge, the less affluent will be further discouraged from borrowing, and parents will become reluctant to borrow on their childrens' behalf. Such a solution will therefore be counter-productive. One alternative solution, at least in the short run, is to be found in a reduction of expenditure on new stocks of adult fiction whilst other categories are maintained in real terms. This will allow most of the social objectives of a public library system to continue to be met. It should also benefit publishers since difficulties in obtaining fiction through library loans will force some would-be borrowers into bookshops, thereby more than compensating for the loss of library sales. This solution will obviously give rise to the complaint

---

*For a more detailed account of these issues see the Library Association Record (September 1979) pages 429-33.

that public libraries will no longer provide the full services which users expect.
Nevertheless something has to give unless of course, the State were to decide to
subsidise the production of quality literature. In Sweden, which has the same level
of library loans proportionate to the population as the UK, and also in Norway, the
State stands ready to purchase library copies of a limited number of quality novels
to the extent necessary to make their production economically viable. However this
idea appears to have little support in the UK.

PUBLIC LENDING RIGHT

Public Lending Right is now part of the law of the land. It may therefore be argued that it is no longer a contentious issue meriting detailed economic analysis.
Nevertheless there are still a good many people who believe that there is no economic justification for PLR, and, to judge by the finance provided by the government,
many others who support PLR in principle are much less enthusiastic when it comes
to the point of having to put it into practice. We have already noted that the
controversy surrounding the Net Book Agreement has never fully died down and one
can anticipate that the same will be true of PLR. In the sections below we therefore propose to set out the economic arguments for and against PLR for the benefit
of any future protagonists in the debate.

A Brief History of PLR*

The battle to establish a PLR lasted from 1951 to 1979, and was waged primarily by
the Society of Authors, the Writers Guild, and later by the Writers Action Group,
assisted by sundry MPs. Bills to establish PLR were introduced on a number of
occasions from 1961 onwards, but pressure only began to appear irresistible after
1975, the year in which the DES published an account of an investigation of technical and cost aspects of PLR. In November 1975 the Queen's Speech included a
promise to introduce PLR, but a year later the Bill came to grief when Messrs Moate,
Sproate and English organised a filibuster in Parliament. However further pressure
resulted in a new Bill being introduced in November 1978 which went to the Lords
in January 1979 and received the Royal Assent on March 22nd 1979. In November 1979
the Government declared that a £2 million fund had been set up to finance PLR, but
pointed out that the need to set up a complex administrative machinery would mean
that no payments to authors would be made until 1982.

The administrative details are not as yet fully decided although a lengthy consultative document was published in January 1980. It is evidently intended that payments will be tied to loans made by approximately 70 outlets representative of the
public library service in the UK. Each outlet in the sample will record all loans,
the outlets being rotated every five years on a phased basis. A PLR Registry head-
ed by a Registrar and advised by a council representing authors, publishers, librarians and local authorities will administer the system. The initial cost of the
system at 1980 prices is assessed at around £100,000 with annual running costs of
£300,000.

The Economics of PLR

Support for PLR is based primarily upon the fact that public libraries make some
650 million loans per annum without any charge to consumers and without needing to

*For a more detailed account see The Bookseller (March 10th, 1979) pages 1148-9,
 and Sutherland (1978) chapter 6.

buy into stock in any one year more than a small fraction of the total number of books in circulation. It is not known exactly how many times on average a library book is loaned out, but a figure of 10 times is generally accepted as a good approximation. Thus an author who has written five books which are stocked, on average, by 200 libraries sells a total of 1000 library copies at, say, £5 a time earning him, say, £500 in royalties spread out over many years. His books will ultimately be read by some 10,000 people (and potentially by five or six times as many). A musician or playright who reaches a live audience on such a scale would expect to be paid vastly more than £500, so why should an author be left out in the financial cold?

The above line of argument is clearly dependent upon the issue of natural justice which very few would wish to deny to authors. However this does not of itself provide an economic rationale for PLR nor for a system of payments based upon library lending. There are, after all, several other ways of ensuring that authors are better rewarded for their endeavours and at a much reduced administrative cost. Ultimately, therefore, we need to clarify the link between lending libraries and authors' incomes.

To begin with we need to analyse the economic characteristics of books. A good can be defined in terms of rivalness and excludability. If by consuming a good an individual thereby prevents all others from consuming it, and if by purchasing a good the owner can thereby deny access to other individuals who refuse to contribute to its price, that good is deemed to be a pure private good. Conversely a pure public good is one where consumption is necessarily collective and where free riders can obtain access without having to pay for their consumption. A book falls into neither category because although its purchaser can deny access to other would-be readers, the act of consumption leaves the book physically intact and thereby available for further consumption. Thus a book is excludable but non-rival over time. This is of course true of most durable goods, but a book is different in that whereas an individual may use his cooker many thousands of times, he is unlikely to want to read a book more than once. The durability of a book combined with the limited satisfaction which it yields to an individual makes it ideally suited for use by a lending agency, whether private or public, or for resale in a second-hand market.

If we turn to consider the remuneration of authors we discover that whereas the act of writing involves a once-and-for-all expenditure of effort this is rarely matched by a once-and-for-all reward. The existence of a royalty system therefore implies either that a lump-sum reward is inequitable because it fixes the reward to the author but not to the publisher, or that there is a commonly held belief in the justice of relating reward to satisfaction provided. This latter argument is of course that which underpins the introduction of PLR. Nevertheless to proceed from this point to the belief that all library loans should result in a payment to an author clearly implies that if the public library system did not exist considerably more copies of any given book would be sold, and that the more a given book is borrowed the more sales are being foregone. This in turn implies that if there were no libraries the private purchaser would not attempt to resell his books, an act which would increase readership but provide the author with no additional payment. Clearly the major difficulty here is that we have no real idea at all of the relationship between potential private purchases of new books in the absence of a library system and total sales given the system as it currently exists. One cannot even take price as a constant in such a comparison because the print run would be different in each case. Thus it is acceptable to argue that consumer satisfaction is enhanced by a public library system in that this results in a book being read more often than would be the case in the absence of the system, but unacceptable to put the difference in the region of ten times as often. Quite clearly the result of shutting down the public library system would be to induce readers to pass on books among themselves to a much greater degree than is currently common practice.

It is therefore highly debatable whether the existence of a public library system
severely damages sales of new books.

Whatever else may be true about the effects of public libraries it is surely not
the case that their existence restrains the volume of publications. As we have
already noted an author expends his entire effort before he learns anything at all
about his ultimate earnings. Given the number of unpublished authors it is fair
to assume that the number, even if not the quality, of publications could easily
be maintained were authors to be paid nothing at all. The supporters of PLR
claim that authors cannot live off their royalties, yet they nearly all soldier on.
Denial of reward for writing might therefore make no difference to literary output,
and even if it did there is still no strong theoretical or empirical justification
for a system of rewards related to library loans.

It is widely accepted that the rewards to authorship are in need of a boost, and it
is not the intention of this section to argue otherwise. But I have sought to explain why the demise of the public library system would not necessarily provide that
boost. A system of reward based upon readership in libraries does not, therefore,
appear to be justified.* Indeed it may be self-defeating because the great majority of library loans are of light fiction, a category in which authors do at least
stand a sporting chance of making a fortune through private purchases. The higher
reaches of literature are frankly going to remain largely unaffected by a system
such as PLR. Other solutions do exist. In Eire certain authors are tax-exempt.
This may be too radical for the UK but the principle of limited tax exemptions
would appear to have much to commend it as an alternative to PLR.

---

*For a technical analysis supporting this conclusion see Cullis and West (1977)

CHAPTER 8

Price Indices

PRICE COMPOSITION

We have now examined the role played by printers, publishers and booksellers in the build-up to the eventual retail price of a book. According to the Price Commission the approximate break down of the typical retail price in 1977 was as follows:

The printer was responsible for 28% of the retail price, of which 21% represented his direct costs, 5% his overheads and 2% his profit margin. The publisher was responsible for a further 42% of retail price, of which 12% represented his direct costs excluding costs of printing, 23% his overheads and 7% his profit margin. The bookseller was responsible for 30% of retail price, of which 25% represented his overheads and 5% his profit margin. Treated cumulatively, therefore, direct costs represented 21% of retail price at printer and binder stage, 40% at publisher stage and 70% at bookseller stage.

PRICE INDICES

The Price Commission chose not to place much emphasis upon price indices because of the difficulties, discussed below, inherent in their compilation. As a result, the relevant sections of the Report are somewhat unhelpful. Indeed, in Table 7.2 of the Report the indices appear to be based simultaneously upon both January 1975 and calendar 1975. Nevertheless, price indices are available going back some fifteen years, and it does seem to be a worthwhile exercise to discover such information as they may yield with a view to establishing the relative importance of the factors which have caused price changes to occur.

The period July 1964 to June 1965 is the most convenient starting point for our purposes since this constitutes the base period for Library Association statistics, and these can be examined in conjunction with the longer-standing series produced by The Bookseller. It is convenient, for reasons explained below, to divide the period 1964 to 1979, this latter year being the most recent for which statistics are currently available, into three roughly equal sub-periods, namely 1964-65 to 1969-70, 1970-71 to 1974-75 and 1975 to 1979. The Bookseller series are produced twice a year, and are based upon all the entries which are listed at the end of each issue of that journal. Table 33 below initially lists the full set of money prices recorded during the entire period under consideration. These have then been adjusted on to a mid-year basis in Table 34 and Table 35 in order to make them fully

TABLE 33   Average Prices Recorded in The Bookseller.   £*

	ALL TITLES		NEW TITLES		REPRINTS AND NEW EDITIONS		NEW CLOTH-BOUND FICTION	
	Money Price	Change % pa	Money Price	Change % pa	Money Price	Change % pa	Money Price	Change % pa
July-Dec 1964	1.38	-	1.46	-	1.10	-	0.79	-
Jan-June 1965	1.38	-	1.46	-	1.09	-	0.86	-
July-Dec 1965	1.49	-	1.50	-	1.34	-	0.87	-
Jan -Dec 1965	1.43	8.3	1.48	5.7	1.21	15.2	0.87	16.1
Jan-June 1966	1.51	-	1.56	-	1.33	-	0.90	-
July-Dec 1966	1.59	-	1.65	-	1.42	-	0.92	-
Jan -Dec 1966	1.55	8.4	1.60	8.1	1.39	14.9	0.91	4.6
Jan-June 1967	1.74	-	1.66	-	1.97	-	0.97	-
July-Dec 1967	1.97	-	1.85	-	2.33	-	0.97	-
Jan -Dec 1967	1.85	19.4	1.76	10.0	2.15	54.7	0.97	6.6
Jan-June 1968	2.05	-	2.11	-	1.85	-	1.03	-
July-Dec 1968	2.17	-	2.15	-	2.22	-	1.10	-
Jan -Dec 1968	2.10	13.5	2.13	21.0	2.05	-4.7	1.07	10.3
Jan-June 1969	2.17	-	2.10	-	2.38	-	1.15	-
July-Dec 1969	2.52	-	2.28	-	3.16	-	1.19	-
Jan -Dec 1969	2.35	11.9	2.20	3.3	2.80	36.5	1.17	9.3
Jan-June 1970	2.72	-	2.43	-	3.33	-	1.25	-
July-Dec 1970	2.83	-	2.44	-	3.89	-	1.25	-
Jan -Dec 1970	2.77	17.9	2.43	10.5	3.57	27.5	1.25	6.8
Jan-June 1971	3.77	-	2.87	-	5.89	-	1.41	-
July-Dec 1971	3.02	-	2.98	-	3.14	-	1.54	-
Jan -Dec 1971	3.39	22.4	2.93	20.6	4.63	29.7	1.48	18.4
Jan-June 1972	3.13	-	3.11	-	3.25	-	1.65	-
July-Dec 1972	3.30	-	3.24	-	3.48	-	1.69	-
Jan -Dec 1972	3.22	-5.0	3.18	8.5	3.37	-17.2	1.67	12.8
Jan-June 1973	3.10	-	3.29	-	2.58	-	1.81	-
July-Dec 1973	3.37	-	3.46	-	3.14	-	1.84	-
Jan -Dec 1973	3.24	0.6	3.38	6.3	2.85	-14.5	1.83	9.6
Jan-June 1974	3.65	-	3.77	-	3.30	-	1.97	-
July-Dec 1974	3.66	-	3.90	-	2.87	-	2.25	-
Jan -Dec 1974	3.65	12.7	3.84	13.6	3.09	7.3	2.12	15.8
Jan-June 1975	4.54	-	4.63	-	4.27	-	2.56	-
July-Dec 1975	4.81	-	5.02	-	4.13	-	2.98	-
Jan -Dec 1975	4.67	27.9	4.82	25.5	4.20	35.9	2.77	30.7
Jan-June 1976	5.28	-	5.43	-	4.76	-	3.07	-
July-Dec 1976	6.42	-	6.23	-	6.93	-	3.42	-
Jan -Dec 1976	5.89	26.1	5.85	21.4	6.00	42.9	3.25	17.3
Jan-June 1977	6.64	-	6.71	-	6.41	-	3.49	-
July-Dec 1977	6.52	-	6.63	-	6.16	-	3.69	-
Jan -Dec 1977	6.58	11.7	6.67	14.0	6.28	4.7	3.60	10.8
Jan-June 1978	7.32	-	7.27	-	7.47	-	4.02	-
July-Dec 1978	7.36	-	7.50	-	6.91	-	4.30	-
Jan -Dec 1978	7.34	11.6	7.39	10.8	7.18	14.3	4.17	15.8
Jan-June 1979	7.65	-	7.82	-	7.03	-	4.57	-
July-Dec 1979	8.06	-	8.22	-	7.53	-	4.77	-
Jan -Dec 1979	7.87	7.2	8.02	8.5	7.30	1.7	4.67	12.0

*Government publications are excluded from these columns

Source: The Bookseller

comparable with those of the Library Association, and then converted into a series
of index numbers. In addition the resultant indices of money prices have been
converted into indices of real prices.

TABLE 34 Price Indices. July 1964 - June 1965 = 100

	July 1964–June 1965		July 1965–June 1966		July 1966–June 1967		July 1967–June 1968		July 1968–June 1969		July 1969–June 1970	
	Money	Real	Money	Real	Money	Real	Money	Real	Money	Real	Money	Real
THE BOOKSELLER												
All Titles	100	100	109	96	120	102	145	121	157	124	190	142
New Titles	100	100	105	93	114	97	136	113	145	114	161	120
Reprint and New Editions	100	100	121	107	154	132	186	155	209	165	294	220
Cloth-Bound New Fiction	100	100	109	96	116	99	122	102	137	108	146	109
LIBRARY ASSOCIATION												
All Titles	100	100	112	99	125	107	148	123	159	125	193	145
Adult Fiction	100	100	109	96	122	104	117	97	116	92	127	95
Adult Non-Fiction	100	100	118	104	131	112	156	130	171	134	205	154
Reference	100	100	109	97	153	131	137	114	153	121	149	112
Children's Fiction	100	100	103	91	107	91	104	86	111	87	130	97
Children's Non-Fiction	100	100	83	74	115	98	98	82	125	99	129	96

The Library Association series are derived from data which, until recently, appeared
in each August edition of the Library Association Record. The series are thus based
upon the entries in the British National Bibliography which records all titles published in Great Britain, and which provides information on prices among other things.
The sub-headings used in The Bookseller and LAR series are not, therefore, directly
comparable. There is also a problem in comparing the 'All Titles' series from 1964
to 1974 , despite the use of this series in both parts of the table, because during
that decade LAR statistics, unlike those of The Bookseller, omitted all material
classified by the BNB as Sd, defined therein as 'a publication, normally of not
more than 48 pages sewn, wire-stitched, or consisting of separate leaves, stapled
or glued together without a cover, and requiring special storage conditions.'

By and large, Sd items are cheap because they are short and cheaply-bound. However,
provided the 'All Titles' series are internally consistent no obvious problem of
comparison presents itself. Unfortunately, the BNB has never used a consistent definition of Sd items. As the Department of Trade and Industry Central Library pointed
out in 1972, many items which should be classified as Sd are classified as non-Sd,

whereas a large number of non-Sd items, especially if defined by length, are classified as Sd. It is possible, therefore, that year-by-year variations in the use
of the Sd category may have introduced a distorting element in to the LAR series,
thereby rendering them less reliable than those of The Bookseller during this period.

If one examines the sub-headings in Table 34 above one detects considerable variance
in the trends depicted. Indeed, certain categories actually fell in real terms
whereas others rose sharply. The overall trend was, however, clearly rising in real
terms. This is somewhat surprising in that this is generally reckoned to have been
a period during which both individuals and institutions were able to expand their
acquisitions in the absence of severe budgetary constraints. Fortunately, we can
resolve this apparent contradiction by reference to Table 35 below in which data
for each LAR category is supplied in three price ranges.

TABLE 35   Average Prices of Books in Selected Price Ranges 1965 - 70. £

	1965-66		1966-67		1967-68		1968-69		1969-70	
	Money	Real	Money	Real	Money	Real	Money	Real	Money	Real
Adult Fiction										
Up to 63p	0.41	0.41	0.38	0.37	0.32	0.30	0.27	0.24	0.27	0.23
63p to £2.10	1.01	1.01	1.04	1.01	1.05	0.99	1.10	0.99	1.19	1.01
Over £2.10	2.63	2.63	2.91	2.81	2.91	2.74	2.83	2.55	3.13	2.64
Adult Non-Fiction										
Up to 63p	0.38	0.38	0.39	0.38	0.38	0.36	0.38	0.35	0.39	0.33
63p to £2.10	1.31	1.31	1.35	1.31	1.34	1.26	1.36	1.22	1.37	1.16
Over £2.10	3.96	3.96	4.61	4.46	5.08	4.78	5.54	4.99	6.36	5.37
Reference Books										
Up to 63p	0.35	0.35	0.36	0.35	0.35	0.33	0.35	0.31	0.38	0.32
63p to £2.10	1.31	1.31	1.27	1.23	1.30	1.22	1.28	1.15	1.31	1.11
Over £2.10	5.38	5.38	6.03	5.83	5.96	5.61	6.70	6.03	6.57	5.55
Child. Fiction										
Up to 63p	0.36	0.36	0.33	0.32	0.30	0.28	0.32	0.29	0.36	0.30
63p to £2.10	0.81	0.81	0.84	0.81	0.85	0.80	0.88	0.79	0.93	0.79
Over £2.10	-	-	-	-	-	-	-	-	-	-
Child. Non-Fiction										
Up to 63p	0.36	0.36	0.54	0.52	0.36	0.34	0.37	0.33	0.40	0.34
63p to £2.10	0.84	0.84	0.87	0.84	0.95	0.89	0.96	0.86	0.94	0.79
Over £2.10	-	-	-	-	-	-	3.19	2.87	-	-
All Categories										
Up to 63p	0.38	0.38	0.37	0.36	0.35	0.33	0.35	0.31	0.36	0.30
63p to £2.10	1.22	1.22	1.25	1.21	1.25	1.18	1.27	1.14	1.29	1.09
Over £2.10	3.96	3.96	4.61	4.46	5.07	4.77	5.51	4.96	6.33	5.35

Source: Library Association Record

The lowest price range in each year accounted for some 20% of all titles published, the middle price range for a further 40%, and the highest, open-ended price range for the remaining 40%. The pattern is plain to see. In every category the 1969-70 real price was at least as cheap as in 1964-65 in the two lower price ranges. Only in the open-ended price range were real prices higher, and this was probably the result not of a general rise in the real price of books in this price range, but of the publication of a comparatively small number of increasingly more expensive titles in the price range '£10 and over'. It therefore seems reasonable to conclude that at least 80% of all books were cheaper in real terms in 1970 as compared to 1965. In this sense , therefore, this period must have represented a golden age for the bibliophile, and in particular the collector of cloth-bound fiction.

The only other identifiable trend during this period was a tendency for the prices of academic books in Dewey classes which were relatively expensive in 1964-65 to rise rather slowly, and for the prices of books in Dewey classes which were relatively cheap in 1964-65 to rise rather sharply.

The price indices covering the second period July 1970 to June 1975 are more difficult to interpret, not least because the Library Association ceased to publish statistics on books in selected price ranges in 1970. The same series as in Table 35 appear below as Table 36, but on this occasion based upon July 1969 to June 1970 equals 100.

TABLE 36   Price Indices.   July 1969 - June 1970 = 100

	July 1970-June 1971		July 1971-June 1972		July 1972-June 1973		July 1973-June 1974		July 1974-June 1975	
	Money	Real	Money	Real	Money	Real	Money	Real	Money	Real
THE BOOKSELLER										
All Titles	126	116	117	100	122	96	134	93	157	92
New Titles	113	104	129	110	139	110	153	107	183	107
Reprint and New Editions	152	140	98	84	93	74	99	69	110	65
Cloth-Bound New Fiction	108	100	129	110	144	114	144	100	195	114
LIBRARY ASSOCIATION										
All Titles	110	101	115	98	105	84	107	75	134	79
Adult Fiction	109	101	131	112	146	115	155	108	190	111
Adult Non-Fiction	108	100	110	94	103	81	106	74	132	77
Reference Books	108	100	108	92	124	98	128	90	164	96
Children's Fiction	105	97	124	106	131	103	152	106	180	105
Children's Non-Fiction	100	92	116	99	118	93	125	87	153	90

The <u>Bookseller</u> indices for 1970-71 are distorted by an extraordinarily high average price for reprints and new editions in Jan-June 1971, which was caused by the pub-lication of a series of very expensive facsimile reprints. The sharp decline in the <u>LAR</u> 'All Titles' real price series reflected what was happening in the largest sub-group 'Adult Non-Fiction', within which individual Dewey classes exhibit very large and apparently random variation from year to year. The much slower decline in the <u>Bookseller</u> real price 'All Titles' series reflected the unusually steady real price of new titles, despite the fact that reprints were becoming extremely cheap in real terms. In both parts of the table we find the prices of fiction books more than keeping pace with inflation, although it is not immediately obvious why fiction and non-fiction should be pulling in opposite directions at this time. Overall, therefore, this half-decade proved critical for cloth-bound fiction, but offered excellent opportunities for the academic buyer.

During the final period under investigation, 1975 to 1979, further data became available in the form of two new price series. The first of these was in the form of a retail price index for books alone, published by the Department of Employment, and which is set out as Table 41 below. The second was published by the Library Management Research Unit at Cambridge University, and covered the 16,000 or so books considered by the LMRU to be academic in content, and hence worthy of being included in the Cambridge University Library main catalogue.

Initially, in Table 37 below, we continue the above price indices on the same basis as before, in this case with July 1974 to June 1975 = 100, but from 1976 onwards we switch on to a calendar year basis in line with recent Library Association data.

TABLE 37 Price Indices. July 1974 - June 1975 = 100

	July 1974-June 1975		1976		1977		1978		1979	
	Money	Real	Money	Real	Money	Real	Money	Real	Money	Real
THE BOOKSELLER										
All Titles	100	100	143	109	160	106	178	109	191	103
New Titles	100	100	136	104	155	102	172	105	187	100
Reprints and New Editions	100	100	167	127	175	116	200	122	203	109
Cloth-Bound New Fiction	100	100	135	103	150	99	174	106	182	98
LIBRARY ASSOCIATION										
All Titles	100	100	144	110	175	116	180	110	211	114
Adult Fiction	100	100	135	103	152	100	164	100	190	102
Adult Non-Fiction	100	100	144	110	179	118	183	112	216	116
Reference Books	100	100	155	118	219	145	228	139	275	148
Children's Fiction	100	100	139	106	147	97	157	96	190	102
Children's Non-Fiction	100	100	132	101	119	78	120	73	137	74

The period covered in the above table is especially interesting in that it includes comparatively recent data. Jan 1975 to Jan 1978 also happens to be the period of coverage in the Price Commission Report. The Report concluded that during this period technical books (on the Commission's own definition), hardback non-fiction and paperback fiction had risen in real terms, whereas hardback fiction and paper- back non-fiction had fallen in real terms.

What the above table does show is a steady rise in the real price for the 'All Tit- les' series, but one which disguises a fair amount of variability in sub-categories. Reprint and new edition prices appear to have made up some of the ground lost during the previous half-decade. Reference books suddenly became rather expensive compared to the decade 1965 to 1975, but childrens' books continued to offer very good value. Fiction prices generally appeared to have stabilised.

A word of caution is, however, necessary at this juncture. When the Library Assoc- iation terminated their July to June series in June 1975, and subsequently went over to a calendar year basis commencing in calendar 1976, they also changed the sample frame. As reported in the Library Association Record (August 1975, page 191), Sd and other limited edition items, hitherto excluded, were to be included in the new series, thereby increasing considerably the number of items included, and lowering appreciably their average price. The old and new series are not, therefore, fully compatible, although one is a subset of the other, and the new series is now a better match with that of the Bookseller. The need for caution arises because as in its submission to the Price Commission the Publishers' Association unhappily failed to notice the change in the sample, and were led to conclude that real prices had fallen in 1976 whereas they had in fact risen by 9% as the above table shows.

TABLE 38   Annual Price Indices. All Titles. 1975 - 1979

	RPI	Retail Prices Books	The Bookseller		Library Association		LMRU	
			Money	Real	Money	Real	Money	Real
1975	100	100	100	100	100	100	100	100
1976	117	117	126	108	128	109	135	115
1977	135	141	141	104	156	116	166	123
1978	146	163	157	108	161	110	179	123
1979	166	180	169	102	189	114	195	118

Table 38 above covers the four series based upon calendar 1975. The retail price index for books shot ahead of the RPI during 1977 and 1978, although the differential subsequently narrowed. The biggest disparity appears to be between the LMRU series and those of the Bookseller and the LA, although the latter is itself consistently ahead of the former. Furthermore, only the Bookseller index shows an increase in real prices during 1978, the other two series doing no better than hold their own, whereas the previous year only the former index shows a decline, the other two rising at an almost identical rate. Whether one should therefore treat the LMRU index as a special case, as was suggested in the PA submission to the Price Comm- ission, is open to doubt. Indeed, in recent years the Bookseller index looks to be the odd man out. It must at any rate be borne in mind that the LMRU series, though covering only academic books, comprise a large proportion of the whole, and may not therefore be as unrepresentative as is sometimes suggested.

Table 39 below contains money price indices for sub-categories covered by the Book-seller, LA, and LMRU,using the same base year as the Price Commission Report. By comparison with the RPI, these suggest that hardback non-fiction has continued to prove very expensive in real terms, whereas the buyer of fiction has been much better placed. The price pendulum is, therefore, now moving in a manner which is inauspic-ious for the academic book buyer, but which looks more optimistic for the future of fiction. Table 39 is based upon calendar 1975 = 100.

TABLE 39   Annual Price Indices.   Sub-Categories.   1975 - 1979.

	THE BOOKSELLER			LIBRARY ASSOCIATION					LMRU		
	New Books	New Edit-ions	Cloth Fict-ion	Adult Fict-ion	Adult Non-Fict-ion	Refer-ence	Child. Fict-ion	Child. Non-Fict-ion	Hard-back	Paper-back	Hard-back/Paper-back
1975	100	100	100	100	100	100	100	100	100	100	100
1976	121	143	117	121	128	138	124	118	141	138	132
1977	138	150	130	135	160	195	131	106	169	159	148
1978	153	171	151	146	163	203	140	107	181	169	179
1979	167	174	169	169	192	245	169	122	-	-	-

We have already noted the Price Commission's reservations about price indices. They point out, in particular, that such indices suffer from being calculated on the basis of titles published rather than taking account of the number of copies sold; that there is an enormous price range between cheapest and most expensive, and that the mix of high-priced to low-priced may change over time; and that the uniqueness of each title makes it impossible to compare it directly with any other title. Another point which may be added is that the indices apply only to new books and reprints, and hence tell us nothing about what is happening to the prices of publishers' back-lists. It is also possible that the average length of books varies from year to year, or that there is a change in production processes.

Under the circumstances it would be unwise to place too much emphasis upon price indices. Nevertheless, these criticisms do not necessarily invalidate the overall trends depicted above. There are, for example, some extremely expensive titles pub-lished in every year, and changes in the price mix from year to year are unlikely to be statistically significant. Nor, for that matter, are changes in trade practice likely to show up other than in the longer term. Thus the indices should prove useful in allowing us to examine the changes which are alleged to have taken place within the publishing industry, in particular those relating to costs and profits, in relation to end-product prices.

Appendix: The Conversion of Money Values to Real Values

TABLE 40   Retail Price Index.   Annual Series

1962	100.0	66.2	39.6
1963	102.0	67.5	40.4
1964	105.3	69.7	41.7
1965	110.3	73.0	43.7
1966	114.7	76.0	45.5
1967	117.5	77.8	46.6
1968	123.0	81.5	48.8
1969	129.7	85.9	51.4
1970	138.0	91.4	54.7
1971	151.0	100.0	59.9
1972	161.7	107.1	64.1
1973	176.6	117.0	70.0
1974	202.9	134.4	80.5
1975	252.2	167.0	100.0
1976	293.8	194.6	116.5
1977	340.2	225.3	135.0
1978	368.2	243.8	146.0
1979	417.9	276.8	165.7

In the above table are three representative series, based respectively upon 1962 = 100, 1971 = 100, and 1975 = 100. They are derived from the Retail Price Index as published in the Department of Employment Gazette. This index was formerly based upon January 1962 = 100. By adding the monthly figures for 1962 and dividing by twelve one obtains a value of 101.6. This then becomes calendar 1962 = 100 as shown in the first column above, and all subsequent calendar years are obtained by dividing the monthly average figure by 101.6. Currently the RPI is based upon January 1974 = 100, and all years from 1974 onwards have been converted on to a compatible basis by taking the new series January 1974 = 100 as equivalent to the old series January 1974 = 190.0.

On a number of occasions in this book it has been necessary to convert a table of money values into, for example, real values based upon 1971 prices. This is done initially by converting the RPI on to a calendar 1971 = 100 basis, as in the second column above, in this case by dividing all of the values in the 1962 = 100 column by a factor of 151.0, the 1971 value in the first column. All money values can then be expressed in terms of constant 1971 prices simply by division using the appropriate year value in the second column.

The conversion of money to real values using the RPI is not altogether satisfactory because one wants to take account solely of movements in the prices of books rather than of prices in general. A retail price index for books does in fact now exist, and is set out in Table 41 below. Unfortunately this is based upon January 1975 = 100, and no compatible series exists for earlier years when the index incorporated other goods such as newspapers as well as books. This problem of compatibility does not, of course exist for the RPI, and I have therefore chosen to use the RPI for conversion to real values throughout this book. The Publishers' Association, on the other hand, prefer to use the price index for books alone, making what they consider to be suitable adjustments for years prior to 1975. As a result their published data on turnover at constant prices is incompatible, though not to any significant degree, with my earlier series, and this incompatibility will apply to our respective versions of any data which has been converted into real terms.

TABLE 41 Retail Price Index. Books. January 1975 = 100

	1975	1976	1977	1978	1979
Jan	100.0	122.1	136.5	173.9	187.2
Feb	101.2	122.8	136.8	174.4	187.9
Mar	101.2	124.3	137.2	174.6	188.6
Apr	105.0	126.9	153.6	174.9	190.6
May	106.4	127.2	153.8	176.0	191.0
Jun	108.2	127.8	154.7	176.3	191.6
Jul	112.5	130.2	159.6	180.3	199.0
Aug	114.1	130.3	159.7	180.5	199.0
Sep	115.4	130.3	161.2	180.5	199.0
Oct	117.9	133.3	170.2	185.6	213.1
Nov	118.0	133.6	170.4	185.6	213.7
Dec	119.2	133.7	170.5	185.7	214.9

Source: Department of Employment

CHAPTER 9

Quantitative Aspects of Journal Publishing

by ALAN SINGLETON

DEFINITIONS

In our discussion of journals we are, for the most part, concerned with learned and scholarly journals published in the UK. However, the available data do not allow us to keep to such a narrow remit. Journals are a sub-group of serials. Although we do not wish to study serials as such, we must spend a little time discussing what they are so that when statistics are presented which refer only to serials we have some idea of what is included.

Since librarians are the people who normally have the job of classifying and coping with published material, it is they who are most concerned with definitions, yet these have proved elusive in practice. Grenfell (1965), Escreet (1971), Osborn (1973) and Carson (1977) discuss the issue at length and we do not wish to do so again except to give two specimen definitions, the first of which shows the tendency of these definitions to define by reference to other undefined items:

Serial: "A publication issued in successive parts, bearing numerical or chronological designations and intended to be continued indefinitely. Serials include periodicals, newspapers, annuals (reports, yearbooks etc), the journals, memoirs, proceedings, transactions, etc., of societies, and numbered monographic serials."

Periodical: "A periodical, as ordinarily understood, is a publication appearing at stated intervals, each number of which contains a variety of original articles by different authors, devoted either to general literature or some branch of learning or to a special class of subjects. Ordinarily each number is incomplete in itself, and indicates a relation with prior or subsequent numbers of the same series...."

In these chapters we are concerned with learned or scholarly journals, which we take to be periodicals largely devoted to the publication of original research and/ or scholarship. They therefore exclude many of the categories of serial such as annual reports, newspapers, magazines, trade journals and abstracts. The difference between serials and journals is illustrated by Singleton (1977) in his study of the holdings list of a large library serving research scientists. Of over 2,000 items listed only about 1,000 were journals in the sense just described. Such journals are the target group of this chapter, and each time we present some data we shall refer to the way in which the group under discussion deviates from this target group. This is necessary because nearly all the data available, fragmentary as they are, do refer to different sets of periodicals, journals and serials and allow little general comparison*.

Within the class of scholarly and learned journals there are three main types, each having its own defining characteristic. For convenience we call these types conventional journals, letters journals and review journals. Most scholarly journals consist largely of papers reporting the results of research. For various reasons, some of which we discuss in the next chapter, special journals have appeared in some fields which present particularly short or even preliminary accounts of research. In these, papers generally appear with less delay than those in conventional journals. Since the first of these journals developed from letters to the editor sections of conventional journals, they are called letters journals. Although these are far less numerous than conventional journals they have grown rapidly over the last twenty years. Singleton (1978) has shown that the field of physics, for example, has at least twenty letters journals.

The other main type of journal is the review journal. In scientific subjects review journals are distinct from conventional journals in that they do not report the results of original scholarly research. Rather a paper in a review journal will normally 'review' a particular topic and the research which has been carried out. They may synthesise previous work and this itself may offer something new, but their main purpose is nevertheless to bring the different strands of a subject together. They vary in type, and attempts have been made to classify them into categories such as critical, evaluative, state of the art and popular. For some purposes it is sufficient to know that they are normally quite long, and although they do not form a large proportion of the literature, probably only a few per cent in most sciences, they are a form of literature which has much in common with the short monograph in the social sciences or humanities. Some conventional journals also include the occasional review paper, as do a number of conference proceedings. Thus, strictly speaking, the review literature should be distinguished from review journals. Most journals, however, are of the conventional type. Most of the statistics in the following sections do not distinguish between these types although their economics are somewhat different.

NUMBER OF JOURNALS

Given the difficulties of definition it is not surprising that the estimates of the numbers of journals and serials differ markedly. Fifteen to twenty years ago there was an increase in interest in estimating their number and predicting the future, and this resulted in a number of varying estimates. One can detect a desire to get to grips with the primary literature and its characteristics, and such studies were concerned not only with numbers but also with contents, country distribution and language, and were often carried out within specific disciplines. Some important studies were those undertaken by Bourne (1962), Barr (1967), Vickery (1968) and Singleton (1978).

Osborn (1973) felt that for "the twentieth century the figures for periodicals are probably in the vicinity of a fourth of the totals for serials of all kinds." Hence he would expect there now to be some 250-300,000 periodicals. Had Price's (1961) extrapolation been accurate there would by now have been well over half a million scientific journals, although he did not take into account the number of journals which had ceased publication. Gottschalk and Desmond, who tried to work to a specific definition and collected lists country by country, came up with a 1961 figure of 35,300 scientific and technical periodicals defined to exclude directories, serial monographs and non-scientific periodicals. Barr felt that this was too high,

---

*For further discussion of definitions see Machlup (1978)

a 1965 total of 26,000 being more likely. Barr felt that the Gottschalk and Desmond estimates might also take insufficient account of the death of journals.

The British Lending Library Division (BLLD) aims to collect all worthwhile serials, and thus provides a more or less stable basis for statistical estimation. However, like most libraries, it is subject to changing policies which can distort its figures. For example, subsequent to the Barr article in 1967 the BLLD changed its scope and now also collects serials in the humanities and social sciences. Recently there has been some change in their definition of serial which again affects the data.

We feel, however, that the BLLD data are probably the best available estimates of the size of the journal literature. The total number of serials 'currently received' at the BLLD up to 1978 was just over 50,000 according to Wood (1979). Of these 8,329 were produced in the UK. This made the UK the second largest producer of serials in the world, with less than 2,000 fewer than the USA but more than twice as many as the third largest producer which is Germany. Since journals are a subset of serials, we can say with some confidence that there are fewer than 8,000 UK scholarly journals. Woodworth (1970) has produced guides to the general British journal literature, and up-to-date figures will become available when a new edition appears towards the end of 1980, but his figures are not readily broken down into types of journal.

We can provide a further example of how the number of scholarly/learned journals is far fewer than might appear to be the case at first sight, if we look at the work of Don King and others (1979) in the USA. They used BLLD holdings data, data from another study by Fry and White (1975), and Ulrich's International Periodicals Directory to estimate the number of scientific and technical journals and periodicals published in the USA in 1977. Their concept of journal was similar to that for the learned and scholarly journals with which we are concerned. Periodicals, however, they took to include bulletins, newsletters and industrial trade periodicals. Using the sources mentioned above they concluded that there were 4,447 scientific and technical journals, and 4,468 other scientific and technical periodicals published in the USA. This evidence suggests that roughly half of the serials in science and technology are scholarly journals, although we would expect the percentage to be higher in the humanities where there are fewer industrial trade journals.

JOURNAL SIZE

Journals have just as great a variation in size as books, ranging from some small annual journals in the humanities up to weekly journals in some sciences where the yearly output will take up several feet of shelf space. Size can be defined in a number of ways. For example a journal's size can be assessed in terms of the number of pages, articles or words which it contains. It can even be measured by the space which it takes up on the library shelf. Each of these measures has been used in the past to aid 'value for money' assessments of the literature, as well as to inform librarians of future space requirements.

However, the fact that most journals continue from year to year introduces some differences which are fundamental to a discussion of their size and economics. Most important here is the fact that the yearly output of many journals increases as the years go by. This immediately poses problems for compilers of statistics of both the price and number of journals. Firstly it means that the size of the literature of a subject might be changing at a much faster rate than would be indicated by changes in the number of journals. In the second place it means that price information is much more difficult to interpret for journals than for books.

If, for example, we plot the price of a group of journals over a five-year period and we find that it has risen faster than general inflation, we cannot draw any real conclusions unless we know how the size of these journals has changed. On the other hand, to restrict ourselves to the same group over a period of five years, during which time other new journals will be appearing, will itself distort the true picture at the end of the five years. The only way to resolve these difficulties would be to have several sets of data, some on average prices and sizes which are based upon a specified set of journals, and others which take an average each year based upon the currently existing journals. Each of these could then be used as appropriate. Unfortunately no such compilation has as yet been attempted. What exists is a mixture of approaches, and interpretation needs to be carried out with some caution. It is unlikely that the collection of such statistics will be materially improved in the near future since none of the 'candidate' sources such as the computerised system either of subscription agencies or of the secondary service databases seems to be set up in ways which could easily provide the required data.

The available data are fragmentary, but are still of some interest not only for the information they present, but also because they show a variety of approaches and interpretations of the problem of size. Wooton (1977) summarised some of the early studies on changes of size of various types of serials in economics, ecology, physics and biology, which used various measures such as numbers of articles, numbers of words and shelf-space occupied. He felt that "All of these gave similar results for the period since 1960: a general increase in size up to 1970, followed by a period of more erratic behaviour, which gives the general impression of roughly constant size or a tendency to decrease."

Wooton reported the results of two surveys of serial size. The first was a random 10% sample of the most used titles at the BLLD, selected in the somewhat vague hope that they would be representative of the holdings of academic libraries. The serials were those so defined by the BLLD after removing irregular reports, monographic series and similar marginal serials. This left 309 serials, and the size of each was measured by the linear shelf space which they occupied. The results illustrate well the difficulties we have mentioned in compiling these statistics, since data for all serials are not available for every year.

Data for the period 1960 to 1974 are only available for 33 UK serials. The changes in size in millimetres of these serials is provided by Wooton as follows:

> 1960: 55.4mm.   1970: 64.2mm.   1974: 61.4mm.

Of more interest, perhaps, are the changes that are introduced when the data are presented for <u>all</u> serials for which data are available, which appears as follows:

> 1960: 56.6mm.(37 serials). 1970: 55.2mm.(62 serials). 1974: 51.2mm.(63 serials).

Thus the effect of including newly-founded journals is to reduce the overall growth in average size. This is hardly surprising given that new journals are likely to start out small. The growth in the literature, however, has been continuing, since, on these figures, the literature is approximated by multiplying the average thickness of the serials by the number of serials under consideration.

It is apparent that such statistics are compiled with libraries in mind. They are considered of more practical interest than counts of numbers of pages, and the sampling is done in order to provide a crude match with the holdings of some academic libraries. When all serials in the sample are used this is again related to the real-life problem of the librarian in managing a serials collection.

Most other studies of size have specialised in either the country of origin or a subject speciality. One of the largest was that by King and others for the USA. They used a mixture of counting through directories and sampling of journals to produce estimates of the number of US scientific and technical journals, and the numbers of articles in these journals from 1960 to 1985.

Their study indicated that life sciences is by far the largest subject field, and it was predicted that it would eventually contain nearly three times as many articles as the next largest fields of physical sciences and social sciences, although in most years social sciences contains more journals. Environmental and life sciences, together with psychology, were predicted to be the fastest growing fields up to 1985. The different size of journals in different subject fields illustrated dramatically the difficulties in estimating the size of the literature by a count of the number of journals alone. There is also the difficulty of comparing statistics compiled in different ways, on different bases, and using different measures. For example, Wooton's 1974 data refer in total to just 119 North American journals, including humanities, compared to King's data on 4,164 scientific and technical US journals. Wooton measured shelf space whereas King estimated and measured the number of articles. We should also stress that King's data have the added uncertainty of being estimates, since most statistical series on books and journals are the result of precise measurement, even if it is not always entirely clear what is being measured.

Wooton also carried out a small separate study on 62 'worthwhile' UK serials, for which he counted the number of pages of text, but not of advertising, in 1960, 1965, 1970 and 1973. The only details given about the selection of this sample are that it was "selected in such a way that the number of commercial serials was equal to the number of serials produced by, or on behalf of, learned societies." Thus we are unable to say how representative this sample is, other than to point to its very small size. The data for text pages are given in Table 42 below.

TABLE 42   Size Changes of 62 UK Serials 1960 - 1973.   Text Pages

	Commercial			Society			All		
	1960	1970	1973	1960	1970	1973	1960	1970	1973
Science & Technology	(22 serials)			(19 serials)			(41 serials)		
Average pages	612	1270	1290	590	817	748	602	1060	1039
Social Science	(6 serials)			(5 serials)			(11 serials)		
Average pages	343	388	451	362	431	450	352	408	450
Humanities	(3 serials)			(7 serials)			(10 serials)		
Average pages	366	377	397	388	408	403	382	399	401
All Subjects	(31 serials)			(31 serials)			(31 serials)		
Average pages	536	1013	1041	508	662	622	522	838	832

Source: Wooton (1977)

The difference between the commercial and the society scientific journals is of some interest, but can scarcely be generalised, especially since one does not know the distribution of change in size within the sample of journals.

The discipline in which the size of the journal literature appears to have received most study is physics. An early review of measures up to 1969 can be found in Anthony, East and Slater (1969), whereas Table 43 below shows the results of a more recent but limited study by Singleton of specific journals over the period 1959 to

1975.

TABLE 43 Changes in Price and Size of Some Physics Journals 1959 - 75*

		No. of Pages	Library Subscription Rate	Price Per Page	Subscription Price Increase	Page Increase
			Dollars	Dollars	%	%
Physical Review	1959	6838	40	0.006		
	1969	25793	100	0.004	150	277
	1975	28022	330	0.01	230	9
Phys. Rev. Lett.	1959	1137	10	0.009		
	1969	3037	30	0.01	200	167
	1975	3525	75	0.02	150	- 16
Nuclear Physics**	1959	2825	60	0.021		
	1969	16374	391	0.024	550	480
	1975	21065	1824	0.09	366	29
Nuovo Cimento	1959	6209	25	0.004		
	1969	7919	48	0.006	92	28
	1975	9500	384	0.02	700	20
J. Chem. Phys.	1959	1720	25	0.015		
	1969	10362	70	0.007	180	502
	1975	10612	165	0.015	135	2
Physical Soc. Proceedings***	1959	1814	35	0.02		
	1969	4648	175	0.038	419	156
	1975	10712	615	0.06	251	130
Philosophical Magazine	1959	1404	47	0.033		
	1969	2643	64	0.024	38	88
	1975	2752	144	0.05	124	4

*1959 and 1969 data taken from Special Libraries, 63, 53-58
**For 1975 refers to Nuclear Physics A and B
***For 1969 and 1975 refers to Journals of Physics A, B and C

Source: Singleton (1976)

The number of pages published each year was counted, and this was compared with changes in subscription price, enabling the change in price per page to be calculated. One problem is that this technique can only be fully accurate where one is measuring the same titles over the period under study, and in this case two of the titles listed changed substantially, splitting into a variety of parts. In addition the table takes no account of any changes in typography or page size which may have taken place.

The proposed use for statistics on journal size and price affects their form. For the librarian, the change in size and price of a library collection is what is most important, and this must take into account the births and deaths of journals as well as changes in size. Wooton used the measure of shelf length occupied because, presumably, this relates to the librarian's concern with storage costs. Such a measure can be combined with price information to give some sort of value for money measure, but not only does this have the drawbacks already mentioned for the price per page measure but it also takes no account of differing page thicknesses of the journals. Since a move towards the use of lighter and thinner paper has been a common cost-saving device over the last few years, a measure of price per unit shelf length is unlikely to make more recent journals appear of good value.

An interesting and different approach is that of Chomet and Nejman (1979), again in physics. Their approach has been to take a considerable number of currently exist-ing journals, and to trace them back over 20 years. This measurement of size then involves the calculation of 'standard' page sizes and the reduction of all journals to this measure. In this way the growth in price and size can be assessed. They chose 150 physics journals which existed in 1977, of which only 48 had existed in 1957. The average price in 1957 was 24 dollars, and in 1977 it was 180 dollars. In constant 1957 dollars the equivalent figures were 24 dollars and 83 dollars respectively. However, when prices were based upon a standard volume this resulted in a rise in cost from 10.7 dollars in 1957 to 20.4 dollars in 1977 when measured in constant 1957 dollars.

As one can imagine this was a very time-consuming study, and one cannot expect to see it repeated across other subject fields. Furthermore, even if this does provide a true indication of changes in cost to the purchaser, it is still difficult to interpret the figures. As the authors admit, a full understanding requires knowledge of trends in the circulation figures of the journals. In particular, we ought to consider the new journals which are such a feature of the sample used. This point for consideration illustrates another major difference between the economics of book and of journal publishing. When a publisher creates a journal he does not expect that the first year's issues will break-even, let alone yield a profit. It may take three, five or even more years to yield a profit. For the first few years the publisher basically aims to achieve substantial annual increases in circulation, and only when this has been achieved does he think about profitability.

Nevertheless, sales will initially have to build up from zero. This means that in the first year the unit cost of each journal to the publisher will probably be very high. Thus there will be some tendency for all new learned journals to be at the high-price end of any scale of prices, and in so doing they will bias any average price index. However, the publisher will not price the journal to try to recover all costs in the first year, and will normally try to make his price comparable with broadly similar well-established journals. Price changes over the ensuing few years may then be much more influenced by how and whether the circulation of the journal changes than by any changes in production costs or exchange rates.

JOURNAL PRICES

Apart from some special studies, usually based upon fairly small samples such as that previously cited by Wooton, there is only one regular series of information of any size about UK journal prices. This is produced by Blackwell's Periodicals Division and appears annually in the Library Association Record. The fact that it is published by a UK source does not mean that it is confined to UK journals, alth-ough there is a UK bias. In 1980, out of a total of 2,007 journals, 877 were from Great Britain, 694 from the USA and Canada, and 436 from other countries. In order to simplify matters all prices below refer to selling prices in the UK.

It is not entirely clear how the sample of 2,007 journals is selected. Blackwell try to ensure that they are 'important' journals insofar as this is defined by being held at a wide variety of libraries. The index is compiled in two sections, namely (1) £0.50 to £25.00 and (2) all titles. Since journals can move over the years out of range (1) and into range (2), we only present data for range (2) below.

TABLE 44   Average Price of Periodicals in the UK*

Year	Price
1972	£14.34
1973	£16.78
1974	£19.78
1975	£23.64
1976	£30.11
1977	£38.28
1978	£41.98
1979	£44.16
1980	£46.80

*Since 1972 the number of journals included has varied from 1,661 to 2,007

Table 44 above shows a marked increase in price in the mid-1970's, and an equally marked levelling off since then. Much of this can be attributed to the changing strength of the pound against the dollar during this period. Table 45 below plots the price changes of journals published in the UK from 1972.

TABLE 45   Average Price of Journals Published in the UK

Year	Price
1972	£11.41
1973	£13.01
1974	£14.16
1975	£16.73
1976	£21.42
1977	£25.27
1978	£29.29
1979	£31.52
1980	£38.56

By comparing these tables we can see that it was the overseas titles which showed the sharpest rises in price between 1975 and 1977. Subsequently, as the pound strengthened against the dollar the price of US journals declined. Table 46 below divides up the world into three sectors in order to show how significant this kind of change can be even in an individual year. The other side of the coin is that UK journals have recently become much more expensive in other parts of the world, and given that the USA represents a substantial share of the world market for many journals, particularly those in science and technology, this is going to provide

TABLE 46   Average Prices of Journals in the UK According to
           Country of Origin

	Number of Titles	Change %	Average Price 1980
Great Britain	877	22.2	£38.56
USA and Canada	694	-1.5	£46.11
Other Countries	436	-1.8	£64.59

many UK journal publishers with a substantial headache.

Included in Blackwell's list of journals is a group which we would not include in considering primary journals. These are the abstract journals. These journals, often called secondary journals, group together abstracts of papers appearing in journals throughout the world. In some large subject areas such as physics, chemistry and biology, such journals are very large and, compared to most primary journals, extremely expensive. Their inclusion can therefore distort an average price considerably, particularly in these subject fields. The reason for their inclusion is simply so that the index will resemble more closely actual library spending. However, they do introduce a major anomaly for anyone examining primary journal prices. The published index should at least point out that abstracts journals are included.

Prices According to Subject Area

Table 47 below details price changes by broad subject division since 1972.

TABLE 47   Average Prices of Journals By Subject 1972 to 1980*

	Humanities and Social Sciences		Medicine		Science & Technology	
	No. of Titles	Price	No. of Titles	Price	No. of Titles	Price
1972	639	£ 6.52	193	£13.32	859	£20.38
1973	635	£ 7.47	193	£15.44	843	£24.10
1974	634	£ 8.60	193	£17.31	834	£28.85
1975	663	£10.20	197	£20.85	893	£34.24
1976	663	£13.03	197	£27.37	892	£43.41
1977	663	£16.31	197	£34.59	892	£55.43
1978	673	£17.65	197	£38.52	892	£61.15
1979	842	£19.12	204	£40.27	961	£66.96
1980	842	£19.89	204	£43.00	961	£71.22

*Prices of all foreign journals converted to pounds sterling

Source: Library Association Record

Science and Technology prices have been increasing somewhat faster than Medicine, and Medicine somewhat faster than Humanities and Social Sciences. This must have been influenced by the relative changes in the number of titles included in each category. It is unclear, however, whether the increases are due to changes in the criteria for inclusion in the table, to the emergence of new journals, or both.

In future we may well see the emergence of more detailed information on prices as a consequence of Blackwell and others putting their records on to computers. Some idea of the kind of information which such an exercise might produce can be gauged by inspection of that already produced by Foxons (1978) in the USA.

We have already remarked upon the consequences of movements in the exchange rate for journal prices expressed in sterling. Other factors may also have a marked impact, for example page charges, learned society membership fees, co-operation between learned societies and commercial publishers and changes in circulation. Many of these may not be directly apparent to the purchaser. Similar caveats also need to be applied to the few studies in specific subject fields which compare the prices of journals from different types of publisher. Singleton (1976) carried out such a study a few years ago for 270 physics journals. He showed that commercial publishers tend to be more expensive, and that this tendency became more marked when cost per page was considered. However, the study included journals which, like those of the American Institute of Physics, were substantially underwritten by the page charge system, a factor which enabled subscription charges to be kept relatively low.

Publishers

There are comparatively little financial data available on the publishers of scholarly and learned journals. In the UK Inter Company Comparisons Ltd produce a regular financial survey of periodical publishers. The latest edition gives financial details on some 285 quoted and unquoted companies gathered from published accounts. Unfortunately, many types of journals are involved, with the result that aggregate statistics are almost meaningless in the context of learned and scholarly journals. Just as importantly, details given are for each company as a whole with the result that the financial details do not refer strictly to journal publication. Since most publishers who publish journals also publish books, the figures can effectively only set upper limits on the size of the journal operation.

Data for some major companies which are known to be active in scholarly journal publishing are given in Table 48 below.

TABLE 48   Turnover and Pre-Tax Profit For Five Commercial Publishers 1977 and 1978. £000's

	1977			1978		
	Turnover	Pre-Tax Profit	Pre-Tax Profit Turnover	Turnover	Pre-Tax Profit	Pre-Tax Profit Turnover
Academic Press	6,422	835	13.0%	8,394	964	11.5%
Blackwell Scientific	5,481	783	14.3%	10,797	1,315	12.2%
Gordon and Breach	944	251	26.6%	-	-	-
Pergamon Press	20,729	3,700	17.9%	24,164	3,362	13.9%
John Wiley	5,306	678	12.8%	5,537	412	8.6%

The figures in the table are based upon accounts deposited at Companies House, and on that basis Blackwell Scientific is currently much the fastest growing of the listed firms. Since these are, in the main, relatively large publishers, the table gives some indication of the size of the scholarly journal publishing operation. This can be seen to be fairly small compared with the largest general publishing groups, some of whom also publish learned and scholarly journals. For example, the turnover of the Pearson-Longman Group in 1978 was over £175 million, with profits of over £25 million.

These figures present a biased picture for another reason. Although commercial publishers do now publish the majority of UK scholarly journals, a substantial number are published by learned societies, professional institutions and the like. There are several hundred such bodies, most of whom publish one or more journals. Most are small, but some of the largest such as The Royal Society of Chemistry, The Institute of Physics, The Institution of Electrical Engineers, and The Institution of Mechanical Engineers have publishing turnovers of well over £1 million, and produce some large and prestigious journals. Many of these societies are registered charities, and hence do not specifically set out to make a profit. This does not mean, however, that their publishing operations do not produce a profit in practice. Profits or surpluses earned in publishing may be used to support other loss-making activities of a society. In the chapters which follow we will explore the relationship between commercial and learned society publishers in more detail.

CONCLUSIONS

We can see in conclusion that the available statistics on journals and journal publishing are somewhat fragmented, and bedevilled by problems of definition. More importantly, the statistics which exist have been gathered with some particular purpose in mind, usually for use by librarians in managing their journal budgets. There is no available store of data on journals which is neutral in this sense.

Subscription agencies are currently able to provide some of the most useful data on journals. Some of the larger agencies now have their records computerised to the extent that they can and do offer tailored information to libraries on their journal holdings. In the near future Blackwell will compile their index of prices using their computerised data on many thousands of journals. This data will, however, be more or less limited to what they need to collect for other purposes. We are unlikely to obtain from these sources any data on the size or number of articles contained in the journals. Nor does it appear that there will be any early standardisation or rationalisation between the indices which are produced. This is because they are produced for different audiences, and it is difficult to see how comparison between the indices would be of any particular interest to those audiences.

The British Library Lending Division has probably the best collection of journals for our purposes. Although it has produced a variety of data over the years, it would seem that, given the limited financial circumstances that are likely to be in existence for some time, it is unlikely to be able to undertake large-scale surveys on a regular basis. Perhaps, however, the BLLD could consider co-operating with the subscription agencies with which it deals, using their computerised facilities in order to produce data on its holdings.

We have seen that, despite all the caveats, there has undoubtedly been an ongoing increase in both the number and price of scholarly journals. The most striking feature of these sample statistics of size, number and price, is that their interpretation is dependent upon the international nature of scholarly journal publishing. This was demonstrated most clearly through the effect of changing exchange rates on UK prices of US journals. Publishers with large home markets, such as US publishers, have a different set of problems to those of publishers who need to export a substantial part of their output, such as UK publishers. The international nature of journal publishing will continue to be a prominent theme in the chapters which follow.

CHAPTER 10

Journal Production

by ALAN SINGLETON

INTRODUCTION

We have just examined such quantitative information as is available on UK scholarly journal publishing. In this chapter we turn to look at the economic role played by the principal participants in the journal publishing system, namely the authors, publishers, agents, purchasers and readers. Of necessity, this will be a largely qualitative account, since data are lacking which would enable us to give a complete picture over the range of subject fields. However, data are introduced where they are relevant, and where they illustrate, albeit in a limited way, some point raised in the discussion.

AUTHORS, EDITORS AND REFEREES

We start with those people who are responsible for creating the scholarly papers or articles, and for deciding which, and in what form, they appear in journals. There is some variation in practice, but most journals have one or more scholarly editors who have the final responsibility for deciding what is published. To do this, they will typically have some help from an editorial board, and/or of other scholars in the field. Depending upon the advice which the editor receives, a paper may be accepted, rejected, or sent back to the author for revision. If, subsequently, an author sends in a revised version, this will once again be refereed. Whether the final decision is to accept or to reject, the whole process may well take several months to run its course.

Considerable effort can be expended by authors, editors and referees, all of whom will form part of the community of scholars having knowledge or expertise in the subject covered by the journal. Thus the publishing decision rests with that group and not with the publisher. This is quite different from book publishing, where, though advice may be received from subject experts, the publisher normally also has to make a commercial decision as to whether or not to publish. A journal publisher will have no say about a particular paper, and, as a consequence, he has less contact with individual authors than a book publisher.

There are other differences between the content of journal papers and of books which have important implications for their economics. In the first place, it is very rare that the author and referees of papers will receive any payment from the publisher, whether it be a learned society, university press or commercial publishing

house. The main exceptions to this are the commissioned reviews which may appear
in conventional or review journals. In fact, these often have more in common with
books or short monographs than the typical journal paper.

Editors will normally receive an honorarium which may be of the order of a few
hundred pounds a year, although a few editors who are paid on a royalty basis do
receive substantial sums. Editorial board members, who will often also act as
referees, can expect little more than a complimentary copy of each issue of the
journal. It is true that scholarly book authors do not normally receive great
financial reward for their efforts, but they do at least receive a royalty of some
kind. It is quite well accepted that the rewards for most authors of journal papers lie not in financial gain, but in (i) the prestige associated with the act of
publication; (ii) the dissemination of the information in the paper which it is
hoped will proceed from publication; (iii) that the act of publication will be
taken to establish priority on a new idea. It has even been argued that research
is not completed until it is published, and this is taken by some US journals to
be a justification for asking the author to pay a charge, based on the length of
the paper, to help pay for the publication of an accepted manuscript. This 'page-
charge' system has not, however, as yet spread to Europe to any noticeable extent.

When looked at from this point of view it may seem a little difficult to explain
why book authors do receive some remuneration. Points (i) and (ii) above certainly
apply to them as well in some measure, yet it is normally felt that the more substantial piece of writing would very often not be undertaken without some financial
reward. In scientific subjects, for example, if prestige is derived mainly from
publication of original research papers in journals, then the writing of a scholarly
book, which is an arduous, time-consuming task, has less appeal. In science books
are rarely used for the reporting of original research results since these require
faster channels of publication, and a greater percentage of the effort typically
goes into the writing of a book than into any research done specifically for the
book.

Academic Authors

Journal publishing is heavily dependent on academics for its source material. Thus
the growth in size and in number of journals depends largely on the ability and
willingness of academics to write, review and edit papers. If the financial support
for academic research declines, then in the long term journals will no longer grow
in size, and it will become more and more difficult for publishers to start new
journals. There were fears that prevailing economic conditions, and the end of the
university expansion of the 1960's, would result in a decline in this respect, and
we have seen in the previous chapter some evidence of a falling off in the growth
of the literature. In the short term, however, other factors can mitigate the
effects of a decline in support for research.

One short-term factor derives from the fact that a reduction in the financial
support for research does not necessarily mean that the researchers will all be
thrown out of work. In countries like the UK there is a dual support system for
academic research, namely through the universities as employers, and through government bodies like Research Councils which give grants for specific projects.
If the grants are reduced in number or size then tenured academic researchers do
not lose their jobs. They will continue to do research, although they may no longer
have resources for new capital expenditure, nor for the temporary employment of
research assistants. It is even possible that time which cannot now be devoted to
the planning of large new projects will be used to write-up for publication much
completed but unpublished work.

As research continues, albeit on a reduced scale, then new subjects or specialisms will appear. Increasing specialisation of research fields may mean that it may be possible to start new journals even in economically difficult times. If the buyers of journals have the same, or even reduced, sums of money to spend on journals, then clearly some established journals will suffer if new ones are introduced. For an individual publisher, however, this can increase the pressure to start new journals in the hope that they will offset any decline in existing journals. Those publishers who cannot be flexible in their publishing programme are likely to suffer.

International Authorship

Most journals have become increasingly international in their authorship. Part of this internationalization can be attributed to the creation of international journals by commercial publishers, but the same trends are apparent in the long-established journals of scientific societies. Thus journals are increasingly dependent upon the international scientific community. While this has some direct economic implications on a small scale, such as increased costs of communication, time lags and translation problems, its major impact may be in its implications for change. For example, the introduction of a page-charge system, or a change in the method of production to camera-ready copy, could be markedly affected by the attitudes and facilities of overseas authors.

Editing and Refereeing

The scholarly editing and refereeing of articles are activities which take time and hence have their associated costs. Most often these are hidden, although large journals may employ professional staff to liaise with authors and referees, and thus take over some of the functions of the traditional editor. Some estimates of overall refereeing and editing costs in the USA can be found in King (1979).

For any particular journal, arranging for refereeing to be carried out may, or may not, cost the publisher money. However, refereeing has another economic implication, namely that since the process causes a number of manuscripts to be rejected, the publisher does not then have to pay for the cost of publishing them. Whether or not this is an advantage to the publisher will depend on the circumstances of the journal in question, and how important quality control through refereeing is felt to be in a particular subject field.

Refereeing practices vary across journals. In addition, there appears to be a marked difference in the proportion of submitted papers that are accepted by journals in different subject fields. Gordon (1978) has carried out a study on some UK journals, and their rejection rates are set out in Table 49 below. This provides evidence to support the above comments about variations according to subject field, and it appears that (geo) physical/chemical journals are at the low rejection end, followed in order of increasing rejection by bio-medical science and mathematics, social sciences and, finally, philosophy. The only anomalies in this pattern are the BMJ and Lancet which have higher rejection rates than other bio-medical periodicals. These two publications are, however, significantly different in being high circulation, general medical journals which serve a different function and audience from the specialist medical publications.

The pattern here is similar to that found in a well-known study of refereeing by Zuckerman and Merton (1971), who argued that "the more humanistically orientated the journal the higher the rate of rejecting manuscripts for publication; the more experimentally and observationally orientated, with emphasis on vigour of observation and analysis, the lower the rate of rejection". It would be tempting to suggest from such figures (i) that there were fewer pages 'available' for journals in scientific subjects and/or (ii) that a substantial proportion of the work in

TABLE 49   Rejection Rate of Papers In a Sample of UK Journals

	Rejection Rate %	Papers Submitted Per Year
Mineralogical Magazine	10-15	70-80
Monthly Notices of the Royal Astronomical Soc.	18	350
Transactions of Faraday Soc.	15-20	600
Journal of Physics (series)	18-30 (average)	300-450
Geophysical Journal	25	170
Journal of Physiology	33	700
Jnl. Geological Society	35-40	100
Palaentology	37	80
Biochemical Journal	40	1000
Jnl. Archaeological Soc.	40	50
Jnl. Pharm. Pharm	40-45	450-550
Jnl. Medical Genetics	45	200
British Jnl. Psychiatry	40-60	500
Bull. Entomological Research	50	120
London Mathematical and Sociological Journal	30	350-380
Mathematika	50	60
Clinical Endocinology	51-52	220-240
Journal of Zoology	50-60	200-270
Journal of Helminthology	60	100
Jnl. Medical Microbiology	60	130-140
Biometrika	60-70	340
Nature	65	7000
Population Studies	75	140
Geographical Journal	75-80	90
British Jnl. Sociology	80	130
British Medical Journal	80-85	4000
The Lancet	83	3700
British Philosophy of Science	85-90	200-250
Economica	90	300
Mind	90	400
Philosophy	92	300

such sciences, including social sciences and philosophy, goes unpublished. Such a
finding might have profound implications for assessing the quality of work in those

fields or the barriers to publication.

However, some crucial data are missing. We cannot be sure how much of the rejected material is eventually published. Most authors are free to offer manuscripts, rejected by one journal, to as many other journals as they wish. Indeed, where journals in similar subject fields are studied, it is possible that some multiple counting would occur of manuscripts rejected by more than one journal.

Overall, the economic implications of the refereeing system will be of major importance only if we consider changing the form of journal publishing. Any new system needs to make provision for the extensive amount of refereeing that takes place. As we have seen, in the social sciences and humanities, it may be that 90% of the papers submitted will be rejected by a journal. If the refereeing had to be paid for this would be an expensive business.

Most publishers are, of course, aware of the economic implications of having a journal which is perceived as of good 'quality'. They may well feel that the refereeing system is a major determinant of the journal's quality. The process and function of refereeing remains a subject of considerable debate, particularly among authors and sociologists of knowledge. We have here considered only the more straight-forward economic implications, and the works cited above also deal with a variety of other aspects.

PUBLISHERS

Another major participant in the journal publishing system is the publisher. We look first at the main types of publisher before going on to consider their role, and interrelationships between the types.

Types of Publisher

The majority of scholarly books are published by commercial publishers and university presses. However, learned society publishers play a much more significant role in scholarly journals. While societies may also publish some books, often through a commercial publisher, many societies see the publishing of a scholarly journal in their subject area as a vital part of the society's function.

Historically, the journal may have acted as a main method of communication with the society's members, as well as a convenient mechanism for the publication of papers presented at meetings or conferences. Typically, the journal will have been received free by members as one of the services provided in return for the member's subscription. There has been a trend in recent years in some societies for the academic element of a society's journal to be separated from the news element, and for only the latter, contained in a bulletin or newsletter to be supplied free to members. This trend has been caused mainly by the increasing financial burden of providing a scholarly journal, in many cases of increasing size, to a large number of members. Furthermore, the removal of parochial member news may render the journal a more saleable commodity in the international market place.

There are few data on how many UK scholarly and learned journals are produced by each type of publisher. We do, however, have some reason to believe that the industry is somewhat more concentrated in the UK and in Europe than in the USA, for which evidence is available in Fry and White (1975), Machlup (1978) and King and others (1979). Sixty four was the largest number of journals published by a single publisher in the Machlup data, whereas in Europe we have publishers such as Pergamon and Elsevier publishing 200-300 titles apiece. Table 50 below indicates who some of the largest publishers are when measured in terms of numbers of journals.

TABLE 50   Largest UK Journal Publishers As Measured By
                           Number of Journals Published

	No. of Journal Titles
Pergamon Press	230
Blackwell's Scientific Publications	67
Academic Press*	63
Gordon and Breach	63
Cambridge University Press	50
Oxford University Press	41
IPC Science and Technology Press	39
Royal Society of Chemistry	39
Wiley - Interscience*	37
Longmans	36
Taylor and Francis	24
British Medical Association**	21

*UK subsidiaries of US companies
**Includes Professional and Scientific Publications

Source: Willings Press Guide and Woodworth (1973).

Nevertheless, there is still a great variety of publishers, a large number of whom publish only one journal. It would appear that the UK scholarly journal industry is relatively less concentrated than many other UK industries, but probably rather more concentrated than in the USA.

Such generalisations can, however, be misleading, since there can be considerable differences between subject fields. In the USA the learned societies dominate in some subject fields. In physics, for example, the American Institute of Physics is by far the largest publisher, claiming to publish 35% of the physics literature in 1970, including translation of Russian literature. Physics is one field where we can provide a comparison between the UK, USA and other parts of the world, as demonstrated in Table 51 below.

TABLE 51   Journals Scanned By Physics Abstracts According To Publisher
                                                                    Type

	Number of Titles	Society	Commercial	Other
World	1680	39.5%	41.2%	19.3%
USA	406	52.7%	41.4%	5.3%
UK	384	31.3%	63.0%	5.7%
Japan	178	77.0%	14.6%	8.4%
The Netherlands	91	4.4%	75.8%	19.8%

The table, published in Singleton (1976), covers the 1700 non-communist journals in physics and related areas which were scanned by <u>Physics Abstracts</u> for inclusion in their 1975 information series. We can see that, overall, commercial publishers produce slightly more journals than learned societies. If, however, we were to consider publications in terms of number of papers, pages or words, then societies are marginally the largest publishers. Table 51 also shows marked differences between the major publishing regions in that the UK and the Netherlands have a very large commercial proportion, whereas the USA and Japan are dominated by their learned society publishers.

We must regard journal publishing as relatively concentrated in the field of physics. The UK journals in Table 51 encompass 63 publishers, with 49% of the papers published in 51 journals either by Pergamon Press or the Institute of Physics. For UK subject areas in general there is no reason to believe that entry into an area is any more restricted than in the USA or elsewhere. The variety of publishers in all fields indicates that the difficulties in starting up journals are largely the straight-forward ones of financing the initial costs, and of spotting and developing a subject area, rather than any rigid control exercised by publishers already in operation in the subject field.

LEARNED SOCIETIES AND CO-OPERATION

Up to now, our discussion of the structure of the journal publishing industry has assumed that each publisher type, whether commercial, learned society or university press, has its own distinct character, and that each type is separate from the others. This is, however, by no means the case. Many learned societies publish their journals through commercial publishers or university presses, and some of them own small, formerly commercial, publishers. Recently a study was carried out by Singleton (1980) which throws considerably more light on learned society publishing of journals, and particularly on their co-operation with publishers.

The study's findings indicated that there are some 675 learned societies and like institutions in the UK. Well over 500 of these publish, or have published for them, one or more scholarly journals. 495 societies responded to the survey. Although 88 of these did not publish a journal, the remainder published just over 500 in total. The distribution of journals per society is given in Table 52 below. As can be seen, the great majority have only one journal, with 45 having more than one.

TABLE 52 Distribution of Number of Journals Produced By or
           With Societies in the UK

Number of Journals	Number of Societies
0	88
1	355
2	29
3	11
4	1
5	1
8	2
9	1

Societies were asked whether they co-operated with a publisher in the publishing of a journal. Of the societies involved in journal publishing, 121 said that they did co-operate with publishers, involving 143 journals, and 280 said that they did not co-operate, involving 352 journals. Those societies in the middle range of size, with a membership of between 1,000 and 5,000, are more likely to co-operate with publishers. It is easy to offer plausible reasons for this. When very small, a society may not be in a subject field of sufficiently wide interest to attract a publisher, whereas when very large, it may well feel that it is in a position to employ its own professional staff to undertake publication. Such generalisations are, however, subject to a number of exceptions.

The distribution of societies across subjects is also of interest, particularly when we consider those who do, and those who do not, co-operate. This distribution, arranged according to the Dewey Decimal Classification, is set out in Table 53 below.

TABLE 53   Subject Areas of Co-operating and Non-Co-operating Societies

Dewey Class	Subject	Number of Co-operating Societies	% of Co-operating Societies	Number of Non-Co-operating Societies	% of Non-Co-operating Societies
0	Bibliography Librarianship	2	1.7	7	2.6
1	Philosophy Psychology	5	4.1	7	2.6
2	Religion	-	-	-	-
3	Social Science Economics Politics	12	9.9	34	12.4
4	Languages	2	1.7	3	1.1
5	Science	31	25.6	48	17.5
6	Architecture Arts	1	0.8	13	4.7
7	Medicine Technology	58	47.9	102	37.2
8	Literature	1	0.8	6	2.2
9	Geography History	9	7.4	54	19.7

As can be seen, almost half of the co-operating societies are in the broad subject area of medicine/technology. This compares with 37% of non-co-operating societies in these fields. A good deal of the co-operation is accounted for by medical societies. Somewhat surprisingly, there are well over 100 medical societies in the UK. Although a number of these do not have journals, of the 59 respondents in the sample that do have journals, 35 co-operate with publishers (29% of all co-operating societies), compared to 24 who do not co-operate (only 9% of all non-co-operating societies).

UKPI - K

The major contrast comes when we consider Dewey Class 9 covering Geography and History. In History, there are 6 co-operating societies compared to 46 non-co-operating societies. Once again, it is relatively easy to suggest plausible reasons for this variation. Subjects in science and technology are generally thought to be of wider international appeal than those in the arts or humanities. If that is the case, then publishers who can claim to have international contacts and marketing expertise will find those subjects attractive where they can hope to put that expertise to good use. Where publishers are involved they usually handle the sales of the society journal to non-members of the society, and this is where they can expect to make their profit. Any subject which may appear to be of parochial interest will be less attractive to a publisher.

Although only four commercial publishers account for 62 of the journals produced in co-operation with societies, more than 50 publishers are involved overall, among whom are other large learned societies. Table 54 below shows the breakdown by type of publisher.

TABLE 54   Breakdown of Co-operative Journals by Publisher Type

Total Number of Publishers	52		Co-operating with	121 Societies
Commercial Publishers	37	(71%)	Commercial Publishers co-operate with	88 societies (72%)
Learned Societies	8	(15%)	Society Publishers co-operate with	14 societies (11%)
University Presses	5	(10%)	University Presses co-operate with	17 societies (14%)
Other Publishers	2	(4%)	Other Publishers co-operate with	2 societies (2%)

143 Journals in Co-operation

Commercial Publishers	co-operate with	106 journals	(74%)
Society Publishers	co-operate with	15 journals	(10%)
University Presses	co-operate with	20 journals	(14%)
Other Publishers	co-operate with	2 journals	(2%)

Source: Singleton (1980)

Singleton interviewed 10 major publishers in the UK who together published more than 500 journals. Something like a third of these were produced in conjunction with UK learned societies, international societies and research institutes. Thus overall, we can see that, although UK scholarly publishers can be divided into broad categories such as commercial, learned society and university press, there is a considerable amount of co-operation, and possibly overlap, between these types when we consider who publishes the journals themselves.

It is difficult to assess the economic implications of co-operation between societies and publishers for the whole journal publishing system. Clearly, it will depend to some extent on the financial arrangements made between society and

publisher. Singleton studied more than 100 of these arrangements, and found that
while there was considerable variety, three main types of arrangement predominated.

(1) <u>Marketing and distribution</u>. Here the publisher acts as a sales and distribution
agent for the society which produces the journal. The journal may be included in
the publisher's catalogue, and appear to the outside world as one of the publisher's
journals, albeit produced in association with a society. Typically, in such circumstances, the publisher will receive a royalty on sales to non-members of the
society.

(2) <u>Commission</u>. Here, typically, the society delegates most publishing functions
other than scholarly editing to the publisher. In most cases, the society retains
overall financial responsibility for the journal, and pays the publisher a commission on the income from sales of subscriptions to non-members of the society. The
publisher typically handles all production, marketing and distribution functions,
pays the bills, and then charges this to the society as well as taking his commission. For successful journals the publisher may take his charges and commission
out of income.

(3) <u>Profit-sharing</u>. This is, perhaps, the most 'intimate' type of relationship
between the partners. Here, in most cases, the publisher takes the financial
responsibility, and undertakes all publishing functions other than scholarly
editing. He may supply free or reduced-rate copies of the journal to members, and
when the accounts for the year are made up, share any profits with the society on
an agreed basis. A large number of journals are born in this way, with society
and publisher coming together to start a journal. The publisher finances the
journal, and stands the early losses, and the society provides the papers and the
scholarly editing and, perhaps, any prestige associated with the society. In his
survey, Singleton found that over 40 journals had been started through co-operation
between a society and a publisher, of which the majority had profit-sharing arrangements.

Thus, in conclusion, we find a range of co-operative arrangements ranging from the
publisher acting as a sort of publishing agent, to the more integrated profit-
sharing agreement.

CHAPTER 11

Journal Publishers

by ALAN SINGLETON

PUBLISHER TYPES AND ROLES

The preceding discussion is essential for a good understanding of the roles of the various types of publisher. All too often opinions on publishers' roles are ill-informed about the relationship between publishers. There are basic differences between types of publisher, which are the commercial, the learned society and the university press, although any generalisations are inevitably subject to a number of exceptions.

The majority of learned societies are also registered charities. This means both that such societies will be non-profit making and that any surpluses derived from publishing will not be subject to tax. Some societies clearly fear that to make a profit on journal publishing would endanger their charitable status. Others rely on such profits to subsidise other activities of the society, in order that the society as a whole does not make a profit, even though its journal publishing definitely does. Some of the larger societies have set up separate companies to handle their publishing. One, the Institute of Physics, has even acquired a former commercial scholarly publisher, Adam Hilger. On the other hand, there are many societies, particularly the smaller ones in the humanities and social sciences, whose journal is supported almost entirely by members' subscriptions and is the largest call on those subscriptions.

UK university presses, with the exception of CUP and OUP, publish relatively few journals between them. Both OUP and CUP publish a considerable number, many in conjunction with learned societies. Although both OUP and CUP have acquired charitable status in the last few years, they are similar to large scholarly commercial publishers in the range of their publishing activities. Like the larger societies they are run by full-time professional staff, although publishing decisions are under the ultimate control of academics.

The Profit Motive

For commercial publishers, almost by definition, the making of a profit is a primary objective for the publishing house as a whole. We should not necessarily assume, however, that each publishing decision is made on commercial grounds alone, although most commercial publishers have responsibilities to shareholders and cannot help but regard publishing as a business.

The notion that a successful commercial publisher should have, as a primary aim, the making of profit, has implications which are responsible for much of the debate on the role of publishers. Some will feel that even the responsible pursuit of profit cannot be congruent with, or complementary to, the dissemination of the results of scholarly research. Whitley (1970a) in a study of British social science journals, displays such an attitude. In choosing 'academic' journals, one of his criteria is that they should be "primarily concerned with disseminating information rather than earning a profit". In our context this appears as a rather muddled statement. However, it does serve a useful purpose since it allows us to separate out some of the issues. It suggests that the journal itself is primarily concerned with either profit or dissemination. Yet it is clear that the 'concern' of any journal is made up of the interests of the editors, the authors and the publishers at the very least. The editors and authors may be concerned with dissemination, the publishers with profit. There seems reason to believe that there are circumstances when these concerns can operate together, and that a profit motive can be allied to a concern for dissemination and produce an 'academic' journal. That is not to deny that the profit motive can on occasion, distort other aims of a journal.

Such a fear does exist among those who might otherwise seek to join with commercial publishers, as is shown in the following quotations.

> "Publishers publish to make money. Societies publish to
> further the aims of that society. The two are incompatible".

> "financial expedience as perceived by such publishers should
> not conflict with the established policy of the society -
> to its deflection, modification or prostitution"...

> "the journal is produced as a service to members - not under
> any circumstances as a commercial venture - we would not
> contemplate any such influences".

Government agencies also on occasion adopt very different attitudes towards society and commercial publishers because of the latters' profit motive. This has shown up most clearly in the USA in the number of page-charges where the Federal Council for Science and Technology, in 1961, instituted a policy of permitting an allowance for page-charges to be included in the allocation of research funds so long as papers were published in non-profit journals.

If the purposes of scholarly journals are defined in terms of the needs to provide recognition to authors and to disseminate the results of research, there is no reason to suppose that this could either always be done in association with a profit motive, or that a profit motive is essential for satisfying those needs. On the one hand it is easy to imagine worthy topics which could not be published at a profit, and on the other hand, the continued existence of genuine non-profit making publishers shows that they can be 'viable'. What is in question in a discussion of the whole journal system is whether the profit motive in scholarly publishing is either acceptable as a complement to other forms, or necessary in some areas where non-profit publishing is found wanting.

GROWTH AND DIVERSIFICATION

Arguments that would have us give an affirmative answer to these questions derive, not directly from the existence of a profit motive, but from its implications, namely the need for growth and diversification. The 'grow or die' syndrome seems as pervasive in the business community as 'publish or perish' is amongst academics. The argument runs as follows. From the need to satisfy shareholders and provide security for the company, a commercial publisher will strive to increase turnover and profit.

Turnover and profit may be increased by increasing the circulation and size of already successful journals, and by finding and exploiting new markets, for the most
part in the remote parts of the world, thereby also achieving an increased dissemination of the results of research. Longer-term security may be found by increasing
the number and range of journal titles, by seeking out developing new fields which
may be either in specialised sub-disciplines, altogether new 'disciplines', or inter
or multi-disciplinary fields. This may be done by the publisher alone, or in co-
operation with (often young) learned societies. Here the publisher can argue that
he has provided a legitimate channel of communication for a new field. It could be
further argued that the commercial publisher is able to do this because, in many
cases, the older, larger learned societies and institutes will not, or cannot, do
so.

The assertion is that these learned societies are more likely to be established
within a discipline controlled by academics from all parts of that discipline. They
are therefore likely to be inflexible in their publishing policy, perhaps because
there exists a 'publication committee' reluctant to take risks, and unreceptive to
the needs of any particular sub-section of their membership. The commercial publisher, it is argued, provides the entrepreneurial flair and the flexibility to
move across traditional subject boundaries.

While this is an over-simplification, there is clear evidence that those in 'new'
disciplines do feel the need to create systems which will establish their field and
thereby distinguish it from the older subjects from which they have sprung. One
such system is a scholarly journal devoted to the new topic. Singleton (1980) found
that in the UK alone, in the last 20 years, more than 150 new societies have been
formed. Of those that have journals, many have started them in co-operation with
commercial publishers. Detailed statistics are not available, but it is clear that
commercial publishers have been responsible for a large proportion of the new journals
to appear over the last twenty years, and that these journals are more often specialist, inter and multi-disciplinary than the established ones.

Those taking a less sanguine view of commercial publishing can, of course, use a
similar argument, arriving at the conclusion that commercial publishers are responsible for the proliferation of journal titles to a wholly unnecessary extent,
and to the detriment of scholarly journal publishing as a whole. A concomitant of
this view is often one that asserts that commercial publishers are mere 'publishers'
in stopping publication of a journal which has not proved its success within a short
period of time, thus further disrupting scholarly communication. Undoubtedly there
is some truth in these assertions as far as some publishers and journals are concerned,
but it cannot be accepted as a reasonable generalisation. Points which imply that
it is unreasonable are as follows:

(i) The number of new specialist societies which are formed independently of commercial publishers is high, thus pointing dramatically to a genuine increase in
specialisation.
(ii) A survey of a number of the largest UK commercial publishers by Singleton
(1980) showed that while they had started many journals in the last ten years, they
had stopped very few.
(iii) It is by no means clear that, in the absence of proliferation, scholarly
publishing in fewer, perhaps much larger, journals would have been beneficial in
either economic or scholarly terms. Once we grant that specialisation has taken
place, we must then question further the wisdom of publishing very large, broad
subject area journals which the specialist community may be forced to buy in order
to obtain the small percentage of papers relevant to them. The potential which
this affords to browse must be set against the overall increase in production costs,
and hence in prices, which would result from the retention of all large 'monolithic'
journals, which itself would lead to an increasing strain on library budgets. In
other words, whereas the small specialist journals will be more expensive in terms

of per page, per article or whatever (since they will have smaller circulations and
therefore higher unit cost, <u>and</u> may be published by a commercial publisher), it
does not follow that this is a more costly way of publishing for any particular
scholarly community, nor that it is a less efficient method of operating the communication system for that community.

(iv) That while commercial publishers are the 'capitalists' when a new journal is
set up, they are by no means entirely responsible for its creation and continuation.
As previously mentioned a scholarly journal needs the support of authors and editors
if it is to survive. In nearly all scholarly journals, no matter who the publisher
is, the scholarly community exercises the editorial control, and provides the bulk
of the papers. If they did not agree to do this, either explicitly by editing the
journal, or implicitly by submitting papers, it could not survive. Arguments which
cast commercial publishers in the devil's role in the proliferation of journal
titles thus have to stretch the argument to suggest that they also prey on the sus-
ceptibilities of academics to temptation in the form of recognition and status
acquired by being either editors or authors.

A more plausible argument is that in the post-war period, particularly in the 1960's,
there was an enormous expansion in higher education scholarly research and in its
specialisation. There was a consequent increase in the amount of material for
scholarly publishing, and of library funds to purchase it. Some commercial publishers seized the publishing opportunity that presented itself and created the new
journals to cater for the new scholars. Learned societies, on the other hand, were
inflexible, and could not readily adapt. In contrast to the new commercial journals,
many of their large scholarly journals were supplied 'free' to members as part of
their subscription and thus, as the journals grew in size and cost these became an
increasing burden on the society, rather than an opportunity.

The activities of several of the larger UK learned societies over the last decade
would support our suggestion that societies have been slow to respond to changing
conditions, and have, in effect, lost out to the commercial houses. In the seven-
ties, the larger societies increasingly divorced their learned journals from their
membership and, while they continued to make the journals available at reduced rates
to members, increasingly relied on institutional sales to support the journals.
They created separate companies, divisions or trusts to run their publishing programmes, and these associated companies have come to have more freedom to expand
their journal programmes in the subject areas in which they publish since some
societies would have been restricted by the terms of their constitution. In short,
they have become more like commercial publishers.

Whichever explanation of the role of the commercial publisher appeals, their importance is now a fact of life. Nevertheless, this does not mean that things will not
change and that there is no cause for concern for the future. We now have to face
the fact that expansion of university and research systems has stopped, at least
for some time. It was always known, of course, that expansion could not go on
indefinitely, otherwise, as Price (1961) put it for science, every man, woman and
dog on the planet would be a scientist within a short space of time. Recently, in
physics, Chomet and Nejman (1979) have claimed to detect that the growth in the
literature has slackened considerably.

It is here where the increasing importance of commercial publishing has its potentially most serious implications. Put crudely, the problem for the commercial
publisher is that he needs to re-stimulate growth by recourse to one or more of the
following options.

(1) Grow by acquisition, either of journals from societies or of other publishers.
(2) Grow through diversification either with new products for the same markets or
     with different products for new markets.
(3) Gain a bigger share of the market.
(4) Become more efficient and lower overheads, perhaps through the use of new

technology.
(5) Cut down on any loss-making goodwill activities.

All these options are open to publishers in good times as well as bad, and, clearly,
not all will have harmful effects. But let us consider some of the possibilities.

Grow by acquisition. We have seen the opinion of the economist Machlup and others
(1978) that scholarly publishing is a relatively unconcentrated activity. Take-
overs and mergers will increase the degree of concentration. If a high level of
concentration was achieved, there would be some danger that entry would become more
difficult, at least for journals of the same form. Scholarly publishing could be
expected to be different from other businesses, in that, unless concentration increased to an extreme degree, the publishing decision on specific papers would
remain with the scholarly community. One could, however, envisage a scenario where
this prerogative disappeared. In general publishing, some, such as Golding (1979)
already regard concentration to have taken place to a considerable degree, with
inevitable implications for the control of the publishing decision.

Grow by diversification. A number of the larger publishers are already trying this
route, particularly through the publishing of newsletters, bulletins, scientific
papers and the like. Some of these, such as expensive bulletins, are aimed at the
same institutional market as the scholarly journals, whereas others, such as the
scientific newspapers, are looking for high circulation amongst individual scientists.

Gain bigger share of the market. One of the options previously mentioned, namely
new products for same markets, also applies here. Other options include more vig-
orous marketing what were previously referred to as 'under-exploited' areas, namely
other countries. Another option is to change the relative emphasis of the publisher's 'product line'. This is already happening in the move from books to journals.
Journals have the attraction of good cash flow and a high degree of 'inertia',
whereby the bulk of subscribers continue from year to year. Some books and journals
are very different from the author's point of view as well as from the publishers'.
These changes could be serious for the scholarly community, and have led, as Singleton (1979) shows, to increased interest in 'do-it-yourself' and 'on-demand' publishing of books.

Become more efficient. A true increase in efficiency should benefit the publisher,
although it may not, for example, benefit all individuals within the publishing
house, since some may, for example, be made redundant, nor other parts of the publishing industry. Other cost-cutting exercises might not lead to increases in
operational efficiency. A move to camera-ready copy, for example, would dispense
with expensive typesetting, but replace it with an additional burden on the author.
A publisher might also regard increased co-operation with societies as a way of
spreading overheads, since, in some cases, society officers will take on some of
the load of, for example, preparing copy. Many other of the 'internal' cost-cutting
exercises are mentioned by Campbell (1980) and we will not discuss them further
here.

To sum up, then, the danger is not that commercial publishers will fail to respond
to expressed needs, but to whose needs they respond. Publishers are obliged to
respond to what markets there are. If the traditional forms of scholarly publishing become increasingly uneconomic from the publishers' point of view, then there
are two dangers:
(i)   that the publishing industry will become excessively concentrated, which may
      threaten the scholarly community's current role in the publishing decision of
      scholarly papers.
(ii) that there will develop an increasing mis-match between the needs of the
      scholarly community for scholarly journals and the needs of a wider community
      or market, part of which will be a section of this same scholarly community,

for a greater variety of product, to the point where the satisfactory performance of the scholarly journal system will be jeopardised.

This being said, it is difficult to imagine that there is a real danger either of
(i) and/or (ii) occurring. In the first place, it is unlikely that they could
occur suddenly. Thus while editorial control remains in the hands of the scholarly
community, entry into the publishing system, determined as it is by prestige of the
product as well as by economic constraints, is likely to remain open. Scholars
would find alternative mechanisms for publishing scholarly journals without commercial publishers, although international communication might suffer if they could
not publish as effectively as the commercial houses. Secondly, it is at least
possible that technological developments will change markedly some aspects of the
conventional system, or at least provide alternative systems of access which would
be used for formal scholarly communication, perhaps independently of conventional
commercial publishers. We return briefly to this topic later in the chapter.

PRINTERS

We will mention only briefly the role of printers in this chapter. Many of the
considerations are the same for journals as for books. Here we merely discuss the
points most relevant to journal publishing.

If scholarly publishing is relatively unconcentrated, so, also, is scholarly printing. If the required typesetting is comparatively uncomplicated then even the
smallest printers can sometimes be used for scholarly journals.

In a survey of societies who publish journals independently Singleton (1980) discovered 250 societies producing 290 journals through 185 different UK printers.
These printers were of all sizes, and spread throughout the country. Commercial
publishers tend not to use the very small jobbing printers for journals, but typically they will still spread the journals around, and not concentrate them at one
printer.

Printers are now very often used for despatch of journal issues, both by society
and commercial publishers. Address labels are supplied to the printer who carries
out the wrapping and addressing. This clearly saves the cost of palletising, of
transport to the publisher, and of providing extra warehousing space.

For the printer, journal printing should be attractive, since, theoretically, it
should provide him with a regular supply of work which should ease scheduling of
the work-load as well as provide a guaranteed income in difficult times. Thus
printers will seek contracts to do at least several issues of a journal. Some
printers offer other services to publishers. In some cases, large printers are
able to purchase paper at favourable rates which can then be stored by smaller publishers. Many small societies benefit from the technical advice that printers can
offer.

SUBSCRIPTION AGENTS

Subscription agents currently play an important economic role in the publishing of
scholarly journals. They have received very little attention from independent researchers, although a number of books and articles exist, such as Katz and Gellatly
(1975), which describe their operation, mainly from the library's or agent's point
of view. However, Singleton and Cooper recently undertook an as yet unpublished
preliminary study of UK agents, on which this section is based.

At the most basic level, the subscription agent places orders with publishers on behalf of libraries or other purchasers for subscriptions to serials, pays the publisher and bills the library. This is, it appears, the limit of the agent's responsibility.

Although many subscription agents are also booksellers, the fact that agents do not, for the most part, physically handle the journals is a most important difference. Rather, publishers drop-ship journals ordered through agents.

Subscription agency is highly concentrated since, in the UK, probably as few as a dozen agents account for 50% of the turnover of scholarly journals. However, there are many hundreds of very small agents, or of booksellers who undertake a very small amount of subscription agency work as a sideline or as a supplementary service to their customers. Thus although entry is easy in that sense, to develop a substantial and successful subscription agency business is very difficult. Profit margins are low and a number of agents make less than 1 to 2% pre-tax profit on turnover, with some currently running at a loss. There has been a tendency for some of the small to middle-sized agents to go out of business, or to be taken over by the large agents, and it looks as if this trend will continue.

The financial basis of the agent's operation is that he receives, or hopes to receive, a discount on the subscription price of the journal. He bills the library at or around the full subscription price, and may add a service or handling charge. Currently, these charges are such that the agent's operating income and profit comes substantially from the discount granted by the publisher, although it is the library which actually makes the payments.

Publishers' discounts are a subject of some debate. Publishers, on the whole, have been reducing discounts over the last decade or so, and, indeed, some now give no discount at all. In such cases, the agent usually makes a higher handling charge to the library. The average discount is a little under 10%, although 10% is the typical discount offered by the large UK commercial publishers. In acting as an ordering service for the library, the agent can reasonably claim to offer economies of scale in ordering, and to reduce the work load of a large library considerably. The agent can also legitimately claim to offer some benefits to the publisher, in providing simpler order processing (since the agent will pay for all of its subscribers with one or a few cheques), guaranteed payment and even the early supply of funds. Nevertheless, there seems little doubt that the agents are essentially the libraries' agents, and that the libraries are the main beneficiaries of their service, whereas the payment for this service is seen to come from the publisher.

Herein lies the dispute about the role of the agent. Some publishers, while granting that agents are useful, feel that the libraries should pay for their services. On the whole, this does not mean that publishers would increase their revenues, since libraries may well be operating on fixed budgets. But it would mean, so they argue, that the cost of the agency service would be more visible to the library, which would then be in a better position to decide on the merits of ordering through agents. In this respect we may note that there is no equivalent to the Net Book Agreement for journals, so there are no constraints on publishers to prevent them from supplying to libraries direct. The current trend is for publishers to reduce discounts, but sometimes offering small increases for specific agency services like the matching of all invoices to renewals. We would expect this trend to continue.

Publishers typically supply 75-80% of their journals through agents, or the 'trade'. The major UK agents deal mainly with the type of journal with which we are concerned, namely the scholarly and learned journals. Some 80-90% of their business is with such journals. Thus, on a rough estimate, this operation costs up to 10% of the total UK turnover of scholarly journals.

Agency work is basically a clerical operation. But to run it successfully requires

considerable business acumen, in part because an agency operates on a small profit
margin in a competitive environment. It has also to cope with substantial cash-flow
and foreign currency problems. Renewals and payments tend to come at the end of
the year, since most scholarly journals are published on a calendar year basis.
Agents thus have to get money in from libraries as early as possible. Publishers
have moved increasingly to a 'cash with order' policy on journals, and have thereby
intensified the problem for agents. In times of high inflation and high interest
rates, delays between expenditure and income can result in considerable additional
expense. On the other hand, many agents are able to adjust any imbalances by supplementary invoices sent to libraries later in the year.

The clerical nature of the agent's work renders parts of it suitable for computerisation, and the larger agents have installed computer systems. This enables them
to offer a wider range of services to libraries, including up-to-date monitoring
of price changes and total journal budgets, as well as computerised claim procedures
and information services. On-line links between libraries and agents are already
at the experimental stage.

The onset of computerisation does, however, raise one or two issues of concern.
In the first place, for a library to take full advantage of an agent's computer
system, it may need to place all of its journal subscriptions through that agent.
At present, few libraries are willing to do this. If the agent-library system is
incompatible with that of a potentially competing agent, then the library may find
it difficult and/or expensive to change agents, thereby reducing flexibility and
competition in the system. Secondly, computerisation involves considerable financial investment, and, as we have mentioned, profit levels in the agency business
are generally low. This means that it is difficult for the small agencies to find
the money to computerise, and they may, therefore, find it increasingly difficult
to compete. Thirdly, many publishers have also been computerising their order-
processing systems, but few agents and publishers have consulted with each other
at the design stage of their systems, and it is therefore possible that an opportunity for introducing more efficient and compatible systems is being missed.

There appears to be little prospect of a direct on-line ordering system being
established, in the near future at least, between libraries and publishers. If,
and when, secure, cheap and error-free debiting systems become available, this
spectre (as far as the agents are concerned) may become a reality, at least for
the major libraries and publishers. This, again, would require that the library
and publisher systems become compatible.

MARKETS AND LIBRARIES

The last parts of the publishing system that we shall consider are the groups who
buy the journals. For the most part, so far as commercial publishing is concerned,
these are libraries of academic, industrial or government institutions. For the
society publishers, as we have mentioned, these groups are also often very important, particularly in scientific and technological subjects.

In many subject areas the government and industrial libraries are significant
elements. However, although there is little published data available, since many
publishers simply do not monitor their circulation figures by sector, we know from
discussions with subscription agents that academic libraries predominate. The
geographical distribution of circulation is very rarely made public, although all
bar a few publishers analyse their markets in this way. A few years ago, Pergamon
did reveal circulation figures in their advertising rates catalogue, and an analysis
of 56 of their journals showed a similar breakdown to that of the Institute of
Physics journals. Although these data refer to 1974, they can still be taken as
fairly typical for a UK scientific journal. The geographical breakdown is given

in Table 55 below.

TABLE 55 Geographical Circulation of 8 Institute of Physics
          Journals and 56 Pergamon Journals

Institute of Physics		Pergamon	
UK and Eire	13%	UK and Europe	36%
Rest of EEC	14%	N. and S. America	41%
Eastern Europe	6%	Asia and Australasia	15%
North America	36%	Rest of World	8%
USSR	4%		
Rest of World	19%		

Source: Singleton (1976)

Asser (1979) of the International Group of Scientific, Technical and Medical
publishers, obtained 30 detailed replies from 158 questionnaires sent out to
publishers. The sample encompassed approximately 400 journals, and data on
exports are given in Table 56 below.

TABLE 56 Exports of Journals 1971-1977 %

Publishers in	1971	1974	1977	Approximate No. of Journals
UK	73.1%	74.9%	75.6%	85
USA	17.9%	19.2%	19.9%	88
Germany	22.0%	23.1%	23.4%	100
Netherlands, Switz-erland & Denmark	96.0%	96.0%	95.7%	79
France	45.0%	43.9%	39.9%	51
				403

Source: Asser (1979)

Table 56 thus makes clear the dependence of UK publishing on overseas libraries,
and hence on exchange rates and overseas attitudes towards price and other changes.

The total circulation figures of journals are also hard to come by, and are often
treated as confidential by publishers. Asser (1979) reported trends in circulation figures for 403 journals. These figures are interesting because they refer
specifically to titles of at least 10 years of age, and the observed trends will
therefore be somewhat less biased by new journals, which one could expect either
to be building up their circulation or to have existed for only part of the period
covered. The results for the journals of seven major countries are given in Table
57 below. The most striking feature of this table is the dominance of the figures
for the USA. The USA represents a large home market, and also, in some fields,
contains very large scientific societies supplying copies to individual members.

TABLE 57   Trends in Total Number of Subscriptions 1971 - 1977

Country	Journals Number	1971	1974	1977	Circulation Mean 1977
UK	85	204,422 (100)	222,738 (108.9)	213,777 (104.5)	2,500
USA	88	948,069 (100)	1,003,107 (105.8)	1,095,423 (115.5)	12,500
Germany	100	300,214 (100)	302,645 (100.8)	302,814 (100.8)	3,000
Netherlands	51	60,521 (100)	61,012 (100.8)	58,049 (95.9)	1,100
Switzerland	7	8,216 (100)	8,100 (98.6)	7,155 (87.0)	1,000
Denmark	21	21,957 (100)	22,168 (100.9)	22,660 (103.2)	1,100
France	51	94,452 (100)	95,215 (100.8)	89,557 (94.8)	1,800
Total	403	1,737,851 (100)	1,714,985 (104.7)	1,789,435 (109.2)	4,400

Source: Asser (1979)

We should remember that Table 57 is based upon a small sample, and one that is not randomly selected. Of more immediate interest is the fact that, for these journals, most countries have shown a modest increase in total subscriptions over the period 1971-1977, although this period is generally believed to have been very difficult for established journals. Note, however, that with the exception of the USA and Denmark, there has been a decline during the period 1974-1977.

King (1979) provides estimates for a much larger number of US journals, and this, to some extent, sheds further light on Asser's data. King found an average figure for the circulation of scientific and technical journals of 6,327 in 1977, over half of which was accounted for by individuals. This average is, however, within a distribution skewed significantly by a relatively few very high circulation journals, namely those of the very large scientific societies. This skewness is shown by the fact that the median circulation is below 3,000. King's figures are roughly in line with another US study performed by Machlup and others (1978), and reported in a journal article by Leeson (1978).

Asser also provides some information on subject areas for the UK. He does not give details either of the number of journals or of subscriptions in each category, and this restricts interpretation of the data. Results are given in Table 58 below. Most noticeable are the differences between medical and physical sciences.

TABLE 58   Circulation Trends of UK Journals in Different
Subject Fields. 1971 = 100

	1971	1974	1977
Life Sciences	100.	106.4	91.8
Medical Sciences	100.	112.9	111.4
Physical Sciences	100.	95.3	85.8
Other Sciences	100.	105.6	108.7

Source: Asser (1979)

Singleton's (1980) survey of learned societies yields circulation figures for a large number of UK journals produced by societies, or in co-operation with publishers. Table 59 below gives the data by subject field. Overall, these journals have a mean circulation of 4,500, with a mode of 1,000 and a mean circulation to members only of roughly 3,500. Thus we again find a markedly skewed distribution, with, in most fields, a median circulation below 2,000. Since, in all these fields, journals have a substantial number of member subscribers, we can be fairly certain that purely commercial UK journals will, on average, have a lower circulation.

TABLE 59   Circulation Data for UK Learned Journals Produced By, or in Association with, Learned Societies 1979

Dewey Class	Subject	Number of Journals	Mean Circulation	Median Circulation
1	Philosophy Psychology	18	1,950	1,500
3	Social Science Economics Politics	51	6,500	1,500
4	Languages	4	2,350	1,450
5	Science	102	3,045	1,950
6	Medicine Technology	168	6,500	2,900
7	Architecture Arts	14	3,700	1,300
8	Literature	7	2,200	2,300
9	Geography History	67	1,600	800

Source: Singleton (1980)

There are relatively few published data which indicate a steady decline in institutional subscriptions, other than that revealed by certain publishers and reported in Koch (1974), Singleton (1976) and Van Tongeren (1976). However, it does seem that several of the very large, established, 'monolithic' journals have experienced a gradual loss of 1-2% per year. The reasons for this cannot be definitely established. Some publishers have claimed that the erosion has been caused by library photocopying and inter-library lending, but equally plausible is the argument that new, specialised journals, as they become established, inevitably cause libraries to readjust their acquisition policies somewhat. This may involve them in cutting out multiple subscriptions, or even single subscriptions to large journals, where such journals are peripheral to the main areas of interest. There will be great pressure to do so if acquisition budgets do not keep pace with rising prices, as has been true in recent years

Nevertheless, journals have typically been treated more favourably than books. Evidence for the USA, supplied by Fry and White (1975), and for the UK, supplied in National Book League annual reports, shows a continuing increase in the proportion of the acquisitions budget spent on journals, apparently at the expense of books. The very large and established journals have in the past generated considerable turnover for publishers, particularly some of the established commercial

publishers, and a gradual decline in circulation can be worrying. The economics
of journal publishing dictates that a lost subscription means a higher price since
overheads have to be allocated over fewer copies. Publishers with such journals
therefore attempt to support the large declining journals with a group of new,
small, specialised journals, priced to make profits even at low circulations. It
appears that this trend will continue.

CONCLUSION

This chapter has examined the traditional journal publishing system as it exists
today. Although the form and contents of journals has changed over the years,
many elements of this system and its economics are similar to those existing soon
after the first scholarly journal appeared in 1665. We should not end this chapter
without at least a mention of the systems which we may see tomorrow, or perhaps
the day after. Although various innovations, more or less radical, have been tried
out, there seems little doubt that conventional hard copy journals will be with us
for a long time yet. But other systems <u>will</u> be developed. The literature is
sprinkled liberally and sufficiently with articles on synopsis, microform, depos-
itory and electronic journals for there to be no need to dwell on them here. Some
of these already exist, and are financially viable. There is little doubt that
others will arise as part of the growing effort to use information technology and
the microelectronic revolution.

Scholarly publishers have understandably been slow to innovate so long as the tried
and true conventional journals continue to make a healthy profit. The issue for
them is not so much a worry that the conventional journal will disappear, since it
clearly will not, but the size of its future role in scholarly communication, and
the organisations which will be involved in these alternative methods. The danger
for them is that the alternative systems could become large-scale, without needing
the traditional publishers' services, expertise and capital. In order to obtain a
share in these developments traditional publishers must be prepared to take some
initiatives rather than adopt a wait and see attitude.

Bibliography

Altbach, P. (1976). Literary colonialism: books in the third world. In Altbach, P., and S. McVey (Eds.), <u>Perspectives On Publishing</u>. Lexington Books, Lexington, Mass. Chap. 8.

Altbach, P., and S. McVey (Eds.) (1976). <u>Perspectives On Publishing</u>. Lexington Books, Lexington, Mass.

American Institute of Physics (1970). <u>A Program For a National Information System For Physics and Astronomy 1971 - 1975</u>. American Institute of Physics.

Anderson, D. (1980). Changes abroad. <u>The Bookseller</u>, <u>3885</u>, June 7th, 2380-2385.

Anthony, L. J., H. East, and M. J. Slater (1969). The growth of the literature of physics. <u>Reports on Progress in Physics</u>, <u>32</u>, 709-767.

Ashworth, W. (1974). The information explosion. <u>Library Association Record</u>, <u>76</u> (4), 63-68.

Asser, P.N. (1979). Some trends in journal subscriptions. <u>Scholarly Publishing</u>, <u>10</u>, 279-286.

Astbury, R. (Ed.) (1967). <u>Libraries and the Book Trade</u>. Clive Bingley, London.

Astbury, R. (Ed.) (1969). <u>The Writer in the Market Place</u>. Clive Bingley, London.

Bailey, A. (1980). Choosing the Book of the Season. <u>The Bookseller</u>, <u>3878</u>, 1725-6.

Bailey, E. (1979). Here be facts. <u>The Bookseller</u>, <u>3831</u>, 2408-2411.

Bailey, H. Jnr. (1975). The limits of on-demand publishing. <u>Scholarly Publishing</u>, <u>6</u>(4), 291-298.

Barker, R. (1976a). International copyright I. <u>The Bookseller</u>, <u>3688</u>, 1522-1528.

Barker, R. (1976b). International copyright II. <u>The Bookseller</u>, <u>3689</u>, 1626-1630.

Barker, R. E., and G. R. Davies (Eds.) (1966). <u>Books Are Different</u>. Macmillan, London.

Barnes, J. J. (1964). <u>Free Trade In Books</u>. Clarendon Press, Oxford.

Barr, D. (1972). <u>Trends in Book Production and Prices</u>. National Central Library, London.

Barr, K. P. (1967). Estimates of the number of currently available scientific and technical periodicals. <u>Journal of Documentation</u>, <u>23</u>, 110-116.

Barron, C. (1978). How Collins was magnified. <u>Management Today</u>, Sept., 107-214.

Bartlett. G. (1975). Books in a siege economy III - bookselling. <u>The Bookseller</u>, Dec. 13th, 2648-2653.

Bartlett, G. (1976a). New prospects for distribution. <u>The Bookseller</u>, <u>3667</u>, 1848-1850.

Bartlett, G. (1976b). Presidential address to Booksellers' Association. <u>The Bookseller</u>, <u>3671</u>, 2146-2152.

Bartlett, G. (1976c). Financial stock control and its importance. <u>The Bookseller</u>, <u>3691</u>, 1820-1828.

Baumfield, B. (1976). Library book funds compared. <u>The Bookseller</u>, <u>3670</u>, 2070-6.

Bell, F. T. (1967). The library supplier. In R. Astbury (Ed.), <u>Libraries and the Book Trade</u>. Clive Bingley, London.

Bell, J. (1970). The proper domain of scholarly publishing. <u>Scholarly Publishing</u>, <u>2</u>(1), 11-18.

Best, M. (1963). In books they call it revolution. <u>Daedalus</u>, <u>Winter</u>, 30-41.

Bingley, C. (1966). <u>Book Publishing</u>. Crosby, Lockwood and Son Ltd, London.

Bingley, C. (1969). Why do book prices go on rising? <u>Library Association Record</u>, <u>71</u>(3), 70-74.

Bingley, C. (1972). <u>The Business of Book Publishing</u>. Pergamon Press, Oxford.

Blackwell, J. (1979). Machine readable codes: working party answers back. <u>The Bookseller</u>, <u>3822</u>, 1392-1393.

Blackwell, R. (1954). The pricing of books. <u>The Journal of Industrial Economics</u>, <u>August</u>, 174-183.

Blond, A. (1971). <u>The Publishing Game</u>. Jonathan Cape, London.

Bohne, H. (1975). The crisis of scholarly publishing. <u>Journal of Canadian Studies</u>, <u>10</u>, 9-15.

Bohne, H. (1976). Why are book prices so high? Scholarly Publishing, 7(2), 135-143.

Book Promotion House (1974). Feasibility Study. Committee Final Report. Book Promotion House, London.

Booksellers' Association (1973). Efficient Book Distribution. Booksellers' Association Service House, London.

Booksellers' Association (1974). Charter Group. Economic Survey. 1972/3. Booksellers' Association Service House, London.

Booksellers' Association (1975). Charter Group. Economic Survey. 1973/4. Booksellers' Association Service House, London.

Booksellers' Association (1976). Charter Group. Economic Survey. 1974/5. Booksellers' Association Service House, London.

Booksellers' Association (1977). Charter Group. Economic Survey. 1975/6. Booksellers' Association Service House, London.

Booksellers' Association (1978). Charter Group. Economic Survey. 1976/7. Booksellers' Association Service House, London.

Booksellers' Association (1979a). Charter Group. Economic Survey. 1977/8. Booksellers' Association Service House, London.

Booksellers' Association (1979b). Machine Readable Codes For the Book Trade. Booksellers' Association Service House, London.

Booksellers' Association (1980). Charter Group. Economic Survey. 1978/9. Booksellers' Association Service House, London.

Boon, J. (1968). Libraries and the Publishers' Association. In R. Astbury (Ed.), Libraries and the Book Trade. Clive Bingley, London. pp. 27-42.

Boon, J. (1975). Books in a siege economy I - publishing. The Bookseller, Nov. 29th, 2516-2520.

Booth, J. (1976). Rationalization and crisis: a quarter century of British publishing. In Altbach, P., and S. McVey (Eds.), Perspectives On Publishing. Lexington Books, Lexington, Mass. Chap. 6, pp. 59-69.

Bourgois, J. M. (1976). The French book trade. The Bookseller, 3679, 2790-2794.

Bourne, C. P. (1962). The world's technical journal literature: an estimate of volume, origin, language, field, indexing and abstracting. American Documentation, 13, 159-168.

Bowen, C. (1973). Considerations of scale in scholarly publishing. Scholarly Publishing, 4(2), 121-124.

Brandom, D. (1978). The challenge of academic bookselling. The Bookseller, 3781, 3090-3093.

Brice, A. (1974). The scholarly monograph and the hereafter. Scholarly Publishing, 5(3), 219-225.

British Library Research and Development Dept. (1978). Complete List of OSTI and BL R & D Reports 1965-1978. British Library Board, London.

British Printing Industries Federation (1979). The Economy and the Printing Industry. British Printing Industries Federation, London.

Broadhurst, S. (1980). The problem with being Penguin. The Bookseller, 3886, 2478-2480.

Brown, I. (1972). The economics of the book trade. Lloyds Bank Review, July, 34-44.

Brown, N. B. (1978). Price indices: US periodicals and serial services. Library Journal, July, 1356-1361.

Campbell, R. (1980). Survival of the fittest: adaptive strategies in journal publishing. In D. P. Woodworth (Ed.), Financing Serials From the Producer to the User. UK Serials Group. Serials Monograph No. 2. Distributed by Blackwell's Periodicals Division, Oxford. pp. 27-39.

Carson, D. M. (1977). What is a serial publication? Journal of Academic Librarianship, 3, 206-209.

Carter, J. (1977). Booksellers' orders and publishers' costs. The Bookseller, 3713, 1354-1356.

Childs, N. (1976). Perils and expense in the concept of a 'self-renewing' stock.

Times Higher Education Supplement, August 13th, 11.
Chomet, S. and E. Nejman (1979). The Periodical Literature of Physics: A First
    Sign of S? Dept. of Physics, King's College, London.
Clark, D. (1980). Distribution is fundamental to the marketing of books.
    The Bookseller, 3883, 2211-2212.
Clasquin, F. F. (1974). The chain enigma for serials and journals. In Spyers-
    Duran, P., and D. Gore (Eds.), Management Problems in Serials Work. Greenwood
    Press, Connecticut and London. pp. 66-88.
Clipsham, M. (1975). Financial planning and cash forecasting. The Bookseller,
    March 22nd, 1832-1837.
Collier, H. (1979). Electronic publishing - a need for perspective. The Bookseller,
    3849, 1542-1544.
Commission of the European Communities (1977). A Study of the Evolution of Concen-
    tration in the Press and General Publishing Industry in the United Kingdom.
    Commission of the European Communities.
Committee on Scientific and Technical Communication (1970). Report of the Task
    Group on the Economics of Primary Publication. National Academy of Sciences,
    Washington D. C.
Compaine, B. M. (1976). Book Distribution and Marketing, 1976-1980. Knowledge
    Industry Publications Inc., White Plains, New York.
Compaine, B. M. (1978). The Book Industry In Transition. Knowledge Industry
    Publications Inc., White Plains, New York.
Cooper, A. (1979a). Average prices of British academic books 1978. Library
    Management Research Unit, University of Cambridge.
Cooper, A. (1979b). Average prices of British academic books January to June 1979.
    Centre For Library and Information Management Report No. 1, University of
    Loughborough.
Cooper, A. (1980). Average prices of British academic books January to December
    1979. Centre For Library and Information Manangement Report No. 2,
    University of Loughborough.
Cooper, A. and J. L. Schofield (1976a). Average prices of British academic books
    1975. Library Management Research Unit Report No. 3, University of Cambridge.
Cooper, A. and J. L. Schofield (1976b). Average prices of British academic books
    January to June 1976. Library Management Research Unit Report No. 4,
    University of Cambridge.
Cooper, A. and J. L. Schofield (1978). Average prices of British academic books
    1977. Library Management Research Unit Report No. 11, University of Cambridge.
Corbett, S. (1980). Mail order into the '80s - bookclubs. The Bookseller, 3892,
    362-366.
Core, G. (1974). Costs and copy-editing. Scholarly Publishing, 6(1), 59-65.
Coser, L. A. (1975). Publishers as gatekeepers of ideas. The Annals of the
    American Academy of Political and Social Science, 421, 14-22.
Cotterell, L. (1976). Book clubs on the march again. The Bookseller, 3695, 2170-
    2171.
Cottrell, R. (1980). A story of high costs and poor profits. Financial Times,
    October 2nd, 23.
Council For Educational Technology (1979). The Use of Copyright Material For
    Educational Purposes. Council For Educational Technology, London.
Coward, B. (1980a). Electronic publishing I. The Bookseller, 3875, 1430-1432.
Coward, B. (1980b). Electronic publishing II. The Bookseller, 3876, 1557-1559.
Cullis, J. G. and P. A. West (1977). The economics of public lending right.
    Scottish Journal of Political Economy, 24(2), 169-174.
Curtis, A. (1979). Hard going for publishers. Financial Times, October 16th, 19.
Curwen, P. J. (1976a). The presses roll on - expensively. Times Higher Education
    Supplement, January 16th, 10.
Curwen, P. J. (1976b). The price of monographs. New Society, 36, 242-243.
Curwen, P. J. (1976c). Minimising the impact of decline. Library Association
    Record, 78(5), 209.

Curwen, P. J. (1976d). The declining fortunes of the stockholding bookseller.
    Times Higher Education Supplement, July 2nd, 17.
Curwen, P. J. (1976e). The reading gap - or why students spend an average of £13
    a year on books. Times Higher Education Supplement, October 8th, 11.
Curwen, P. J. (1977). The economics of academic publishing in the UK. Journal of
    Industrial Economics, XXV(3), 161-175.
Curwen, P. J. (1978a). Academic books: the exception to the rule about 'real prices'.
    Times Higher Education Supplement, May 26th, 11.
Curwen, P. J. (1978b). Prices report that is "not worth the paper it is written on".
    Times Higher Education Supplement, July 28th, 12.
Curwen, P. J. (1979). The Price Commission Report on books - a short critique.
    Journal of Industrial Economics, XXVII(3), 295-299.
Davies, G. R. (1976). Before and after price control. The Bookseller, 3695, 2160-
    2166.
Davies, G. R. (1977a). Early selling; only publishers can stop it. The Bookseller,
    3714, 1482-1485.
Davies, G. R. (1977b). International bookselling and market problems. The Book-
    seller, 3732, 39-43.
Davies, G. R. (1978a). Bookselling in Europe (I). The Bookseller, 3797, 2486-2487.
Davies, G. R. (1978b). Bookselling in Europe (II). The Bookseller, 3798, 2618-2621.
Davies, G. R. (1978c). Bookselling in Europe (III). The Bookseller, 3799. 2716-2719.
Davies, G. R. (1979). Euronet: a trap for the unwary? The Bookseller, 3826, 1856-
    1858.
Davies, W. (1976). Library priorities in a situation of stress. The Bookseller,
    3690, 1732-1736.
Davinson, D. (1976). Small libraries are the problem in the public sector.
    Times Higher Education Supplement, August 13th, 11.
Day, K. (1977). Matching supply with demand. The Bookseller, 3739, 1558-1559.
Denniston, R. (1979). The academic publisher. The Bookseller, 3840, 388-396.
Department of Education and Science (1972). The purchase of books by public libraries.
    Library Information Series No. 1. HMSO, London.
Department of Education and Science (1975). Public Lending Right: An Account of An
    Investigation of Technical and Cost Aspects. HMSO, London.
Department of Education and Science (1977). Maintaining library services: a study
    in six counties. Library Information Series No. 8. HMSO, London.
Department of Employment and Productivity (1970). Publishing and printing.
    Manpower Studies No. 9. HMSO, London.
Department of Trade and Industry, Business Statistics Office (1968). Report On the
    Census of Production 1963, Part 118. HMSO, London.
Department of Trade and Industry, Business Statistics Office (1972). Report On the
    Census of Production 1968, Part 143. HMSO, London.
Department of Trade and Industry, Business Statistics Office (1973). Report On the
    Census of Production 1970, Part C143. HMSO, London.
Department of Trade and Industry, Business Statistics Office (1974). Report On the
    Census of Production 1971, Part PA489. HMSO, London.
Department of Trade and Industry, Business Statistics Office (1975). Report On the
    Census of Production 1972, Part PA489. HMSO, London
Department of Trade and Industry, Business Statistics Office (1976). Business
    Monitor Quarterly Statistics 1975, PQ489. HMSO, London.
Department of Trade and Industry, Business Statistics Office (1977). Business
    Monitor Quarterly Statistics 1976, PQ489. HMSO, London.
Department of Industry, Business Statistics Office (1978). Business Monitor
    Quarterly Statistics 1977, PQ489. HMSO, London.
Department of Industry, Business Statistics Office (1979). Business Monitor
    Quarterly Statistics 1978, PQ489. HMSO, London.
Department of Industry, Business Statistics Office (1980). Business Monitor
    Quarterly Statistics 1979, PQ489. HMSO, London.
Dessauer, J. P. (1974). Book Publishing: What It Is, What It Does. R. R. Bowker
    Co., New York and London.

Dessauer, J. P. (1976). Economic review of the book industry. Publishers Weekly,
    July 26th, 35-58.
Dessauer, J. P. (Ed.) (1979). Quarterly review of business and finance. Publishers
    Weekly, October 8th, 31-37.
Eble, K. (1974). Scholarly publishing and academic reward. Scholarly Publishing,
    6(1), 19-25.
Educational Publishers Council (1979). The Supply of Books To Schools.
    Publishers' Association, London.
Epstein, J. (1963). A criticism of commercial publishing. Daedalus, Winter, 63-
    67.
Escreet, P. K. (1971). Introduction to the Anglo-American Cataloguing Rules.
    A. Deutsch, London.
Evans, C. (1979). The Mighty Micro. Gollancz, London.
Fairlie, R., and M. Corby (1979). Not dead yet: a reply to "The Mighty Micro".
    The Bookseller, 3845, 1008-1011.
Farr, D. (1978). Sales - a few suggestions from 'an ordinary author'.
    The Bookseller, 3783, 3310-3311.
Farrer, D. (1975). The role of a publisher's editor. The Bookseller, July 19th,
    182-183.
Farrow, D. (1975). Thoughts for the academic publisher. The Bookseller, April 19th,
    2174-2175.
Ferguson, G. (1976). US books in Australia after the Market Agreement ends.
    The Bookseller, 3675, 1686-1690.
Financial Analysis Group Ltd (1974). The Book and Magazine Publishing Industry.
    Financial Analysis Group Ltd, Winnersh, Bucks.
Financial Times (1979). Financial Times survey - the printing industry.
    Financial Times, January 23rd, 11-14.
Findlater, R. (Ed.) (1971). Public Lending Right. A. Deutsch, London and Penguin
    Books, Harmondsworth.
Ford, J. (1977). Staff: the largest single expense. The Bookseller, 3743, 2047-
    2050.
Foxons (1978). Periodical prices: 1976-78 update. F.F. Clasquin Library Journal,
    October, 1924-1927.
Franklin, N. (1975). Utility production to cut costs. The Bookseller, September
    13th, 1660-1661.
Franklin, N. (1977). After the Consent Decree. The Bookseller, 3732, 46-47.
Fry, B. M., and H. S. White (1975). Economics and Interaction of the Publisher-
    Library Relationship in the Production and Use of Scholarly and Research
    Journals. Final Report. US Office of Science Information Services. National
    Science Foundation.
Gabriel, M. (1974). Surging serial costs. The microfiche solution. Library
    Journal, October 1st, 2450-2453.
Gade, S. (1979). Easing the flow of books to Europe. The Bookseller, 3814, 380-
    382.
Godfray, T. (1976). BA delivery survey. February-March 1976. The Bookseller,
    3672, 2238-2241.
Godfray, T. (1977). BA delivery league table 1977. The Bookseller, 3726, 2510-
    2515.
Godfray, T. (1978). Publishers' delivery times: no sign of improvement.
    The Bookseller, 3788, 432-439.
Godfray, T. (1980). BA delivery survey report. The Bookseller, 3870, 793-799.
Goff, M. (1976). 'Book flood' moves to Bradford. The Bookseller, 3679, 2788-2790.
Golding, P. (1978). The international media and the political economy of publishing.
    Library Trends, Spring, 453-467.
Golding, P. (1979). Creativity, control and the political economy of publishing.
    Mimeo available from the Centre For Mass Communications Research, University
    of Leicester.
Gordon, M. (1978). A Study of the Evaluation of Research Papers By Primary Journals
    in the UK. Primary Communications Research Centre, University of Leicester.

Graham, F. (1980). A librarian's view of copyright. The Bookseller, 3871, 9-10.
Graham, G. (1974). Book supply is not an isolated problem. The Bookseller,
    June 29th, 2828-2832.
Graham, G. (1976). New mediums and old problems. The Bookseller, 3686, 1302-1304.
Graham, G. (1977a). A rich smorgasbord of American publishing. The Bookseller,
    3716, 1684-1686.
Graham, G. (1977b). Publishers, librarians and photocopying. The Bookseller,
    3744, 2148-2151.
Graham, G. (1978a). Spring rituals. The Bookseller, 3783, 3298-3300.
Graham, G. (1978b). Measuring the performance of British publishing.
    The Bookseller, 3793, 1949-1950.
Graham, G. (1979a). Reproaches from the Third World. The Bookseller, 3813, 253-
    256.
Graham, G. (1979b). European incursion into the American STM market.
    The Bookseller, 3825, 1762-1765.
Graham, G. (1979c). Report from Singapore. The Bookseller, 3848, 1414-1415.
Graham, G. (1980). The cry of an endangered species. The effect of new technology.
    The Bookseller, 3876, 1560-1562.
Grenfell, D. (1965). Periodicals and Serials: Their Treatment in Special Libraries,
    2nd ed. Aslib, London.
Gretener, C. (1978). Selling British books in Europe. The Bookseller, 3778,
    2806-2810.
Grice, E. (1979). The millions they owe to the diary of a nobody. Sunday Times,
    December 30th, 5.
Guttsman, W. L. (1976). Why a national library system should be a network not a
    pyramid. Times Higher Education Supplement, August 6th, 11.
Hall, J. (1974). Science journals in a prices jungle. Nature, 247, 417-419.
Hall, J. (1976). Notes on a government enquiry. The Bookseller, 3695, 2530-2533.
Hall, J. (1977). Little comfort for publishers in Franki Report. The Bookseller,
    3711, 420-424.
Hall, T. (1976). Micro publishing becomes a challenge. The Bookseller, 3692,
    1918-1920.
Hamilton, A. (1969a). The top twenty publishers I. The Author, Spring, 22-27.
Hamilton, A. (1969b). The top twenty publishers II. The Author, Summer, 79-83.
Hamilton, A. (1970). Little publishers. The Author, Spring, 29-32.
Haslam, D. (1975). Books in a siege economy II - library statistics.
    The Bookseller, December 6th, 2586-2589.
Hepburn, P. (1975). What book promotion to whom? The Bookseller, May 31st, 2702-
    2706.
Heslop-Harrison, J. (1978). Learned society publications in the United Kingdom.
    In Commission of the European Communities, The Future of Publishing By Scient-
    ific and Technical Societies. Proceedings of a Seminar Held In Luxemborg,
    April 1978.
Hewison, J. (1976). Australian trade practices law. The Bookseller, 3661, 1312-
    1314.
Hill, A. (1979). Building an empire. The Bookseller, 3847, 1282-1286.
Hill, F. (1976). Small presses feel the squeeze. Times Higher Education Supple-
    ment, March 19th, 13.
Hill, L. F. (1978). An insight into the finances of the record industry.
    Three Banks Review, 118, 28-45.
Hochland, E. (1978). Teleordering and book distribution - a personal view.
    The Bookseller, 3787, 340-342.
Hochland, E. (1980). Facing the problems of UK book distribution. The Bookseller,
    3900, 1250-1255.
Hodder-Williams, M. (1978). Teleordering costs and benefits - a publisher's view.
    The Bookseller, 3772, 2186-2189.
Hopkins, P. (1975). A cycle of deprivation in academic publishing. Times Higher
    Education Supplement, July 4th, 11.

Horvitz, P. M. (1966). The pricing of textbooks and the remuneration of authors.
    American Economic Review, Papers and Proceedings, May, 412-420.
Hughes, N. (1977). Does the trade still want the Net Book Agreement?
    The Bookseller, 3736, 462-466.
Hurt, R. M., and R. M. Schuchman (1966). The economic rationale of copyright.
    American Economic Review, Papers and Proceedings, May, 421-439.
Ingram, P. (1976). The high cost of publishing. Times Higher Education Supplement,
    October 29th, 7.
Inter Company Comparisons Ltd (1978). Financial Survey. Periodical Publishers.
    England and Wales, 4th ed. Inter Company Comparisons Ltd, London.
Inter Company comparisons Ltd (1979a). Financial Survey. Booksellers, 1st ed.
    Inter Company Comparisons Ltd, London.
Inter Company Comparisons Ltd (1979b). Business Ratio Report. Book Publishers,
    2nd ed. Inter Company Comparisons Ltd, London.
Johnson, A. (1977). OCR in the Highlands. The Bookseller, 3741, 1795-1796.
Johnston, D. (1978). Copyright for books, designs and other works.
    The Bookseller, 3787, 352-353.
Jones, T. L. (1968). The university press. In R. Astbury (Ed.), Libraries and
    the Book Trade. Clive Bingley, London. pp. 81-92.
Jordan Dataquest (1978). Book Publishing. Jordan Dataquest, London.
Joy, T. (1964). The Truth About Publishing. Pitman, London.
Kachergis, J. (1976). New technology; new solutions. Scholarly Publishing, 7(2),
    157-160.
Katz, W., and P. Gellatly (1975). Guide to Magazine and Serial Agents.
    R. R. Bowker Co, New York and London.
King, D. W., and others (1977). Statistical Indicators of Scientific and Technical
    Communication (1960-1980), Vol. 5: An Update. King Research Inc., Maryland.
King, D. W., and others (1979). The Journal In Scientific Communication: The Roles
    of Authors, Publishers, Libraries and Readers In a Vital System. King Research
    Inc., Maryland.
Kleinman, P. (1977a). Book advertising in a changing world. The Bookseller, 3722,
    2162-2164.
Kleinman, P. (1977b). Don't let poor David starve. The Bookseller, 3744, 2182.
Kleinman, P. (1978). Teleordering: the revolution will now start next week.
    The Bookseller, 3807, 3460-3462.
Koch, A. W. (1974). Copyrighting physics journals. Physics Today, 27, 23-28.
Lacy, D. (1963). The economics of publishing, or Adam Smith and literature.
    Daedalus, Winter, 42-62.
Lane, M. (1970). Books and their publishers. In J. Turnstall (Ed.), Media
    Sociology. Constable, London.
Lane, M. (1975). Shapers of culture: the editor in book publishing. The Annals
    of the American Academy of Political and Social Science, 421, 34-42.
Latham, J. E. (1979). Publishers' publicity - a personal approach.
    The Bookseller, 3845, 1014-1016.
Lea, P. W. (1976). Trends in scientific and technical primary journal publishing
    in the USA. Report 5272 HC. British Library Research and Development Depart-
    ment, Wetherby, W. Yorks.
Leeson, K. W. (1978). The economic viability of scientific and scholarly journals:
    a look at the recent trends in circulation, income and cost. Journal of Research
    Communication Studies, 1, 19-36.
Letts, J. (1979). Opening Pandora's box: book clubs ten years on. The Bookseller,
    3829, 2202-2206.
Leventhal, L. (1979a). UK publishers edging into the American market.
    The Bookseller, 3813, 259-261.
Leventhal, L. (1979b). Three ways into the US. The Bookseller, 3826, 1860-1863.
Library Association (1979). The effect of cuts in public expenditure on public
    libraries in England and Wales. Library Association Record, 81(9), 429-433.
Lightfoot, M. (1976a). The catch in the net. The Guardian, March 16th, 15.

Lightfoot, M. (1976b). The distribution of books: weak link in the publishing
    chain. In Altbach, P., and S. McVey (Eds.), Perspectives On Publishing.
    Lexington Books, Lexington, Mass. Chap. 7, pp. 71-79.
Line, M., and B. Williams (1976). Alternatives to conventional publication and
    their implications for libraries. Aslib Proceedings, 28(3), 109-115.
Line, M., and D. Wood (1975). The effect of a large-scale photocopying service on
    journal sales. Journal of Documentation, 31(4), 234-245.
Livesey, F. (1980). Publish or be damned. Times Higher Education Supplement,
    September 12th, 10.
Longworth, A. (1975). Books in a siege economy IV - libraries. The Bookseller,
    December 20th, 2706-2710.
Lusty, R. (1976). The future role of the publisher. The Bookseller, 3692, 1910-
    1914.
Lusty, R. (1977). Musing among the shelves. The Bookseller, 3755, 3131-3132.
Lusty, R. (1980). Are books becoming redundant? The Bookseller, 3887, 2579-2581.
Machlup, F. (1976). Our libraries: can we measure their holdings and acquisitions?
    AAUP Bulletin, Autumn, 303-307.
Machlup, F. (1977). Publishing scholarly books and journals: is it economically
    viable? Journal of Political Economy, February, 217-229.
Machlup, F., and others (1978). Information Through the Printed Word. The
    Dissemination of Scholarly, Scientific and Intellectual Knowledge.
    New York U. P., New York.
Macrae, J. (1980). Beginning again. The Bookseller, 3872, 1072-1073.
Manheim, F. T. (1975). The scientific referee. IEEE Transactions On Professional
    Communication, PC - 18, 190-195.
Mann, P. (1971). Books, Buyers and Borrowers. A. Deutsch, London.
Mann, P. (1973). Books and Students. National Book League, London.
Mann, P. (Ed.) (1976). Books and Undergraduates. National Book League, London.
Mann, P. (1977). Problems in scholarly publishing. The Bookseller, 3717, 1766-
    1768.
Mann, P. (1978a). Author-publisher relationships in scholarly publishing.
    British Library R & D Report No. 5416. British Library Board, London.
Mann, P. (1978b). Scholarly authors and their publishers. The Bookseller, 3774,
    2408-2409.
Mann, P. (1978c). Teachers and publishers talk books. The Bookseller, 3780,
    2994-2995.
Mann, P. (1978d). When scholarly publishing means money. Times Higher Education
    Supplement, December 1st, 13.
Mann, P. (1979). Americans as book readers. The Bookseller, 3814, 388-390.
Mann, P., and J. Burgoyne (1969). Books and Reading. A. Deutsch, London.
Marland, M. (1979). N.B.L. report on school book provision. The Bookseller, 3830,
    2290-2292.
Marriott, M. (1979). Machine-readable codes. The Bookseller, 3861/2, 2692-2694.
Mason, J. (1980). Publicising children's books. The Bookseller, 3872, 1102-1103.
Matarazzo, J. (1972). Scientific journals: page or price explosion? Special
    Libraries, 63, 53-58.
May, J. (1976a). The economic possibilities within retail bookselling.
    The Bookseller, 3672, 2253-2257.
May, J. (1976b). Wholesaling, teleordering and stock control. The Bookseller,
    3692, 1906-1909.
May, J. (1977). The public still needs the net book system. The Bookseller,
    3738, 1435-1438.
McCarthy, P., and N. Barker (1974). Publishing. Problems and paradoxes.
    The Bookseller, November 16th, 2636-2640.
McGregor, C. (1977). Economic performance in publishing. The Bookseller, 3742,
    1915-1918.
Meadows, A. J. (1978). Current problems in the commercial publishing of scholarly
    monographs in the United Kingdom. Journal of Research Communication Studies,
    1, 125-137.

Mogridge, S. (1979). The case of cassettes v books. The Bookseller, 3815, 523-524.

Moore, N. (1977). Statistics concerning academic libraries. British Library R & D Report No. 5335. British Library Board, London.

Morgan, J. P. (1973). Government publishing and bookselling. In Proceedings of the 20th Annual Conference and Study Course. Library Association, London.

Morin, A. J. (1966). The market for professional writing in economics. American Economic Review, Papers and Proceedings, May, 401-411.

Morley, D. (1963). Self-Help for Learned Journals. Oxford U. P., Oxford.

Morris, D. (1977). The economics of the Net Book Agreement. A Re-Evaluation. Discussion Paper No. 53. Dept. of Industrial Economics, University of Nottingham.

Moss, E. (1980). Mainly about money. The Bookseller, 3872, 1070-1071.

Mumby, F., and I. Norrie (1974). Publishing and Bookselling, 2nd ed. Jonathen Cape, London.

Nash, M. (1976). Books On-Demand - An Economic Comparison of the Academic Book Publishing Industry and the Micropublishing Industry. Oxford Microform Publications.

Nasri, W. (1976). Crisis In Copyright. Marcel Dekker Inc., New York and Basel.

National Book League (1977). University Library Expenditure 1969-1975. National Book League, London.

National Book League (1978). University Library Expenditure 1970-1976. National Book League, London.

National Book League (1979). University Library Expenditure 1971-1977. National Book League, London.

Neavill, G. (1976). Role of the publisher in the dissemination of knowledge. In Altbach, P., and S. McVey (Eds.), Perspectives On Publishing. Lexington Books, Lexington, Mass. Chap. 5.

Neuburg, V. (1973). The reprint trade. Retrospect to forecast. Journal of Librarianship, 5, 28-36.

Neville, C. O. Jnr. (1973). Pricing, licensing, microform publishing and copyright as a source of income. In R. A. Day and others (Eds.), Economics of Scientific Publications. Council of Biology Editors, Bethesda, Maryland.

Nieuwenhuysen, J. P. (1975). Competition in Australian Bookselling. Melbourne U. P., Melbourne, Australia.

Noble, D. H., and C. M. Noble (1974). A Survey of Book Reviews: October-December 1973. Noble and Beck Ltd.

Nolan, K. (1976). Production man's nightmare. The Bookseller, 3686, 1314.

Norkett, P. (1980a). Company profile: Pentos - giant on a growth curve. The Bookseller, 3878, 1742-1745.

Norkett, P. (1980b). The problem with being Penguin. The Bookseller, 3886, 2475-2478.

Norrie, I. (1976). Can the novel still sell? The Bookseller, 3673, 2312-2314.

Norrie, I. (1979). My own and other sacred cows. The Bookseller, 3845, 1076-1079.

Orlov, A. (1975). Demythologizing scholarly publishing. The Annals of the American Academy of Political and Social Science, 421, 43-53.

Osborn, A. D. (1973). Serial Publications: Their Place and Treatment in Libraries. American Library Association.

Packard, D. (1973). Can scholars publish their own books? Scholarly Publishing, 5, 65-74.

Parnell, M. (1968). The local bookshop. In R. Astbury (Ed.), Libraries and the Book Trade. Clive Bingley, London. pp. 173-182.

Parsons, I. (1976). The changing face of the book trade. The Bookseller, 3674, 2384-2387.

Parsons, I. (1980). The publishing of books. The Bookseller, 3867, 474-482.

Paton, G. (1976). The effects of inadequate stock control. The Bookseller, 3694, 2090-2093.

Philipson, M. (1974). The quality of scholarly publishing and scholarly writing today. Scholarly Publishing, 6, 9-18.

Phipps, P. (1980). Read any good books lately? The Bookseller, 3901, 1330-1333.
Plant, M. (1965). The English Book Trade, 3rd ed. Allen and Unwin, London.
Political and Economic Planning (1951). Economics of book publishing. Planning, XVIII, 21-43.
Political and Economic Planning (1956). Publishing and bookselling. Planning, XXII, No. 392.
Powell, W. W. (1978). Publishers' decision making: what criteria do they use in deciding which books to publish? Social Research, 45, 227-252.
Pratten, C., R. M. Dean, and A. Silberston (1965). The Economies of Large Scale Production in British Industries. Dept. of Applied Economics, Occasional Paper No. 3, Cambridge University Press, Cambridge. Chap. 2.
Price, D. J. de Solla (1961). Science Since Babylon. Yale U. P., New Haven, Connecticut.
Price Commission (1978). Prices, Costs and Margins in the Publishing, Printing and Binding of Books. HC527. HMSO, London.
Primary Communications Research Centre (1977). Scholarly Publishers' Guide: New Methods and Techniques. Primary Communications Research Centre, University of Leicester.
Primary Communications Research Centre (1980). Societies and Publishers: Hints on Collaboration in Journal Publishing. Primary Communications Research Centre, University of Leicester.
Printing Trades Journal (1976). Production in the printing industry remains at low level. Printing Trades Journal, June, 24-27.
Prior, A. (1979). How serials agents can help libraries cut costs. In D. P. Woodworth (Ed.), Financing Serials From the Producer to the User. UK Serials Group. Serials Monograph No. 2, Distributed by Blackwell's Periodicals Division, Oxford. pp. 44-55.
Publishers' Association (1969). The price of books. Library Association Record, 71(3), 75-76.
Publishers' Association (1978). Submission to the Price Commission. Publishers' Association, London.
Publishers' Association (1979). Statistics Collection Scheme and Business Monitor. Publishers' Association, London.
Putnam, J. B. (1973). The scholar and the future of scholarly publishing. Scholarly Publishing, 4(3), 195-200.
Range, P. (1976). Distribution costs and performance. The Bookseller, 3673, 2322-2323.
Rimmer, A. (1978). A student at the Dutch Centraal Boekhuis. The Bookseller, 3795, 2244-2249.
Ringer, B. (1976). The demonology of copyright. In Altbach, P., and S. McVey (Eds.), Perspectives On Publishing. Lexington Books, Lexington, Mass. Chap. 4.
Roberts, E. H. (1968). The book trade and the role of the library. In R. Astbury (Ed.), Libraries and the Book Trade. Clive Bingley, London. pp. 183-194.
Rosenthal, T. G. (1975). Quality and quantity: publishers and public demand. The Bookseller, May 31st, 2694-2701.
Russak, B. (1975). Scholarly publishing in Western Europe and Great Britain: A survey and analysis. The Annals of the American Academy of Political and Social Science, 421, 106-117.
Santinelli, P. (1976). Alternatives to rising book costs. Times Higher Education Supplement, October 8th, 23.
Schmoller, H. (1968). The paperback revolution. In R. Astbury (Ed.), Libraries and the Book Trade. Clive Bingley, London. pp. 13-26.
Schofield, J. L. (1978). Research support for investment in library buildings. Library Association Record, 80, 9.
Shatzkin, L. (1963). The book in search of a reader. Daedalus, Winter, 105-115.
Shils, E. (1963). The bookshop in America. Daedalus, Winter, 92-104.
Shugg, R. (1963). The professors and their publishers. Daedalus, Winter, 68-77.
Silberston, A. (1972). Economies of scale in theory and practice. Economic Journal, 82, 369-391.

Singleton, A. (1975a). International publication: changing patterns. Physics Bulletin, August, 354-355.

Singleton, A. (1975b). Do Institute members publish? Physics Bulletin, November, 490-491.

Singleton, A. (1976). Publishing at the crossroads? Physics Bulletin, September, 399-403.

Singleton, A. (1977). Scientific journal budgeting: where does the money go? Aslib Proceedings, 29, 127-132.

Singleton, A. (1978). Letters and letters journals in physics. Journal of Research Communication Studies, 1, 47-67.

Singleton, A. (1979). On-demand publishing. Aslib Proceedings, 31, 561-582.

Singleton, A. (1980). Learned Societies, Journals and Co-operation with Publishers. Primary Communications Research Centre, University of Leicester.

Sissons, M. (1977). British books in world markets. The Bookseller, 3714, 1486-1490.

Skeoch, L. A. (1964). The abolition of Resale Price Maintenance: some notes on the Canadian experience. Economica, 260-269.

Skilton, C. (1968). The independent publisher. In R. Astbury (Ed.), Libraries and the Book Trade. Clive Bingley, London. pp. 73-80.

Smith, D. C. Jnr. (1975). The bright promise of publishing in the developing countries. The Annals of the American Academy of Political and Social Science. 421, 130-139.

Smith, D. C. Jnr. (1976). A case for on-demand publishing. Scholarly Publishing, 7(2), 169-178.

Smith, G. (1977). Book boom born in a traffic jam. Sunday Times Business News, September 4th, 55.

Smith, R. (1980). British printing in the 1980's. Part 2. The Bookseller, 3874, 1316-1319.

Sturrock, P. (1976). Measuring the effectiveness of mail promotion. The Bookseller, 3676, 2548-2549.

Sutherland, J. A. (1978). Fiction and the Fiction Industry. University of London, The Athlone Press.

Sweeten, C. (1977). Fleeing the main frame monster. The Bookseller, 3719, 1948-1949.

Teague, J. (1976). Libraries after the watershed. Times Higher Education Supplement, October 8th, 20.

Temple Smith, M. (1968). The general publisher. In R. Astbury (Ed.), Libraries and the Book Trade. Clive Bingley, London. pp. 43-72.

The Bookseller (1976a). The book trade in 1975, January to June. The Bookseller, 3655, 88-96.

The Bookseller (1976b). The book trade in 1975, July to December. The Bookseller, 3656, 162-169.

The Bookseller (1976c). How academics see publishing. The Bookseller, 3663, 1524-1527.

The Bookseller (1976d). The low value order problem. The Bookseller, 3676, 2542-2544.

The Bookseller (1977a). The book trade in 1976, January to June. The Bookseller, 3707, 40-45.

The Bookseller (1977b). The book trade in 1976, July to December. The Bookseller, 3708, 121-129.

The Bookseller (1977c). The prospects for wholesaling I. The Bookseller, 3710, 314-316.

The Bookseller (1977d). The prospects for wholesaling II. The Bookseller, 3711, 412-418.

The Bookseller (1977e). B.A. charter seminar. The Bookseller, 3716, 1676-1682.

The Bookseller (1977f). The long road to the B.A. Promotion House. The Bookseller, 3726, 2520-2521.

The Bookseller (1978a). The book trade in 1977, January to June. The Bookseller, 3759, 39-43.

The Bookseller (1978b). The book trade in 1977, July to December. The Bookseller, 3760, 120-124.

The Bookseller (1978c). Booksellers in the High Street. The Bookseller, 3766, 1582-1583.

The Bookseller (1978d). P.A. submission on Whitford report. The Bookseller, 3769, 1896-1899.

The Bookseller (1979a). The book trade in 1978, January to June. The Bookseller, 3811, 38-42.

The Bookseller (1979b). The book trade in 1978, July to December. The Bookseller, 3812, 150-153.

The Bookseller (1980a). The book trade in 1979, January to June. The Bookseller, 3863, 52-55.

The Bookseller (1980b). The book trade in 1979, July to December. The Bookseller, 3864, 150-154.

The Bookseller (1980c). PLR: the consultative document. The Bookseller, 3864, 139-147.

The Bookseller (1980d). Teleordering: PA and BA presidents ask members to decide its future. The Bookseller, 3893, 492-495.

Thin, A. (1974a). Why booksellers need libraries. The Bookseller, June 15th, 2674-2677.

Thin, A. (1974b). Inflation - what it is doing to booksellers. The Bookseller, October 26th, 2398-2399.

Thompson, J. (1977). University libraries under siege. The Bookseller, 3736, 455-459.

Thompson, R. S. (1979). An economist's case against PLR. Library Association Record, 81(4), 174-175.

Times Educational Supplement (1977a). Read any good books lately? Times Educational Supplement, November 18th, 8-9.

Times Educational Supplement (1977b). Why crisis is just around the corner. Times Educational Supplement, November 25th, 10-11.

Tunstall, J. (Ed.) (1970). Media Sociology. Constable, London.

Turfrey, M. (1980). Sales boom for children's books? The Bookseller, 3872, 1076-1077.

Turnbull, A. (1979). The uncreating word. The Bookseller, 3825, 1766-1770.

Turner, B., and P. Richardson (1978). Growth in further education is a challenge for booksellers. The Bookseller, 3794, 2090-2093.

Unwin, S. (1960). The Truth About Publishing. Allen and Unwin, London.

Urquhart, D. (1976). University libraries: the case for a national lending system. Times Higher Education Supplement, September 17th, 8.

Usborne, P. (1979). Spotting a gap in the American market. The Bookseller, 3822, 1400-1402.

Van Tongeren, E. (1976). The effect of a large-scale photocopying service on journal sales. Journal of Documentation, 32, 198-206.

Vaughan, S. (1977). Books in an age of uncertainty. The Bookseller, 3708, 132-134.

Vickery, B. C. (1968). Statistics of scientific and technical articles. Journal of Documentation, 24, 192-196.

Wace, M. (1968). Educational publishing for schools. In R. Astbury (Ed.), Libraries and the Book Trade. Clive Bingley, London. pp. 93-104.

Wagner, N. (1976). Scholars as publishers. A new paradigm. Scholarly Publishing, 7, 101-112.

Wall, R. (1977). Alternatives to Whitford. Library Association Record, 79(9), 465-466.

Walsh, R. (1978). Australia: publishing and its future. The Bookseller, 3791, 1660-1664.

Walsh, R. (1979). Australia '78: much activity, and some change. The Bookseller, 3813, 264-267.

Ward, A., and P. Ward (1979). The Small Publisher. Oleander Press.

Ward, M. L. (1977). Readers and Library Users. Library Association, London.
Weinberg, L. (1975). The photocopying revolution and the copyright crisis. The Public Interest, Winter, 99-118.
White, D. (1977). Which part is profitable? The Bookseller, 3743, 2050-2052.
White, H. (1978). New Zealand and the closed market. The Bookseller, 3763, 442-444.
White, H. (1979). New Zealand booksellers' inward mission to the UK. The Bookseller, 3854, 2086-2087.
Whitestone, P. (1977). Paying for copying in the USA. The Bookseller, 3739, 1570-1571.
Whitford Report (1977). Copyright and Designs Law. Cmnd 6732, HMSO, London.
Whitley, R. D. (1970a). The formal communication system of science: a study of the organisation of British social science journals. The Sociological Review, Monograph No. 16, September, 163-179.
Whitley, R. D. (1970b). The operation of science journals: two case studies in British social science. The Sociological Review, 18, 241-258.
Williams, J. (1979). French book pricing: new system - new problems. The Bookseller, 3850, 1696-1698.
Willings Press Guide (1980). Thomas Skinner Directories. IPC Business Press.
Wilson, A. (1968). The chartered bookseller. In R. Astbury (Ed.), Libraries and the Book Trade. Clive Bingley, London. pp. 163-172.
Winter-Goodwin, B. (1976). The case for wholesaling. The Bookseller, 3671, 2154-2156.
Wood, D. N. (1979). Serials at the British Library Lending Division. Interlending Review, 7, 18-19.
Wood, D. N., and J. Ferguson (1974). Statistics of social science periodicals. British Lending Library Review, 2, 92-95.
Wood, E. G. (1977). British Industries: A Comparison of Performance. McGraw-Hill (UK), Maidenhead.
Woodley, L. (1979a). Bookselling in Australia. The Bookseller, 3830, 2294-2298.
Woodley, L. (1979b). Australian inward mission. The current scene. The Bookseller, 3850, 1688-1690.
Woodward, A. M. (1976). Editorial Processing Centres: Scope in the United Kingdom. British Library Research and Development Department.
Woodworth, D. P. (1970). A Guide to Current British Journals. Library Association, London.
Woodworth, D. P. (1973). A Guide to Current British Journals, 2nd ed. Library Association, London.
Woodworth, D. P. (Ed.) (1980). Financing Serials From the Producer to the User: Proceedings of the UK Serials Group Conference, Loughborough, UK, April 1979. UK Serials Group.
Wooton, C. B. (1977). Trends in size, growth and cost of the literature since 1955. British Library Research and Development Report No. 5323 HC. British Library Board, London.
Yamey, B. S. (1963). The Net Book Agreement. Modern Law Review, November, 691-699.
Ziegler, P. (1976). Can the novel still sell? The Bookseller, 3673, 2314-2319.
Zifcak, M. (1977). Net Book Agreement. An Australian view. The Bookseller, 3744, 2156-2157.
Zifcak, M. (1978). Do booksellers need resale price maintenance? The Bookseller, 3787, 332-335.
Zifcak, M. (1979). Australian inward mission. Book promotion. The Bookseller, 3850, 1690-1694.
Ziman, J. M. (1968). Public Knowledge. Cambridge U. P., Cambridge.
Zuckerman, H., and R. K. Merton (1971). Patterns of evaluation in science: institutionalisation, structure and functions of the referee system. Minerva, 9, 66-100

Author Index

Anthony, L. J. 118
Asser, P. N. 114, 115
Bailey, H. Jnr. 54
Barker, R. E. 43
Barr, K. P. 115
Bourne, C. P. 115
Campbell, R. 140
Carson, D. M. 114
Chomet, S. 120, 139
Corby, M. 56
Cullis, J. G. 103
Davies, G. R. 43
Dean, R. M. 61
East, H. 118
Escreet, P. K. 114
Evans, C. 56
Fairlie, R. 56
Fry, B. M. 116, 130, 146
Gellatly, P. 141
Golding, P. 140
Gordon, M. 128
Graham, G. 14
Grenfell, D. 114
Hall, J. 59
Hepburn, P. 81
Hill, L. F. 47
Hughes, N. 41
Hurt, R. M. 57
Katz, W. 141
King, D. W. 116, 117, 118, 128, 130, 145
Koch, A. W. 146
Leeson, K. W. 145
Line, M. 58

Machlup, F. 115, 130, 140, 145
Merton, R. K. 128
Morris, D. 49
Nash, M. 54
Nejman, E. 120, 139
Nieuwenhuysen, J. P. 48
Norrie, I. 41, 48
Osborn, A. D. 114
Pratten, C. 61
Price, D. J. de Solla. 139
Ringer, B. 57
Schuchman, R. M. 57
Silberston, A. 61
Singleton, A. 54, 114, 115, 119, 123,
    132, 134, 135, 138, 140, 141, 144, 146
Skeoch, L. A. 47
Slater, M. J. 118
Smith, D. C. Jnr. 54
Sutherland, J. A. 101
Van Tongeren, E. 58, 146
Vickery, B. C. 115
West, P. A. 103
White, H. S. 116, 130, 146
Whitestone, P. 59
Whitley, R. D. 137
Wood, D. 58, 116
Wood, E. G. 2, 3
Woodworth, D. P. 116
Wooton, C. B. 117, 118, 120
Yamey, B. S. 45, 47
Zifcak, M. 48
Zuckerman, H. 128

Subject Index

Associated Book Publishers   20, 29
Academic Press   123, 131
Advances   26
Allen and Unwin   20, 73, 95
Authors   25, 34
   and on-demand publishing   54
   bestselling   37
   conflict with publishers   25
   remuneration of   101-3

Backlist   17
Bertelsmann   85
Bertrams   72-3, 95
Bestsellers   26, 35, 36, 37, 45, 48
Bibles   6-13
Billings   63
Bingley, Clive   67
Blackwell   55
Blackwell Scientific   123-4, 131
Blackwell's Periodicals Division   121
Blanket licensing   59
Books
   economic characteristics of   102
Book clubs
   and the NBA   46-7
   future prospects of   85
   history of   84-5
   simultaneous   85
Book Club Associates   85
Book promotion   25, 79-83
   aims of   81-2
   by booksellers   82
   in newspapers   82
   on television   81
Book Promotion House Feasibility Study
   80-1, 116-7
Book reviews   81
Book of the Season   82-3
Bookseller
   see The Bookseller
Booksellers' Association   41, 74, 87
   delivery league table   73, 93-5
Booksellers' Association Service House
   82-3
Booksellers' Association Trade Practice
   and Distribution Committee   73
Bookselling
   competition in   87
   discounts in   24, 42-6, 82, 87-8
   financial performance of   88-92
   small-order surcharges in   92-3
   structure of   87
   wastage in   88

Bookshops
   see Stockholding bookshops
Bookwise   72-3, 95
Book Trade Capacity Committee   64
Bowes and Bowes   87
British Lending Library Division   116-7
   and reprography   58
British Market Agreement   75-7
British National Bibliography   106
British Printing Industries Federation
   60-1, 63-4, 66-8
Business Monitor   4, 6-15, 38, 60, 79
Butterworth   20, 29

Cambridge University Press   131, 136
Camera-ready copy   54
Capacity in printing   64-5
Cape   20, 37
Capital expenditure
   by libraries   97
   in general publishing   2, 3
   in printing   64
Cash-and-Carry   73
Cassell   20, 29
Census of Production   1, 2, 64
Charter Economic Survey   88-92, 99
Charter Group   87-92, 99
Childrens' books   6-12, 13
   cost multiplier for   23
   prices of   27, 106-111
Closed markets   76-7
Collins   17, 18, 20, 21, 37, 63
Competition
   in book publishing   16-8, 27
   in bookselling   87
   in printing   65
Concentration ratios in publishing   22
Conglomerates   37, 61
Consent Decree   76-7
Consumers' expenditure   15
Copyright   25, 56-9
   economic rationale of   56-7
   in Australia   59
   in the USA   59
   law of   58-9
   reprography and   57-8
Copyright Act 1956   58
Corgi   20, 81
Costs
   in bookselling   88-90
   in printing   65
   in publishing   22-6
Cost multipliers   23-4

Credit collection 30
Crisis in book publishing 33, 78
  and on-demand publishing 55

David and Charles 20, 85
Delivery
  speed of 72-3, 93-5
Department of Education and Science
  100, 101
Department of Employment Gazette 112
Department of Industry
  Business Monitor 4, 6-15, 38, 60, 95
  wholesale price index for printing 67
Discounts 24, 42-4, 45-6, 82, 87-8
  and bookshop costs 46
  and risk 46
  and school books 95
  and service 46
  and wholesaling 72
Distribution 71-5
  in America 77
  in Australia 74-6
  in Germany 73-4

Economies of scale
  in printing 63
  in publishing 17-8
Educational contractors 95
Elasticity of demand 25-7
Electronic books 56
Elsevier 130
Employment
  in general publishing 2-5
  in printing 60-1
Exchange rates 68-9, 78
  and journal prices 122-3
Exports 8-11, 37
  and exchange rates 69
  percentage total receipts earned by
    8-9
  problems with 77-9
  real value of 78-9
  to America 79

Fiction 6-12, 13, 33
  bestselling 37
  elasticity of demand for 26
  highbrow 37
  in libraries 100
  numbers of 33
  prices of 106-111
Financial performance
  of book publishers 27-30
  of booksellers 88-92
  of journal publishers 123-4
  of printers 65-7
First-copy costs 23
Foyles 85

Franki Report 59
Futura Publications 20, 29, 35

Gardners 72-3, 95
Gordon and Breach 123, 131
Granada 77
Gravure 62-3
Gross output 2-3, 5
Guiness Superlatives 29

Hamlyn 20, 83
Hammicks 72, 95
Hardbacks 6-13, 33-4
  exports of 10
  in home market 10-12
Hardback publishers
  bestsellers of 36-7
  profitability of 28
Heinemann 20, 29, 36
Heron Books 85
High St bookselling 82
Hodder and Stoughton 77
Hodges Report 73
Hutchinson 20, 77, 82
Hyping 36

Indent 76
Innovation in publishing 53-6
Inspection copies 54
Institute of Physics 132, 136, 144
Inter Company Comparisons 27-30, 123-4

Jordon Dataquest 27
Journals
  abstract 122
  circulation of 144
  conventional 115
  definition of 114-5
  expenditure on 98
  exports of 144
  geographical spread of 144
  in life sciences 118
  in medicine 133
  in physics 115, 118-9, 120, 123, 131-2
  in psychology 118
  in social sciences 118
  letters 115
  new 138-9
  numbers of 115-6
  prices of 120-3
  reprography and 57-8
  review 115
  size of 116-20
  subscriptions to 145
  trends in number of subscriptions to
    145
  turnover of 13

Journal publishers
   commercial 118, 123, 128, 130, 132,
      134, 136, 138, 140-1
   concentration among 131, 140-1
   efficiency of 140
   financial performance of 123-4
   growth and diversification among
      137-41
   profit motive of 136-7
   rejection rates among 128-30
   society 118, 128, 132, 134, 138
   university press 130, 132, 134
Journal publishing
   authors in 126-8, 130, 137, 139
   editors in 126-8, 137, 139
   referees in 126-8, 130

Kodansha 20, 21

Learned societies 118, 124, 128, 130,
   132, 136, 146
   in co-operation with printers 141
   in co-operation with publishers 132-5,
      138
Leisure Circle 85
Letterpress 62, 64
Libraries 33-4, 96-101
   and bookclubs 84
   and journals 119-20, 138-9
   and microform 55
   and NBA 44, 98-9
   and reprography 58
   and subscription agents 142-3
   charges for services of 99-101
   expenditure by local authority 97-8
   expenditure by university 98
Library Agreement 43, 96
Library Association 100
   book price statistics 104, 106-11
   journal price statistics 120-3
Library Association Record 100, 106-11,
   120-3
Library Management Research Unit 109-11
Library suppliers 44, 96
Libri 73-4
Liquidity in publishing 29, 30, 47
Literary Guild 84-5
Litos 73-4
Longmans 20, 131
Low-value orders 73

Macmillan 20, 22, 29, 33, 77
Manufacturing costs 23
Menzies, John 73, 87
Michael Joseph 20, 29, 36
Microchips 56
Microform 54-6
   and libraries 55
   and user resistance 55

economics of 55
   publishers of 55
Midways 35
Mills and Boon 20, 29, 49, 81
Mitchell Beazley 81
Monographs 32
Monopoly power in publishing 18
Mystery Guild 84

National Book Council 80
National Book Fair 80
National Book League Report on School
      Books 95
National book sale 43, 47
National book week 80
National Income and Expenditure 'Blue
      Book' 3, 15
Net Book Agreement
   and book prices 50
   and journals 142
   and libraries 98-9
   and number of titles 49-50
   and stockholding bookshops 50-1
   book clubs and 46-7
   content of 42-5
   critique of 45-51
   history of 41-2
   in the 1890's 47
   remainders and 46-7
   risk and 46
   terms of 51-2
Net output 2, 3, 5
New English Library 20, 29
New Fiction Society 84
New Scientist 68
Non-fiction 13, 87
   in libraries 100
   prices of 106-111
Non-net books 95-6, 99

Octopus 20, 36, 81
Odham's 85
Offset lithography 62, 64
Omnibus edition 36
On-demand publishing 53-5, 140
Over-capacity in printing 66
Overheads in publishing 23, 27
Oxford University Press 18, 20, 27, 75,
   131, 136

Paperbacks 6-13, 33-6
   exports of 10
   in home market 10-12
   rights 37
Paperback publishers
   profitability of 28
Paper prices 28, 65, 67
Penguin 34-5, 75, 77
Perfector process 62

Pergamon Press 20, 22, 29, 123, 130-1, 132, 143-4
Periodicals
  defined 114
  numbers of 115-6
Photocomposition 62
Price Commission 1, 8, 79, 110, 111
  and bookshops 87-8
  and printing 63-7, 69
  and school books 95
  attitude to price indices 104
  critique of Report 38-40
  Report 27-8
Price indices for books 104-113
  drawbacks to 111
Prices of books 43-4, 104-113
  in Australia 48
  in Canada 47
  in France 48
Prices of journals 120-3
  average for UK 121
Printers' International Comparisons
      Scheme 68-9
Printing
  and Price Commission Report 65-7
  capacity in 64
  competition in 65
  costs and prices in 67-70
  expenditure on plant and machinery in
  64
  financial performance in 65
  of journals 141
  sales and employment in 60-1
  scale of production in 61-2
  size of firms in 61
  specialisation in 63
  standardisation in 63
  technological change in 62-3
Print runs 26, 30, 31
Productivity
  in general publishing 3
  in printing 68-70
Profits
  in bookselling 88-92
  in printing 65-7
  in publishing 24-5
Promotion of books 25, 79-83
  aims of 81-2
  by booksellers 82
Public Lending Right
  economics of 101-3
  history of 101
Publishers' Association 9, 13-5, 39,
  41-3, 58, 69, 74, 95, 110
  and book clubs 84
  and library sales 99
Publishers' Association Sales Statistics
  13-5

Publishing of books
  competition in 16-8, 27
  credit collection in 30
  crisis in 33, 55
  delivery in 93-5
  economies of scale in 17-8
  financial accounts in 27-30, 39
  first-copy costs in 23
  in the USA 35
  liquidity in 29
  manufacturing costs in 23
  monopoly power in 18
  overheads in 23, 27
  pricing policy in 26-7
  profits in 24-5, 28-9, 30
  profit sharing in 26
  return on capital in 28-9, 39
  stockturn in 29

Quartet Books 34

Rand McNally 20, 21
Reader's Union 84
Record industry 47
Reference books
  prices of 106-111
Remainders
  and the NBA 46-7
Reprint Society 84
Reprography 33, 53,
  and copyright 57-9
Retail price index 110-12
Retail price index for books 109-10,
  113
Returns 35
Return on capital employed
  in printing 65-6
  in publishing 28-9
Rights 34, 35, 37, 77
  and book clubs 85
Rotary press 62
Royalties 6, 7, 9, 11-12, 23-6, 102

Sale-or-return 42, 46
Sangam 20, 21
Scale of production in printing 61-2
School textbooks 6-12, 13, 95-6
  cost multiplier for 23
Secker and Warburg 37
See-safe 87
Serials
  defined 114
  in humanities 118
  in science and technology 118
  in social science 118
  numbers of 115-6
  size of 117
Simpkin Marshall 71-2

Single copy orders 71-2, 92-3, 99
Size distribution
  of printing firms 61
  of publishing firms 21
Small order surcharges 92-3
Smith, W. H. 36, 72-3, 74, 83, 87
  book clubs 84
Society of Authors 58, 101
Software Sciences 74
Specialisation
  in bookselling 92
  in printing 63
Standardisation in printing 63
Stockholding bookshops 42-4, 49, 50-1
  and library sales 99
  and microchips 56
  and microform 55
  and on-demand publishing 54
  and the NBA 49-51
  discounts given to 87-8
  financial analysis of 87-92
  technical and scientific 91-2
  theological 91-2
Stockturn 29, 45-6, 89, 92
  and wholesaling 72
Stock valuation 30-1
Subscription agents 141-3

Taylor and Francis 131
Technical and scientific books 6-12,
  13, 31-3
  elasticity of demand for 26, 32
  exports of 32
  in Price Commission Report 38-40
  prices of 27, 32
  print runs for 31-2
  promotion of 32
  shelf life of 32

Technological change in printing 62-3
Teleordering 73-5
  difficulties with 74
The Bookseller 9, 18, 33, 48, 59, 63,
  67, 73, 76, 86, 92, 101
  price indices 104-111
Titles published 18-20, 44
  and consumer detriment 49-50
Trade paperbacks 35
Traditional markets 75
Turnover
  of general publishing 4, 6-13, 23, 28
    export 8-11
    home 10, 12
  of printers 60-1

Value added 2

Wages and salaries
  in general publishing 2-5
Warehousing 72
Web offset 62-4
Webb and Bower 36, 82
Whitford Committee Report 58-9
Wholesalers 71-3
  and discounts 72
  and speed of delivery 73, 93-5
  and stocks 72-3
Wildwood 34
Wiley 123, 131
World Distributors 29
Writers Action Group 101
Writers Guild 101